Another Chance
to Be Real

Another Chance to Be Real

Attachment and Object Relations Treatment of Borderline Personality Disorder

Donald D. Roberts and Deanda S. Roberts

JASON ARONSON
Lanham • Boulder • New York • Toronto • Plymouth, UK

Published in the United States of America
by Jason Aronson
An imprint of Rowman & Littlefield Publishers, Inc.

A wholly owned subsidiary of
The Rowman & Littlefield Publishing Group, Inc.
4501 Forbes Boulevard, Suite 200, Lanham, Maryland 20706
www.rowmanlittlefield.com

Estover Road
Plymouth PL6 7PY
United Kingdom

British Library Cataloguing in Publication Information Available

Library of Congress Cataloging-in-Publication Data

Roberts, Donald D., 1939–
  Another chance to be real : attachment and object relations treatment of
borderline personality disorder / Donald D. Roberts and Deanda S. Roberts.
     p. ; cm.
  ISBN-13: 978-0-7657-0553-2 (cloth : alk. paper)
  ISBN-10: 0-7657-0553-2 (cloth : alk. paper)
  ISBN-13: 978-0-7657-0554-9 (pbk. : alk. paper)
  ISBN-10: 0-7657-0554-0 (pbk. : alk. paper)
  1. Borderline personality disorder—Treatment. 2. Attachment behavior.
3. Object relations (Psychoanalysis) I. Roberts, Deanda S., 1942– II. Title.
  [DNLM: 1. Borderline Personality Disorder—therapy. 2. Object Attachment.
3. Psychotherapy—methods. WM 190 R643a 2007]

  RC569.5.B67R62 2007
  616.85′852—dc22   2007022381

Printed in the United States of America

Contents

Introduction: Attachment   1

1 Normal Development and the Real Self   9

2 Borderline Personality Disorder Development and the False Self   31

3 Compassionate Attunement: Igniting the Self   51

4 Stance, Neutrality, and Frame With the Borderline Patient   65

5 Listening and Speaking to the Borderline Patient:
   An Invitation to a Secure Separation   77

6 Psychotherapy: Another Chance to be Real   97

7 Terri: Destitute and Desperate for Help   117

8 Susan: Immobilized, Helpless, and Hopeless   125

9 Laura: Tormented and in Trouble   145

10 Practical Considerations   153

11 Now and Then, Here and There, Change Happens   163

   References   167

   Index   175

   About the Authors   179

Introduction

Attachment

Seven or eight years ago, we came upon an article in a mental health journal.[1] It was written by an ethologist, Helga Fischer-Mamblona (2000), and it was the story, the developmental journey, of a goose. Feli was one of the flock whose social behavior was being investigated by Konrad Lorenz's team of researchers; the geese lived in a seminatural environment at the Max Planck Institute, Seewiesen, Germany. Feli was separated from the flock at birth and lived the first 10 days of her life sequestered away from visual and auditory stimulation. She then spent 8 weeks in a pen constructed so that she could see through the top but not make visual contact with the other geese. Stimulation during this period was limited to the heating lamps in her pen and by the replacement of her food and water bowls.

As we understand it, goslings from birth onward vocally "greet" their mothers, fathers, and siblings and repeatedly seek proximity and contact with them. According to Fischer-Mamblona's article (2000), this process of initiating contact and becoming attached in the first days of life is the most critical stage in a goose's social development. Even in isolation, Feli engaged in a gosling's normal greeting and complaining behaviors. But unlike her peers, she had no social context. There were no other geese within her visual field at all, no mother goose to interact with. As the author describes it, Feli seemed confused by this situation. She began to scurry around in a disorganized and directionless way, making weak and pathetic sounds into the vacant space of her pen. At first, she was unresponsive to any changes in her environment. But in time, she came to "greet" any changes that she observed, like the replacement of her food dish or the ons and offs of the warming lights.

1

At the end of 8 weeks, when she had acquired her feathers, Feli was allowed to leave her pen and explore her environs. She was frightened when she first saw the other geese, and if one approached her, she hurriedly returned to the safety of her pen. The researchers began to move her feed bowls progressively closer to the other geese; with this help, she gradually became desensitized to them. Eventually, she became able to eat in the presence of the others, although if one approached her, she still took refuge in her pen.

According to the article, goslings during the second spring of their lives typically leave their families and are attracted to their peers, seemingly looking for company and making social contacts. Feli observed this behavior and was fascinated by it. In fact, she sometimes shed her anxiety and ran to join in. But the other geese didn't recognize her as a member of the flock. They considered her behavior a violation of good goose manners and, as the observers expected, promptly chased her away. As this repeatedly happened, Feli's fear and anxiety intensified, and her tendency to flee the other geese increased.

Feli was faced with a knotty dilemma. If she approached another goose, she was aggressively rejected; but if she withdrew to her pen, she lived in complete isolation. Both her attachment and separation behaviors had negative consequences. Apparently in response to this quandary, when a goose approached, Feli began to groom her feathers, an expression of her desire to engage socially. But, simultaneously, she vigorously shook her head, a manifestation of her dread of being close to another goose. Her observers thought that these incongruous behaviors served to regulate the anxiety stimulated by her predicament. At first, she preened and shook every time that a goose approached her, because this elicited her conflict between approaching and fleeing. But over time, the dilemma resolved itself after a fashion; the urge to flee, stimulated by her fear of attachment, overpowered her desire to attach, and Feli seemed to resign herself to being alone. She became increasingly withdrawn and apathetic.

In their second year of life, geese become sexually mature, and this intensifies attachment urges. But in Feli's case, advances by other geese merely caused her to withdraw. On occasion, a shy male would court her from a distance, but instead of reciprocally approaching him, her response was only to shake and preen. Her odd behavior discouraged the other goose from coming nearer. This pattern persisted for 2 years.

But in Feli's fourth year, something curious happened. A particularly shy and cautious male approached her. This time, she did not retreat or resist, and she mated for the first time and produced a nestful of eggs. Observers noted that although she appeared to provide all of the usual maternal ministrations, she still tended to flee when another goose came near, and she would (if necessary) vacate her nest. But she did manage to tolerate the 4-week incubation period, and one gosling hatched.

Feli's gosling immediately attempted to seek proximity to her mother. But Feli did not respond to the gosling's approach behavior. She withdrew physically, preening and shaking and ignoring the gosling's cries of distress. The next day, the gosling was found dead.

Feli laid eggs again the next year. This time, the eggs were sterile. The observers replaced them with fertilized duck eggs, which are less sensitive than goose eggs and require a shorter incubation period. The ducklings hatched, but once again, Feli did not respond to their approach behavior, preening and shaking instead. Again, she abandoned the nest in response to their pestering. Even after she returned, she was unresponsive to the distressed appeals of the cold and hungry ducklings. A few days later they, too, died.

In her sixth year, Feli once more laid sterile eggs; again, these were replaced with ducks' eggs. When the ducklings hatched, she again resumed her preening and shaking and—a familiar sight by now—seemed altogether apathetic to her "offspring." But this time, the outcome was quite different. These ducklings were relentless in their efforts to be close to their "mother." Several times a day, they would greet her and snuggle up to her. Feli responded with her preening and shaking ritual, but these ducklings could not be deterred, and they persisted in nibbling her feathers and making efforts to get close. Feli tried to bite them—unanticipated behavior in a mother goose, according to the author. For a while, even these persistent ducklings resigned themselves to the situation and got through the nights by keeping each other warm. Inexplicably, though, during this time, Feli's ritualized preening waned. One rainy night, the ducklings returned to their mother for warmth—and this time, she gave it to them.

This was a pivotal event. From then on, Feli responded, albeit hesitantly at first, to her ducklings' greetings. In fact, she began to demonstrate most of the typical maternal behaviors of geese: She accompanied the ducklings down to the water to feed; she bathed them; she tended to their feathers. In response, the ducklings pursued her when she left them to graze, and they approached her for warmth and protection. In short, an attachment was realized—for the first time in Feli's life.

This account has a bittersweet conclusion. An older gander approached Feli, who this time did not retreat into ritual or distance. She actually obliged, and the two remained a pair long after the ducklings had become independent. During the 4 years that Feli and her gander were together, they had their own goslings and reared them successfully. When the flock moved to Konrad Lorenz's lab in Austria, the pair lived together there for 2 more years. But one day, Feli mysteriously disappeared. Shortly after that, the gander flew away and was reportedly shot and killed by a hunter in Switzerland. A sad conclusion to an otherwise heartening story.

The author concludes her account of Feli's life by emphasizing that the first stage of development is the most critical: "If a gosling does not learn in its first days to attach itself to the mother, to follow her, to greet her and run to her if scared, thus taking refuge, then all the next phases cannot be accomplished" (Fischer-Mamblona, 2000, p. 16). She points out that attachment and what she calls *escape* (i.e., separation) are basic motivations of animals and people alike and that difficulties with escape inevitably result if escape is not grounded in attachment. That is, the mother figure is at the center of the infant's responses both to its urges to attach and its urges to separate; a secure attachment is requisite to healthy separation and individuation.

Fischer-Mamblona (2000) creates of Feli's developmental journey a poignant picture of the critical importance of early development. Extrapolating to the human realm, she underscores what we have known all along: that early developmental experience is crucial in the shaping of later personality structure and dynamics. And it is early attachment experience in particular that influences the developmental pathway so strongly. We propose in this book that early experience with primary caretakers is formative in the development of the borderline personality disorder and that a developmental perspective, informed by attachment theory, offers the most useful approach to the diagnosis and psychotherapy of this disorder. Fischer-Mamblona concludes in her article:

> The example of the goose Feli may be used to show therapeutic possibilities. The ducklings stimulated her motherly instinct and thus activated her attachment behavior, which had never been challenged before in that way. Her fear of closeness was reduced by the insisting brood, so that step by step Feli became habituated to them. This is exactly what happens in therapy: a climate of trust is created by slow habituation between patient and therapist and, thereby, fear is constantly reduced. Only then can transference be created and by this the beginning of a new attachment. By slowly changing the developmental levels the therapist can dig through different layers of pain and traumatization until reaching initial pain of insufficient attachment. (2000, p. 19)

In 1992, PBS aired a series entitled *Children*, which included some stunning research footage filmed by psychologists. The investigators started with the assumption that a child is well prepared from birth to engage in intimate interaction with his or her mother, and they attempted a microanalysis of that relational process. With two cameras side by side, the researchers were able to provide split-screen images of the interactions of a child and his or her caregiver.

In the first film, we see 2-month-old Zoey gazing at her mother from her infant seat. Her mother, on the other half of the screen, looks back adoringly. Zoey yawns and stretches. Her mother says softly, "Oh, such a busy day. Such a busy day!" Zoey looks back and smiles—a big smile. "Are you my sweetness?" her mother coos. Wiggling and smiling, Zoey responds as if joy were exploding in every part of her body. "You are," says the mother with soft glee. "You are the sweetest girl I know. Yes, you are!" Zoey smiles and then looks away. Her mother sees her attention shift. "What do you see?" she asks quietly. "Over there? Hmm?" She does not demand eye contact or attention. But soon Zoey looks back. And smiles. And her mother smiles in response. Over these few moments, there is a remarkable correspondence as their affective states fluctuate in quality and intensity.

One might expect that a child would respond to her mother, as Zoey did in this film. It is not necessarily so obvious to the intuition that the mother would take her cue from the infant. But using this observational technique, the researchers were able to demonstrate that the communication process between mother and baby is mutual and reciprocal. That is, Zoey's mother follows Zoey's lead. And through these interactions, Zoey learns something very important—that, though small and weak, she is not powerless. In fact, through repeated interactions of this sort with a caring adult, she discovers that she can affect and even alter her world. In return, the infant's smile gives the parent encouragement and invites her into an ever-deepening relationship with her baby. As we discuss later, it is likely that this process of "mutual-gaze regulation" is an important experiential ingredient for attaining optimal development of the self and one's emotions.

A father and his 4-month-old son Stephan were also filmed with this split-screen technique. Stephan's father had been asked to participate in what is called "still face" research. That is, he was instructed to interrupt the mutual-gaze process by turning his face and eyes away from Stephan and by avoiding his son's efforts to make eye contact. In a matter of just a few seconds, Stephan would become strikingly agitated, sad, or remote. But as soon as engagement with his father was restored, he relaxed once more and involved himself in the mutual interaction process.

Then there was 4-month-old Matthew, filmed in intimate interaction with his mother. She was singing, "Patty cake, patty cake," to her infant son, and their shared pleasure and delight were almost palpable—until the researchers suddenly flooded the room with the orchestral music of Mozart. Startled and afraid, Matthew immediately looked to his mother. When he saw that she was not alarmed, his anxiety vanished, and they were able to resume their play. Her peaceful presence seemed to help allay his fears and enable him to return to his former joyful affective state.

There on the screen, it was possible to see the minute but palpable incremental interactions that shape an infant's evolving capacity for attachment to others—the seeds of relationships. And it is the attachment styles that grow from them, we believe, that are internalized as characteristic ways of being with one's self and with others. In other words, the way that the self and the personality develop is significantly influenced by the quality of these early relationships with primary caregivers. Relationships influence the development of the self; the personality evolves in the crucible of early relationships and, especially, early attachment experiences.

Of course, many babies never have consistent relational experiences of the kinds that we saw with Zoey and Matthew and even Stephan (when his father was allowed to look at him). The result is often a developmental detour or arrest. When the parent cannot take cues from the baby, respond to the baby's emotional state in helpful ways, allow the baby to disconnect and reconnect at will, or restore relatedness when it is disrupted, the baby may never learn to relax and trust his or her connections with other people. For instance, what if a baby's parent behaved naturally, and frequently, the way that Stephan's father did briefly on the instructions of the researchers. Instead of Stephan's expanding into a comfortable and joyous sense of himself and his powers, Stephan may take refuge in alternative behavior in his need to solicit the attachments that are vital to his security and yet are not reliably available in response to the ordinary baby repertoire. In more severe instances of this kind of mismatch, the alternative behaviors and strategies may solidify into what we call a *personality disorder*.

How, then, do parents nurture, from birth, the healthy, authentic selves of their children, in all of their potential? How do we as psychotherapists find and free the Zoey, the Stephan, the Matthew in our patients? How does the person whose early experience comprised abuse, neglect, or indifference, whose early experience did not include attentive and responsive parents or reliable attachments, discover his or her genuine identity?

More pointedly, what can these stories of Feli and Zoey teach us about the psychotherapy of patients with borderline personalities, one form of attachment disorder?

Attachment theorists, and Fischer-Mamblona (2000) of the Feli story, take the position that a poor attachment experience in an individual's earliest years arrests the developmental process in childhood and continues to constrain it far into the future. But they believe, too, that a new attachment experience can initiate a trajectory of healthy development even after development has been thwarted. A new relationship, a particular quality of attachment experience, can resolve the developmental impasse and free the person for unencumbered growth.

The story of Feli goes only so far toward understanding the complex psychological and developmental wounds of human beings, and a goose's biography is not likely to be the last word on personality disturbances. But Feli's tale does give us a springboard for articulating how we understand attachment theory and its relevance to the development and diagnosis of the borderline personality disorder. It also offers a taking-off point into what we consider the necessary integration of attachment research with self theory and the object relations perspective. We believe that the resulting model of psychotherapy is refined and enriched by all three contributions.

Attachment theory and research have added a robust new dimension to our understanding of personality development and psychotherapy. Theoretically influenced by client-centered psychotherapy (originally formulated by Rogers [1957]), which was in vogue when we were in training, we looked for years to the quality of relationship offered to the patient for treatment effectiveness. And we conducted therapy on the assumption that a new, healthier relationship with a therapist, a new attachment experience, would be healing for the patient. But in time, we came to question this assumption, especially in the treatment of personality-disordered patients. We thought that we were missing something, that our effectiveness was being limited by our failure to recognize something important about personality structure and function.

We turned to psychodynamic models of treatment, in an effort to enhance our understanding of the person and to improve the efficacy of our treatment. In the literature on object relations theory especially, we began to discover ways to conceptualize what had been lacking in our theoretical orientation—a refined portrayal of the intrapsychic experience of our patients. We read voraciously the writings of Guntrip (1961, 1968), Fairbairn (1952), Winnicott (1958, 1965, 1986), and Kernberg (1975, 1980, 1984), among others.

But it was Masterson's view of personality development (1976, 1981, 1985, 1988, 1993, 2000) and his model for treating the personality disorders that we found most helpful in our clinical work. Masterson (2000) integrated developmental theory, object relations theory, and self psychology with attachment theory and neurobiology and constructed a model of treatment based on his understanding of personality disorder as the outcome of early developmental arrest. He delineated what he came to see as the characteristic intrapsychic structure for the borderline, narcissistic, and schizoid disorders and the structural and technical variables that are indispensable to effective psychotherapy with personality-disordered patients. In this book, we confine our discussion to the borderline disorder. Our clinical experience has convinced us that Masterson's integrated model refines and enriches the earlier models that contributed to it, and we write this book to make that model accessible to clinicians.

In the following pages, we describe an integrated model of normal development and contrast it with the stunted developmental processes that result in borderline personality disorder. We also discuss diagnostic criteria for the disorder based on this developmental paradigm. Finally, we propose a treatment approach grounded in this understanding of borderline character pathology.

NOTE

1. The *we* in the text refers to both of us. When we speak in our individual voices, we use *I* and identify the speaker as either *DDR* or *DSR*.

1

Normal Development
and the Real Self

Human development is a complex phenomenon—part biology, part experience, and part mystery. As psychotherapists, we look to understand both the patient as a person and the developmental course that has shaped his or her personality. The model of optimal healthy development that we have found most useful is a blend of neurobiological research, attachment research, object relations theory, and self theory.

I (DDR) pause at the door of the waiting room as I prepare to welcome my next client. Her name is Terri, and I first met her several years ago, when she was a teenager. Now she's 22—5 years have come and gone. I know that she is unmarried, that she has two children, and that her life since high school has been difficult. But I can't yet answer the most important question of all—who is she?

I open the door, and there she is. She's slouched in the larger chair, the only really comfortable chair in the room, with a leg over one of its arms, and she is chewing gum and mindlessly turning the pages of *People* magazine. She's wearing jeans cut off into shorts, an oversize Metallica T-shirt, and worn sandals; there's a small blue backpack and sweatshirt next to the foot that's still on the floor. Shiny but slightly disheveled black hair frames a soft, pretty face and large dark eyes. There's a silver stud in her nose and a conspicuous tattoo on her calf. She sees me. She grins broadly and warmly, scoops up her shirt and backpack, and bounds across the room to greet me with a disarming familiarity.

What's going on here? I find myself wondering. She seems pretty nonchalant about our first meeting in more than 5 years—and she hardly knows me. What does her effusiveness mean? She's reading *People*—why not *Newsweek* or *The New Yorker*? How is she experiencing this encounter? What is she feeling? About herself? About me? And again, who is this person?

9

In the consulting room, Terri sits with her back to the window and smiles radiantly once more. Again this strikes me as odd behavior, considering that she—this is something I do know—has experienced great disappointment and turmoil in recent years. Why is she really here? As if in answer, she blurts through her smile, "Boy! Have I ever f—— up my life since I last saw you!" To meet her again in this surprising way, seems to me both a mystery and a privilege. But how little I know about her . . .

NATURE AND NURTURE

How do people become who they are? The once perennial nature–nurture debate seems to have run its course; it has become clear that neither genetics nor environment alone satisfactorily explains personality development. Recent research suggests that both are salient in the developmental process and that they affect each other in a delicate interactive relationship.

There is no question that constitutional factors significantly influence the development of personality. According to LeDoux (2002), "genetic factors are in fact known to influence a variety of individual or personality characteristics, including how outgoing, fearful, or aggressive one is, as well as the likelihood that one will develop depression, anxiety, or schizophrenia" (pp. 3–4). One resource suggests that genetics account for 25 percent to 33 percent of the variance of personality traits among people (Klein, 1998), whereas Siegel (1999) points out that "genetic studies of behavior commonly note that fifty percent of each of the personality features measured is attributable to heredity" (p. 19). But it is apparent that even this strong genetic sway over the development of personality leaves ample room for the effects of environmental and experiential variables.

Even brain development is conditioned by experience. In Siegel's words (1999), "the brain's development is an 'experience-dependent' process" (p. 13). Although genes contain all of the connectional possibilities for a brain's structure, it is genes and experience together—particularly, relational experience—that combine to determine what specific networks of synaptic connections actually form. As Siegel says, infants are born with "a genetically programmed excess in neurons" (p. 14), and experience ordains the conditions under which specific genes are expressed. According to LeDoux (2002), "most systems of the brain are plastic, that is, modifiable by experience. Which means that the synapses involved are changed by experience" (p. 8).

At birth, the infant's brain is the most undifferentiated organ in the body (Siegel, 1999). According to Schore (1994), it will increase in weight from 400 g to 1,000 g during the first year of life; this means that experience plays an enormous role in influencing postnatal brain development and, ultimately, personality patterns. Siegel (1999) writes,

For the infant and young child, attachment relationships are the major environmental factors that shape the development of the brain during its period of maximal growth. Therefore, caregivers are the architects of the way in which experience influences the unfolding of genetically preprogrammed but experience-dependent brain development. Genetic potential is expressed within the setting of social experiences, which directly influence how neurons connect to one another. Human connections create neuronal connections. (p. 85)

Simply stated, parents and the experiences they provide have a direct effect on a child's brain; the development of neural networks has to do with how relationships are experienced.

So, experience—especially, interpersonal experience—directly influences how neurons connect to one another, how they strengthen existing connections, and how they create new synaptic connections (Schore, 1997; Siegel, 1999). Vaughan (1997) has referred to this process of the development of new synaptic links as *arborization*. But interpersonal experience also affects a "pruning" process; whereas certain neurons are strengthened through experience, others are allowed to die off through lack of experience (Siegel, 1999).

In this regard, Siegel (1999) reminds us of neurobiologist Donald Hebb's (1949) axiom of brain development: "Neurons that fire together at a certain time wire together" (p. 70). Siegel elaborates,

Any two cells or systems of cells that are repeatedly active at the same time will tend to become associated so that activity in one facilitates activity in the other. . . . These associated linkages make it more likely that items will be activated simultaneously during the [memory] retrieval processes. (p. 27)

Memories of the experiences of life, then—behaviors, emotions, and images—coalesce over time into a more or less stable and organized sense of self (or not). So, one's internal world, including mental representations and models of relationships, has a neuronal substrate. (Remarkably, there is evidence that some plasticity of the neural structure of the brain persists throughout the life span [Schore, 1994, 2001b; Siegel, 2001]. This is good news; no matter our age, there is still hope!) This substrate, in turn, influences the evolution of the specialized neuronal circuits within the brain that are responsible for such processes as memory, emotion, and self-awareness.

Of particular relevance to the neurobiological development of the self is the brain's limbic system. It is situated neatly between the brain stem and the cortex. The brain stem is most essential to the maintenance of life-sustaining functions—such as breathing, swallowing, and heartbeat—whereas the cortex is the source of capacities for reasoning, planning, speaking, writing, and, probably, volition. The limbic brain is the seat of emotional life and, as such, is the origin of abilities for social communion, nurturance, empathy, communication, and play. Without the limbic system, there would be no emotional connections with others—no relationships. But as suggested, "most of the nervous system (including the limbic brain) needs exposure to crucial experiences to drive its healthy growth" (Lewis, Amini, and Lannon, 2000, p. 89).

Equally important, for our purposes, is the development of the right orbitofrontal cortex. Residing within the prefrontal lobe, approximately behind the eye, this is the only cortical structure that has direct access to the subcortical limbic structures that play a crucial role in emotional, motivational, and relational processes (Schore, 1994). In this regard, Masterson (2005) proposes that "a center emerges in the prefrontal orbital cortex in the right brain for the control of emotion and emotional relationships, and is, therefore, a neurobiologic center of the self" (p. 10). It has been suggested (Masterson, 2005; Schore, 1994; Siegel, 1999) that most of the growth and differentiation of this particular brain structure occurs between the ages of 10 and 18 months (before the development of the conscious, rational left brain) and that it is enormously influenced by the interactive experiences with the primary caregiver. So, this center of the self forms nonconsciously, prerationally, and neurobiologically—in relationship.

Of course, it works the other way around, too—nature affects nurture, and the relational experience between child and parents are shaped by the child's own temperament. Certain temperaments predictably evoke certain responses from caregivers (Appelman, 2001; Siegel, 1999), which in turn influence personality development and corresponding brain structure. In addition, there appears to be a recursive quality to infant development whereby particular personality presentations or styles are reinforced by the interpersonal environment. "In this way, behavior itself alters genetic expression, which then creates behavior" (Siegel, 1999, p. 19).

Early personality development, then, appears to be an exquisite process of mutual creation, or co-construction. It involves complex interplay between genetically derived temperamental factors and the relational context provided by the infant's significant caregivers.

A REAL SELF

But how in this process of co-creation do children learn to perceive, to think, and to feel—about themselves, about others, about relationships? Fundamental to our understanding of the developmental process is the concept of a real self, which is present from birth on. The notion of this real self, distinct from a false or defensive self, is a bedrock concept of Masterson's theory (1985, 1988, 1993) of the etiology and treatment of the personality disorders. Stern (1985) has elaborated on the idea, commenting that "infants begin to experience a sense of emergent self from birth" (p. 10). His contention, based on infant research, is that

> during the first two months the infant is actively forming a sense of an emergent self. It is a sense of organization in the process of formation, and it is a sense of self that will remain active for the rest of life. (p. 38)

Winnicott's earlier notion (1965) of a "true self" is somewhat analogous:

> At the earliest stage the True Self is the theoretical position from which come the spontaneous gesture and the personal idea. The spontaneous gesture is the True Self in action. Only the True Self can be creative and only the True Self can feel real. (p. 148)

These three different conceptions, each based on the observation of infants, share the belief that there is an identifiable individual self from the start, which is in the process of increasing separation and differentiation.

Optimally, one would be free to experience and express this real self. This is what Masterson (2000) refers to as self-activation: "the capacity to identify one's unique individuative wishes and to use autonomous initiative and assertion to express them in reality and to support and defend them when under attack" (p. 27; see also, Masterson, 1985). E. Greenberg (2004) states that "self-activation refers to the awareness of, and expression of, aspects of the real self" (p. 32). Difficulties with self-activation are expressed in an individual's not knowing what he or she wants to do—or in having an awareness of what is desired but not being able to initiate it—or in being able to initiate a real-self activity but not being able to persevere to its completion

ATTACHMENT AND SEPARATION

There is no guarantee that this real self will develop optimally over the years. The vicissitudes of the developmental process result in a range of outcomes. Horner (1994) suggests that "the intrinsic self," as she calls it, may be "forced into hiding or distorted expression during the formative years" (p. 362).

What variables account for differences in the quality and realization of the real self, supporting the experience and expression of the real self or encouraging it into hiding? We propose that the developmental tasks pertinent to optimal growth and elaboration of the real self require a healthy attachment experience and a healthy process of separation. This suggests two parallel but interrelated lines of development: the capacity to be emotionally close and the capacity to be autonomous. Blatt and Blass (1990, 1996) have discussed these developmental lines, which they call the need for relatedness and the need for self-definition, and Holmes (1996) has addressed a correspondence with the fundamental needs of adults for intimacy and autonomy.

Some students of development emphasize the attachment line of development (Ainsworth, 1967; Bowlby, 1969, 1973, 1980; Fonagy, 2001a), whereas others accentuate the separation line (Kernberg, 1976; Mahler, 1968, 1979; Mahler, Pine, and Bergman, 1975; Rinsley, 1982). It is our contention and that of Masterson (2004) that each of these lines represents crucial developmental tasks for optimal development of the real self. Departing from an earlier emphasis on the separation process, Masterson stated,

> Attachment theory describes how the mother's affect regulation function mediates the expression of genetic influences and provides a vital environmental support for the development and wiring of the neurons in the prefrontal orbital cortex that will become a center for the self, which will then regulate the individual's affect and affective relationships. (p. 13)

Auerbach and Blatt (2001) succinctly describe the dialectical relationship between these two lines of development: "An increasingly differentiated, integrated, and mature sense of self is contingent on establishing satisfying interpersonal relationships, and, conversely, the continued development of increasingly mature and satisfying relationships is contingent on the development of a more mature self-concept or identity" (p. 431). In other words, healthy, secure attachment is a prerequisite for healthy separation; a pathological, insecure attachment is not apt to provide the sense of safety necessary for a child's psychological separation from the mother. Viewed from this perspective, all personality disorders are fundamentally disorders of attachment and only secondarily disorders of separation.

Attachment theorists hypothesize that people are hardwired to seek relationships and that the quest for emotional attachment to a significant other is the common goal of human life. They understand attachment behavior as a function of an innate psychoneurobiological system that impels infants to seek proximity to their parents or other primary caregivers, particularly under conditions of stress, and to establish communication with them (Bowlby, 1969, 1973, 1980; Karen, 1994). So, in attachment theory, as in object relations theory, the infant's drive to establish contact, connection, and relationship with another is of motivational primacy (Greenberg and Mitchell, 1983).

This built-in need for relationship is significant. First, a behavioral attachment system of this kind enhances the infant's odds for survival; as Vaughan (1997) puts it, it is "sensibly Darwinian" (p. 86). Second, the interpersonal relationship established through attachment enables the immature mind of the infant to make use of the mature mind of the mother[1] for the development of such capacities as emotion regulation, reflective function, and interpersonal relatedness (Tronick, 1998). (As we amplify shortly, important capacities are developed through mutual and reciprocal "right brain to right brain" communication between mother and infant [Schore, 1994, 2000, 2001b; Siegel, 1999, 2001].) Third, a secure-enough attachment experience supports the emergence and elaboration—the *experience* and elaboration—of the real self.

To measure security of attachment (a concept fundamental to attachment theory), Ainsworth and colleagues (1978; see also, Karen, 1994) designed an experimental procedure termed the *strange situation*. All infants typically manifest distress and protest upon separation from their mothers, but they manage it depending on the nature of their attachment. Researchers conducting strange situation studies observe children's responses after standardized separations from and reunions with their primary caregivers, and they have identified four distinct attachment styles: one of secure attachment and three of insecure attachment (Ainsworth et al., 1978; Main and Solomon, 1986). These four patterns of behavior are ways of reestablishing attachment to the mother when it has been interrupted so that the infant can regain access once to her soothing and protective attributes.

All infants are distressed by separation from their mothers whether another ("strange") adult is present or not; however, upon reunion with their mothers, securely attached infants demonstrate a confidence in the restoration of attachment, whereas the insecurely attached do not. Securely attached infants are able to use their mothers as a source of comfort under conditions of stress and as a "secure base" (Bowlby, 1988) from which to explore the environment under conditions of perceived safety. They cry and protest when separated, but when the mother returns, secure children seek her proximity, use her presence for soothing and reassurance, and shortly return to normal playful and exploratory behavior.

Insecurely attached infants of the avoidant style appear to be unperturbed by the mother's departure, and they fail to show acknowledgment of her reappearance, as if they were entirely independent and self-reliant. However, measurements of physiological distress throughout the separation–reunion sequence suggest that avoidant infants are in fact significantly distressed (Dozier, Cue, and Barnett, 1994; Spangler and Grossman, 1993). This implies that the avoidant attachment style does not indicate an absence of stress in separation but that it is actually a strategy, a learned albeit unconscious habitual technique acquired for dealing with that stress.

A resistant pattern of insecure attachment has also been identified in some babies. These infants show distress at the mother's departure but react with extreme ambivalence when she returns. That is, there is an oscillation between clinging and rejection in response to the returning mother, and they seem unable to use the mother for soothing and re-regulation.

Finally, in the disorganized pattern of insecure attachment, approach and avoidance behaviors are evoked by the mother's return after separation, inconsistently and unpredictably. It appears to be a dreadful, almost tortured, reunion for the child and a confusing one for the mother. It appears that a coherent pattern of attachment fails to develop.

The conditions of the infant–parent relationship determine how attachment style develops. When the mother is sufficiently consistent, the infant can develop a reliable strategy for attaching, detaching, and reattaching. This enables harmonious, nonambivalent interaction with the parent and facilitates the development of affect regulation. But infants whose primary caregivers are not reliably or predictably available are likely to develop the less effective strategies for attachment, displayed in the three insecure attachment styles described—avoidance, ambivalence, or disorganization. It is significant that research has determined that these attachment styles and strategies of infancy tend to remain relatively stable through the life span (Sroufe and Flesson, 1986, 1988).

AFFECT ATTUNEMENT

Attunement and Attachment

What is the mother's role in all this? According to attachment research and theory (Bowlby, 1969, 1988), an emotionally available primary caregiver is requisite to a secure attachment experience—a caregiver who attunes relatively consistently and accurately to the needs and mental states of the infant. Siegel (1999) emphatically states that "parental sensitivity to signals is the essence of secure attachments" (p. 70). And Winnicott (1958) refers to the *primary maternal preoccupation* of the mother, which provides the relational, rhythmic, and affective context necessary for attunement to the infant. He also emphasizes the contingent aspects of self-development: "There is no such thing as an infant, meaning of course that wherever one finds an infant one finds maternal care, and without maternal care there would be no infant" (p. xxxvii). Development is a process of mutual co-creation, wherein mother and infant together achieve repetitive states of *affective synchrony* (Feldman, Greenbaum, and Yirmiya, 1999) that support—or *scaffold*, a term from Jerome Bruner's lexicon (1983)—the development of the real self.

Particularly important is the mother's attunement to the affective experience of her infant (Stern, 1985). Optimally, in the emotional transactions between a mother and her infant, the parent is emotionally sensitive and responsive to the child's affect states. As Stern (1985) has said, "the sharing of affective states is the most pervasive and clinically germane feature of intersubjective relatedness" (p. 71). This requires that the parent be relatively attuned to the affective crescendos and decrescendos of the infant and able to follow the fluctuations of her infant's affective experience. It is a relational dance that needs to be good enough—not too stimulating, too invasive, or too neglectful. Needless to say, not all parents can do this. Beebe and Lachmann (1994) suggest,

> Infants who will later become securely attached have mothers who stimulate with a mid-level range of intensity, contingency, and reciprocity. Infants who will later become insecure-avoidant have mothers who are overstimulating, intrusive, high intensity, noncontingent, or overly contingent. Infants who will later become insecure-resistant have mothers who are underinvolved, detached, or inconsistent; who fail to respond; or who attempt to interact when the infant is not available. (p. 137)

The notion of the mother's following the affective contours of the infant's experience may seem counterintuitive, given that it is commonly assumed that the infant generally responds in synchrony with the mother's affective experience. But the reality is that, with affect attunement, it is the mother who follows, as well as invites and amplifies, the infant's self-experience. Bowlby (1988) has said, "She lets him call the tune and by a skillful interweaving of her own responses with his creates a dialogue" (p. 7). This calls to mind the videotape of the *mirroring gaze transactions* (Beebe and Lachmann, 1994) between Zoey and her mother that we reference earlier. When Zoey smiled at her mother, her mother responded in a loving tone, "Oh, I see you, my little girl. I see you smiling . . . " And Zoey smiled even more.

Significant in this regard is the finding that affect attunement is a psychobiological process that is largely nonverbal, alogical, and outside of conscious awareness (Schore, 2003). In fact, it seems to involve a mutual and reciprocal "right brain to right brain" communication between the mother and her infant, an "interactive 'transfer of affect' between the right brains of the members of the mother–infant . . . dyads" (Schore, 2000, p. 9). According to Lewis et al. (2000), "the limbic brain is another delicate physical apparatus that specializes in detecting and analyzing just one part of the physical world—the internal state of [others]" (p. 62). Cued by a variety of implicit indexes of affect states—facial expression, gesture, quality of vocalization, eye contact, inflection, rhythm, prosody, and so forth—the mother's limbic brain system apperceives the infant's affective state and communicates it via her own affectivity back to the limbic brain of the infant. Siegel (2001) suggests, "The sharing of nonverbal signals creates a joining of two minds at a basic level of 'primary' emotions. [In this way] each person may come to 'feel felt' by the other" (p. 78), a fundamental condition for the achievement of a secure attachment and for the support and consolidation of the real self.

Attunement and Affect Regulation

A parent who is attuned to the affect states of the infant can amplify or modulate that child's emotional experiences. For example, Beebe and Lachmann (1988a, 1988b, 1994) describe studies of mothers and infants in which both members of the dyad, through mutual facial mirroring, increased or decreased their levels of engagement and their degrees of positive affect. The researchers suggest (Beebe and Lachmann, 1994) that "this matching provides each partner with a behavioral basis for knowing and entering into the other's changing feeling state" (p. 136).

It is possible for the parent to amplify positive states too much. For example, it has been determined that the parent can contribute to the infant's arousal level through exaggerated mirroring responses, reflecting an incrementally intensified affective experience (Beebe and Lachmann, 1994). In such a case, the child becomes overstimulated and hyperaroused. However, positive states can be modulated so excessively that the child becomes emotionally inhibited.

Optimally, though, the mother's mirroring of positive feelings, such as pleasure, joy, excitement, and curiosity, may not only help the child delineate feeling states but also tend to heighten arousal and support a more robust experience of the feeling.

Responses of incrementally decreased affectivity may serve to facilitate the down regulation of excessive arousal. A child who is hyperaroused or overstimulated or is experiencing such dysphoric feelings as fear, anxiety, or sadness can be comforted and soothed by the parent's sensitive attunement to such affect states. For instance, we recently witnessed at a grocery store a mother talking to her obviously distressed son, probably 3 or 4 years old. "Oh, yes, I see you're upset. It's okay. Mommy will help. It's okay. Ohhh, it's okay. You can calm down . . . " And in a brief time, he did.

As Stern (1985) has said, an infant seeks an optimal level of excitation: the highest level that is still pleasurable. Displeasure occurs above a certain level of excitation, and disinterest, below a certain level. The range of excitation varies across infants, with each playing an active role in the regulation of excitation—gaze aversion helps to diminish the level of stimulation, and gaze resumption and facial behaviors invite higher levels of stimulation. Field (1981) has noted that gaze aversion on the part of the infant is not only a form of self-regulation but also an act that typically initiates a mutual process of regulation. Beebe and Lachmann (1994) support this point:

> If the mother can use the infant's gaze away to lower her level of stimulation while the infant is reregulating his arousal, and if the infant can likewise use the mother's lowering of stimulation so that he then looks back at her, adequate mutual regulation will be established. (p. 139)

In this case, the mother responds as if she were thinking, "I see that you need to look away. Okay, I'll look away too so that you can calm down."

Both Sroufe (1996) and Schore (2000) have considered affect regulation a central component to the attachment process. In Schore's words, "attachment represents dyadic (interactive) regulation of emotion. The baby becomes attached to the psychobiologically attuned regulating primary caregiver who not only minimizes negative affect but also maximizes opportunities for positive affect" (p. 8). The infant establishes a secure emotional attachment to the extent that dyadic regulation of affect occurs with the caregiver. This regulation of affect includes both the up-regulating joy system as well as the down-regulating system that soothes.

Schore (2000) goes on to say that brain morphology is changed as a result of this interactive process of affect regulation: "The emotion communicating transactions within the attachment relationship are instrumental to the experience-dependent maturation of the developing brain" (p. 8). Specifically, it is the limbic system and the right orbitofrontal cortex that have been identified as the neurobiological site of affect regulation (Lewis et al., 2000; Schore, 1994, 2000, 2003; Siegel, 1999, 2001); the orbitofrontal system, then, is "an executive of limbic arousal" (Schore, 2003, p. 43).

The child learns affect regulation and frustration tolerance in the context of a sufficiently secure attachment relationship, in which the attachment figure can attune to the child's affective experience and help the child to down-regulate when frustrated, angry, anxious, or otherwise hyperaroused. Interactions such as these, which are relationally mediated, develop in the child a capacity to adaptively manage the inevitable affective ups and downs of life. At a neurobiological level, "the right brain stores an internal working model of the attachment relationship that encodes strategies of affect regulation that maintain basic regulation and positive affect even in the face of environmental challenge" (Schore, 2003, p. 45). So experience-dependent, affect-regulating cortical circuits, formed early in life, establish the probability (or, in certain cases, the improbability) that the right orbitofrontal cortex will be activated under conditions of high arousal.

Attunement and Internal Representations of Self and Others

There is evidence that the quality of the attunement relationship influences the process of attachment, by shaping how representations of the self and others are internalized and incorporated into a template of relationships (Stern, 1985). These images of the self and of others color one's self-perception and that of other people and hence shape expectations for the relationship. Not surprisingly, Beebe and Lachmann (1994) suggest that such "representations result from interactions. We hold a dynamic process model of representations in which a schema is constructed of the expected moment-to-moment interplay of the two partners" (p. 131). These internal relational models, which form out of consciousness in the first 18 months, define a person's views of self, others, and relationships. A child whose mother has provided sufficiently accurate and consistent attunement over time is likely to develop a self-representation that is valued, a representation of others as being interested in him or her and basically benign, and an anticipation of mutual and reciprocal interaction with others.

Beebe and Lachmann (1994) propose further that the development of such relationship templates is influenced most robustly through the interchange of fully expressed affect between mother and child—an intensely joyful full gape smile or a crying face, for example. These "interaction structures are organized through heightened affective moments, in which the infant experiences a powerful state transformation" (p. 147). Both the content and the affective coloration of developing internal models of relationships are significantly influenced by moments of high affective charge.

The experience of being known, informed by a good-enough attunement process, critically facilitates the infant's secure attachment to the mother. It also promotes the progressive development of the capacity for regulation of affect states. Finally, this attunement experience provides the relational environment for the evolution of positive internal representations of self, other, and relationships.

Attunement and the Real Self

An adequate attunement process ignites and supports the development of the real self of the infant. Mahler (1968) suggests that the mother's availability "facilitates the optimal unfolding of innate potentialities" (p. 49) and that "the primary method of identity formation consists of mutual reflection" (p. 19). Sander (2000) calls this a *recognition process*: "Recognition refers to a moment . . . in which one comes to know oneself as being known by another, a moment of shared awareness" (p. 14). Lyons-Ruth (2000) elaborates that "the task of coming to know oneself through the way one experiences being known, lies at the heart of self-organization" (p. 89). Siegel's notion of "feeling felt" (1999) and Fonagy's concept of awareness of "a mind with my mind in mind" (2001b) are also ways of describing a connection that supports self-clarification and self-consolidation. Indeed, these are different ways to describe a process through which the self, in the experience of repetitive moments of shared affect exchange with the parent, is ignited into awareness.

Similarly, Masterson (1976, 1981, 1985, 2000) posits that the emergence and evolution of the real self are contingent on the mother's ability to provide the emotional conditions for secure attachment and, eventually, support for age-appropriate psychological separation. Optimally, the mother provides many opportunities for real-self (i.e., authentic) experience and expression and few where regression or false-self (i.e., defensive) adaptations are necessary. Authentic expression is the condition of attachment that is internalized and enacted in life; the resulting internal relational model derives from the caregiver's way of supporting and encouraging the experience and expression of the real self. In other words, genetic, temperamental, and situational factors aside, basic support and encouragement for the development of the infant's real self come from the relationship with the primary caregiver. More simply, the experience and expression of the real self form the fruit of a healthy attachment relationship, the organic expression of a good-enough relational environment.

DISRUPTION–REPAIR CYCLE

The experience of accurate attunement alone is not sufficient for the ignition and evolution of a healthy, autonomous self. Several theorists (among them, Hoffman, Marvin, Cooper, and Powell, 2006; Schore, 1999b; Siegel, 2001; Tronick, 1989) have suggested that optimal development is built on repeated disruptions of an attuned relationship, which is then followed by repair. This disruption–repair cycle, in which the mother's inevitable occasional misattunements to the infant are satisfactorily "repaired," is critical to the achievement of a stable, coherent sense of self and effective autonomous affect regulation in that it gives the infant the opportunity to develop an internal model of repair. Even in the best of circumstances, there will be disruptions of connection between infant and caregiver; all mothers are, at times tired, stressed, preoccupied, or simply confounded. In optimal conditions, they respond promptly enough and are successful enough most of the time. As the cycle of occasional failure and then success is repeated over and over again, "the infant develops a representation of himself or herself as effective, of his or her interactions as positive and reparable, and of the caretaker as reliable and trustworthy" (Tronick, 1989, p. 116).

In other words, a model of interactive repair is internalized by the infant and becomes available for the management and attenuation of experiences disruptive to the attachment relationship. Although the inevitable miscoordinated communications or interactive errors may well evoke anxiety and fear about not being connected, these feelings can be experienced as transient, tolerable, and manageable by the securely attached infant.

It is this recurrent disruption–repair interaction that prepares the self for healthy separation. Experiences of misattunement and the consequent relational ruptures are prototypical separation experiences for the infant (Tronick, 1989). As such, they afford opportunities for the development of autonomous affect regulation and are gradually internalized as a model of rupture and repair that is available for the management of future separation experiences.

The infant who has experienced sufficiently accurate and consistent attunement and who has internalized a model of rupture and repair is likely to establish a secure attachment—and that infant will also have a relatively secure sense that communication and connection with others are possible. These, then, provide a secure base from which the developing child can gradually separate and individuate:

> Provided the parent is known to be accessible and will be responsive when called upon, a healthy child feels secure enough to explore. At first these explorations are limited both in time and space. Around the middle of the third year, however, a secure child begins to become confident enough to increase time and distance away—first to half days and later to whole days. As he grows into adolescence, his excursions are extended to weeks or months, but a secure home base remains indispensable nonetheless for optimal functioning and mental health. (Bowlby, 1988, p. 122)

ATTACHMENT AND NONATTACHMENT EXPERIENCES

Because no parent can always be perfectly attuned, there will be times when the child "feels felt" and times when she or he does not; experiences of attunement alternate with experiences of misattunement. Therefore, there are two distinct experiences of self and other in relationship—an attachment experience and a nonattachment experience (Klein, 1998), or an experience of attachment and an experience of disrupted attachment.

When the mother is experienced as frustrating or absent, the child experiences anxiety about the trustworthiness of the relationship. If secure attachment has afforded the child a secure emotional base and the expectation of repair, he or she experiences the anxiety of disrupted attachment as being tolerable and transient, as a 3-year-old explained to his grandmother: "I was naughty, but now I'm okay. I'm happy. We are okay."

In this kind of healthy development, the two disparate experiences of self and other blend into one integrated and coherent internal model of relationships that includes both attachment and nonattachment experiences. Both the self-representation and the representation of the other include positive and negative characteristics, gratifying and frustrating traits, satisfying and disappointing behaviors. But there is also the sense that both the self and the other are predominantly good and that the relationship between them is durable. In other words, these are whole object relations.

Object Relations Units

Theorists have described these internalized templates, the child's experience of who others are, who he or she is, and what makes relationships work, in different terms and from slightly differing points of view. Bowlby (1988) calls them "internal working models of self and attachment figure in interaction" (p. 171), whereas Stern (1985) refers to "representations of interactions that have been generalized" (p. 97). Kernberg (1976) writes of "internalized object relations represented by a certain affect, object-representation, and self-representation" (p. 29). Similarly, Masterson (1976) refers to these models of relationship as internal "object relations units" (p. 57), each of which comprises a self-representation, an object representation, and an affective experience linking the two.

Whatever they are called, these templates reflect the internalized conditions of attachment, the "deals," conscious or not, that are struck with the mother to ensure attachment (Klein, 1998). Optimally, the mother has attuned relatively consistently to the real self of the child such that attachment is ensured as long as the child is expressing his or her real self. But not every mother can do this; thus, attachment strategies may be required that disallow real-self experience. Common strategies include passivity, compliance, dependence, overachievement, idealization of the mother and deference to her wishes, or the maintenance of a safe distance. In other words, attachment may be possible in some cases but at the cost of authenticity. We examine these situations in detail in the next chapter.

In the best of circumstances, then, the self of the child emerges from infancy with an internal working model of relationships in which the object acknowledges, affirms, approves of, cares for, and is protective of the child. Correspondingly, the self-representation of the child with an optimal developmental experience feels loved and valued. Furthermore, this internal relational paradigm contains a model of rupture and repair that results in the expectation that misattunements and other forms of interpersonal disruption will promptly be repaired. Finally, this child's internal working model is supportive and encouraging of real-self experience; the internal object acknowledges, affirms, and applauds the expression of the real self. The recursive self system begins its life.

These internal working models of relationships are formed very early in life, and largely out of consciousness. They are products of *implicit procedural learning*, and they are encoded in *implicit procedural memory* (Lyons-Ruth, 1998; Lyons-Ruth et al., 1998). *Explicit semantic memory*, what we usually mean by "memory," is the symbolic representation of facts, events, or ideas in language. *Implicit procedural memory* is the "in your bones" memory; the right-brain memory; memory that is preverbal, preconceptual, prereflective, and preconscious; the sort that enables you to get on a bicycle after many years and still know how to ride. *Implicit relational memory* is the operational memory of the implicit procedures of attachment—how to "be" with others, how to relate, how to attach. Lyons-Ruth (2001) refers to implicit procedural memory as a nonconscious "knowing how," in contrast to "knowing what." In the case of relational memory, it is a procedural knowing how one has to be to connect with and relate to others. Schore (2003), writing of internal relationship schemas, states from a psychoneurobiological perspective, "Affective experiences with caregivers are thus imprinted and stored in early-forming procedural memory in the orbital prefrontal system and its cortical and subcortical connections as interactive representations" (p. 20). Because implicit relational memory is not conscious, it is activated reflexively, often nonverbally, and usually without awareness of the underlying attachment motive. So, our internal object relations units, working models of relationships, operate largely out of our awareness as well.

It is notable that there is some evidence that these object relations units, these internal working models of relationship, persist over time. For instance, Lyons-Ruth (1991) and Berlin and Cassidy (1999) cite studies suggesting that attachment behaviors in infancy and early toddlerhood are predictive of behaviors in preschool. In fact, the demonstrated association of infant–parent attachment with parenting styles and with adult affectional relationships provides evidence that these internal models may endure over the entire life span (Berlin and Cassidy, 1999). This is not to suggest that they cannot be changed. But the tenacity of these models and their manifestations in relationships can be seen in everyday life and in psychotherapy; we discuss the implications of this persistence in following chapters.

THE CAPACITIES OF THE REAL SELF

In the course of normal development, the real self is sufficiently supported and sufficiently enjoyed such that it can be safely experienced and expressed. Under those circumstances, as Masterson (1985, 1988) suggests, the capacities of the real self can develop. These include

1. the capacity to experience deeply a wide range of feelings, both pleasant and unpleasant;
2. the capacity to expect appropriate entitlements, such as experiences of mastery and pleasure;
3. the capacity for self-activation and self-assertion, including the ability to identify one's own unique individuality, wishes, dreams, and goals and to be assertive in expressing them autonomously;
4. the capacity for the acknowledgment of self-esteem, because one cannot always depend on others to shore up one's self-esteem;
5. the ability to soothe painful affects;
6. the ability to make and follow through with commitments, despite obstacles or setbacks;
7. the capacity for creativity, the ability to be creative in altering old, familiar patterns of living and replacing them with new and more successful ones;
8. the capacity for intimacy, which requires the capability of entering into a close and open relationship with another person with a minimal experience of abandonment or engulfment;
9. the ability to be alone, to be alone without feeling abandoned; and
10. continuity of self, the capacity to recognize that the real self persists over time and circumstance (Masterson, 1988, pp. 42–46).

REFLECTIVE FUNCTION

We believe that reflective function, or *mentalization* (Fonagy, 2001b; Fonagy and Target, 1996a, 1996b, 1997), may be considered an additional capacity of the self. According to Fonagy, Gergely, Jurist, and Target (2002),

> reflective function . . . is the developmental acquisition that permits children to respond not only to another person's behavior, but to the children's conception of others' beliefs, feelings, attitudes, desires, hopes, knowledge, imagination, pretense, deceit, intentions, plans, and so on. . . . By doing this, children make people's behavior meaningful and predictable. (p. 24)

Siegel (2001) refers to *mindsight*, "the capacity of one mind to 'perceive' or create representations of the mind of oneself or of another" (p. 82). In short, reflective function is the capacity to imagine and recognize the reality of separate minds. As it becomes available, the process of reflection gives the normally developing child awareness of and some access to the inner worlds of others—the fact that other people do have internal worlds and that these are made up of feelings, desires, attitudes, beliefs, and intentions. The child can enter into the experience of another; the other's behavior becomes more meaningful and more predictable, and empathy then becomes a possibility.

Reflective function also enables the child to reflect on his or her own experience in an effort to understand it and to make reasoned decisions based on this understanding, rather than just to react to it unreflectively. Our nearly 5-year-old grandson recently asked his aunt if she was going to have a second baby. When she said that she probably would sometime, he replied, "You better think twice about it, because since my sister came, I don't get as much attention." In terms of reflective function, he demonstrated the capacity to experience his disappointment about less attention, reflect on his feelings, generalize them to this new situation with his 3-month-old cousin, ask an interested question of his aunt, make a self-assertive comment to her that reflected his own experience, and do so in a self-regulated fashion. (Wish we could do as well!)

Fonagy and Target (1996b) have proposed four reasons that reflective function is of such significance. First, it enables the child to understand others' behaviors in terms of thoughts and feelings and thus render them meaningful. Second, reflective function enables the child to distinguish the difference between inner reality and outer reality. That is, the behavior of another person toward the child is not necessarily a reflection of the reality of that child. For example, a critical response to a child does not mean that the child is bad; rather, the other's behavior might well be a function of an emotional state quite independent of anything having to do with the child (e.g., "Mom is having a bad day"). Third, communication with others is severely limited without the capacity for reflective function because conversation is a collaborative process that depends on an awareness of the perspective of the other person. Fourth, reflective function is requisite to a richer and more meaningful interpersonal life—to a richer and more meaningful life in general—because the quality of relational experiences imbues life with meaning and satisfaction.

But infants are not born with this capacity to reflect on the dynamic complexities of internal affective experience, nor are they aware of the independent psychological experience of other people. These capacities are learned in the context of an attachment sufficiently secure that it acknowledges and appreciates the existence of separate minds (as opposed to one that insists on one-mindedness as the condition of attachment) and that allows for self-experience and self-clarification in the safety of that relationship. Schore (2003) says that these capacities develop neurobiologically through "the emergence, at 18 months, of a 'reflective self'" (p. 21), which depends on the maturation of the cerebral cortex at about that time.

According to Fonagy and Target (1996a, 1996b), reflective function is learned in a secure relationship with an attachment figure who, in his or her own attunement to the affective experience of the child, helps the child to develop "a theory of mind." Fonagy, Target, and Gergely (2000) suggest,

> The parents' capacity to observe the child's mind facilitates the child's general understanding of minds through the mediation of secure attachment, [because] a secure attachment relationship provides a congenial context for the child to explore the mind of the caregiver, and in this way to learn about minds. (p. 5)

For instance, consider the following exchange, between a child and mother:

CHILD: Are you mad at me, Mommy, or at Karin? Or are you mad at both of us? Why?

MOMMY: Yes, I am—at both of you. It's frustrating for me when I am on the phone and you keep calling my name. Please wait until I get off.

CHILD: But I get mad when you talk on the phone.

MOMMY: I know. Thanks for telling me, but I would like you to wait until I finish my phone call.

The mother transmits her belief that the child's behavior is a reflection of feelings, thoughts, attitudes, perceptions, and desires; the child becomes aware, implicitly or explicitly, of her acknowledgment of him as a thinking, feeling, intentional being. By focusing on the subjective facet of the dyadic experience, the parent communicates the dual sense that the internal world is important privately and that it can be shared with others as well. The repetition of such relationally mediated procedures builds into the self an ability to reflect on internal experience and the internal experience of others. In the words of Target (2001), "the child depends on the attachment figure to discover his own subjectivity" (p. 4). It is not surprising, then, that attachment security with the mother is a robust predictor of effective reflective function at later ages (Fonagy, 2001a, 2001b; Target, 2001).

Because a securely attached relationship allows for differences to be experienced and expressed, it demonstrates to the child, in both attitude and behavior, an acceptance of differing cognitive, affective, and perceptual experiences. Explicitly or implicitly, the caregiver communicates, "I can see that you are happy, excited, angry, afraid, sad, worried, etc., and that is okay." This is another way that the sense of "feeling felt" (Siegel, 2001) is induced in the child, that the experience and expression of the real self is supported, and that the capacity for self-reflection is enhanced.

In the same way, children learn to reflect on the experience of others—an equally important achievement. The parent lets the child know how she feels and why, and she makes herself available to talk about it and work things out. When the parent communicates this attitude, whether implicitly or explicitly, the child develops a growing awareness of separate but interfaceable minds (Bretherton and Bates, 1979). In this ease with differences, reflective function becomes available for self-regulation and for healthy relationships in which differences are acknowledged and respected. But it is not always with ease that these differences are managed, because affect must be metabolized by the parent and returned in words understood by the child in moments that are safe enough to invite the child's experience (anger, fear, sadness, etc.) to be expressed and considered. (The nuances of these sorts of procedures are thoroughly explicated in *Parenting From the Inside Out* [Siegel and Hartzell, 2003].)

Other adaptive functions are dependent on early attachment experiences. According to Fonagy et al. (2002),

> there is unequivocal evidence from two decades of longitudinal research that secure attachment in infancy is strongly associated with the precocious development of a range of capacities that depend on interpretive or symbolic skills, such as exploration and play, intelligence and language ability, ego resilience and ego control, frustration tolerance, curiosity, self-recognition, social cognitive capacities, and so on. Attachment security foreshadows cognitive competence, exploratory skill, emotion regulation, communication style, and other outcomes. (p. 130)

Reality perception, for instance, develops in a relationship in which the immature mind of the child can make use of the mature mind of the mother. In a relationship of trust, questions can be asked, and reality can be defined without fear of relational rupture. The capacity to tolerate a realistic, complex view of others in turn diminishes the need for defenses that distort reality. Splitting, projection, projective identification, and denial are detrimental to the perception of reality and, for this reason, are maladaptive; the ability to tolerate a realistic view of others makes such wholesale defenses less necessary.

Consider another example: The ability to tolerate frustration and contain impulsive reactions is mediated by early attachment experience and its influence on the development of the right orbital prefrontal cortex. According to Schore (1994), the maturation of the orbitofrontal cortex, largely dependent on early attachment experience, enables "the auto-modulation of hyperactive behaviors and hyperaroused states" (p. 230). And the capacity for effective regulation of affect, both autonomously and in interaction with others, has been considered a by-product of a secure attachment (Fosha, 2000; Schore, 1994).

In moments of shared affectivity, both in pleasure and in the repair of painful disruption experiences, the self grows. In the safety of feeling seen and known and regulated by a trusted other, self capacities form and become self-activated. Relationally established, neurobiolgically wired, and recursively maintained, the healthy-enough self is being prepared for life.

But such ideal circumstances are not always available for developing children—so it was for Terri. In the next chapter, we describe the way that unfavorable conditions can influence development and painfully replicate themselves in later life.

NOTE

1. Throughout this book, *mother* will be used as a shorthand for *primary caregiver*.

2

Borderline Personality Disorder Development and the False Self

When development does not take place under optimal conditions, ideal outcomes may not be realized, and of course, it is the nonideal outcomes that psychotherapists usually end up dealing with. We do not suggest that insecure attachment is synonymous with psychopathology. We do contend, however, that all personality disorders reflect insecure attachment strategies and that they are the result of severe attachment and separation deviations. The attachment experience of a child with an inadequately attuned parent or with a parent who cannot engage constructively in disruption–repair experiences is likely to be less secure and reliable than that of more fortunate children, and an insecure attachment does not provide robust support for the experience and expression of the real self. It is also likely to encourage maladaptive internal working models of relationships and so limit the development of adaptive ego and relational capacities.

The *Diagnostic and Statistical Manual of Mental Disorders* (American Psychiatric Association, 1994, fourth edition; hereafter, *DSM–IV*) takes a primarily descriptive approach to diagnosis. Many psychotherapists, however, tend to think about psychopathology structurally. Klein (1989a) puts it,

> Each personality disorder has a unique intrapsychic structure, which the therapist should be able to map out. This internal, representational world consists of a host of internalized objects—both self and object representations—as well as the relationships between and among these objects—internalized object relationships. (p. 12)

Given the basis of the quality of internal images of the self and others and how they relate to each other, Masterson (1989, 2000) divides the

31

DSM–IV personality disorders into four categories—borderline, narcissistic, schizoid, and antisocial—each with a distinctive intrapsychic structure. He understands the narcissistic and related disorders to operate from an internal model in which mirroring, idealization, and adoration are the basis for feeling connected to another. People with schizoid disorders, fearful that closeness means being controlled or appropriated, maintain their attachments at a relatively safe, comfortable distance. In the antisocial personality disorders, the lack of attachment—emotional detachment from others—dictates relational style. And the child destined to develop a borderline disorder has internalized a paradigm of relationships in which helplessness, compliance, and clinging are the primary conditions of attachment. Masterson (1981, 1988, 1993, 2000) believes that different intervention strategies for each of the personality disorders are required for maximum effectiveness in psychotherapy. In this book, we focus on the borderline personality disorder.

CASE STUDY: TERRI

These structural considerations were on my mind as I (DDR) sat down with Terri for that first reunion session. I knew that she was now 22, unmarried, unemployed, and the mother of two boys. I knew that she had recently separated from Daniel, the father of her second child, that she was living on welfare with her sons, and that Daniel was also unemployed and had been subsisting on Terri's welfare benefits for the last year.

But what was she all about? What was important to her? What motivated her? What did she believe in? Who was she? I knew I would not be able to answer those questions right away, but I could ponder them in the context of what I already knew regarding her early history and what she told me of her recent years as our hour together unrolled.

RELEVANT FAMILY HISTORY AND PAST HISTORY

The youngest of three children, Terri was adopted at birth into an upper-middle-class family. The other two were boys (both biological children) and Terri's adoptive parents, who had longed for a daughter, were delighted by her arrival. They said that they considered her "quite special" for the first 2 years of her life but that, afterward, she had been an almost continuous source of frustration and disappointment. Terri was an insecure child and had suffered from severe separation fears. At the same time, she did not easily accept the conservative, restrictive, and achievement-oriented values of her family. In spite of her documented high intelligence, she did not consistently try in school, and she often failed to complete assignments. In her extracurricular activities, too—Campfire Girls, music and dance lessons—her interest waned rapidly after an initial period of enthusiasm.

Terri's view of it was that her mother was anxious and overprotective. Terri acknowledged that her mother meant well and was tenaciously committed to giving her children the love and the family life that they needed, to compensate for their early abandonment. But Terri experienced her mother as a primarily controlling woman who needed Terri to be dependent on her. When Terri didn't comply with these expectations, her mother turned to criticism and emotional withdrawal.

Terri's father was the source of warmth in the family, but he seemed to be controlled by his wife. He was a mostly ineffectual parent, reluctant to set limits for the children or impose expectations on them. But he was Terri's favored parent—partly because he expected little from her, aside from closeness—and she felt much affection for him. She was "Daddy's little girl" if she stayed close to him. And she looked to him for connection, comfort, and soothing—he was apparently her primary attachment figure.

According to Terri, both of her brothers were "good kids." They behaved themselves growing up and were successful in their lives; they had earned college degrees, married, and established themselves in respectable careers. Nonetheless, Terri always believed that her parents had been more emotionally invested in her than in her brothers, and she came to experience this as more of a burden than a benefit. It felt to her that their acceptance and approval were contingent on her closeness and compliance. This belief revealed the insecure conditions of attachment that Terri had internalized ("I have to stay close and do what they say").

Terri did graduate from high school, although it wasn't certain that she would until the very last minute. The day after commencement, she took off with a boyfriend. Thus began a painful 3-year odyssey as Terri moved from city to city following a series of exploitative men. She would make herself dependent on them and then leave them when she realized that they weren't going to take care of her after all. She abused drugs and sold them; she shoplifted and was arrested for it; she spent brief times in jail; she had two abortions and two babies; she never worked; she ended up on welfare. In desperation, she returned to her hometown, where her welfare caseworker arranged for her to attend a vocational school to develop clerical skills. The caseworker helped Terri find suitable care for her children and recommended psychotherapy as well, pointing out that the state would provide some modest funding for treatment. Terri had seen me several times during her tumultuous adolescence and had maintained occasional telephone contact since then. Now she called me again, and we arranged for weekly psychotherapy.

PRESENTING COMPLAINT

Terri wasn't really thinking in terms of goals when she came in for that first session. She had concerns, though. She knew that she had a pattern of "screwing things up" when they started to go well. She knew that she was too dependent—she got panicky when other people weren't around, but when they were around, she let them take her over, leaving her with no motivation or sense of competence of her own. She knew that her own fears kept her from doing her best by her kids; in fact, she didn't even really know what was best for her or what really mattered to her. Her life was aimless. Terri's own summation of herself was that she had no self-esteem.

This was a realistic appraisal, but it didn't tell us much about how this had come to pass, let alone how to proceed. Terri was a bright and talented person who grew up within the structure, safety, and apparent security of a conservative upper-middle-class family. Yet, it was clear that the problems of attachment and separation that brought Terri to my waiting room—the aimlessness, the dependency, the self-destructiveness, the lack of self-esteem—were characteristic structural and behavioral reflections of the developmental detour called *borderline personality disorder*. What had gone wrong?

INSECURE ATTACHMENT AND BORDERLINE PERSONALITY DISORDER

Bateman and Fonagy (2004), Fonagy (2000, 2001a), Fonagy et al. (2000), and Dozier, Stovall, and Albus (1999) have suggested that personality disorders in general and the borderline personality disorder in particular are fundamentally attachment disorders. Our own theoretical interest lies in the influence of attachment vicissitudes on object relations. The borderline disorder may be seen as a form of insecure attachment that has not been reliable enough to support a secure separation and individuation process. The patterns of behavior that develop under such circumstances and later appear as characteristically "borderline" reflect early strategies (successful or not) by which an insecurely attached infant attempts to reestablish an interrupted attachment and regain access, although at some cost, to its soothing and protective attributes. A story such as Terri's lets us investigate how a severely insecure attachment may underlie the development of the borderline personality disorder.

Attachment insecurity in borderline personality disorders derives in part from an inversion of the healthy attachment paradigm. The primary caregiver's agenda takes precedence over the needs of the child, requiring that the child relinquish self-initiative and spontaneity and instead resonate with the parent's needs and expectations (Masterson, 1976, 1981). That is, the child with a nascent borderline personality disorder is forced to attune to the mother and follow her lead to stay connected. The result is an attachment experience that is not secure enough—that is too conditional—to support the emergence and flowering of the child's real self.

The mother who cannot attune regularly to the real-self experience of her child is also likely not to be able to provide consistent repair experiences following relational disruptions. Her child will not internalize the expectation or experience that reunion (i.e., restoration of the attachment) will occur after rupture. A child for whom attachment is insecure is likely to find it hard to separate psychologically from the mother and develop a clearly and reliably individuated sense of self. He or she remains hypervulnerable to threats to attachment posed by rejection, separation, abandonment, self-activation, and even awareness of the needs of the self. Misattunements and other manifestations of separateness, instead of being experienced as transient, tolerable, and manageable, are experienced as permanent and intolerable and are likely to plunge the borderline patient into severe anxiety, depression, or despair (Klein, 1998). Relational repair is an enactment of the survival-driven need to stay attached, but for the borderline-disordered person, it comes at a cost. If the only way for the child to reconnect after the disruption of a relationship is to focus on the mother and comply with her wishes, the child's own feelings and urges must be ignored.

The mothers of these children are rarely deliberate in their encouragement of dependence and passivity. Often, the mother may be aware of the disruption herself and share with her child the need to restore connection. But her own emotional limitations make it hard for her to find a way to manage this, short of demanding compliance from the child. Many of these mothers are painfully vulnerable to separation themselves. The discomfort of their own abandonment feelings when a child begins to individuate is precisely why they press so hard for reconciliation, but it is a reconciliation on the mother's own terms. For the child, this means that separation and authentic self-expression must be avoided, and when reattachment occurs, it is not in the context of the child's real self. Distress is calmed, and the dysregulated self of the child is regulated, but with each occurrence, the brain is more firmly wired for an alive but second-rate attachment. Although the borderline attachment is forming, the self of the child is being sacrificed.

SEPARATION SENSITIVITY

People with personality disorders experience characteristic attachment-related vulnerabilities. Cooper, Hoffman, Powell, and Marvin (2005) identified three such distinct vulnerabilities, based on Masterson's (1981, 1993, 2000) and Klein's (1989d) differential diagnoses of the personality disorders:

1. *separation sensitive,* which in a rigid and pervasive form is border-line personality disorder;
2. *esteem sensitive,* which in a rigid and pervasive form is narcissistic personality disorder; and
3. *safety sensitive,* which in a rigid and pervasive form is schizoid personality disorder.

Furthermore, Cooper et al. (2005) contend,

> Safety-sensitive persons have learned that the cost of being connected in a relationship is to abandon one's sense of self and be swallowed up by the other. On the other hand, the cost of having a sense of self is to be isolated. Since neither is bearable, individuals who are safety sensitive are constantly seeking a compromise between the two. However, the compromise keeps them neither in nor out of relationship and therefore is itself not satisfying. (p. 10)

In other words, the schizoid person must be neither too close nor too far interpersonally. This is what Klein (1995) and Masterson (2000) have referred to as the "schizoid dilemma."

In contrast, esteem-sensitive people fear that "who they are as a person is not enough to make them lovable. Therefore, to protect themselves from abandonment they must prove that they are special through performance and achievement" (Cooper et al., 2005, p. 10). And separation-sensitive individuals "believe that to avoid abandonment, they must focus on what others want, need, and feel, while disavowing their own wants, needs and feelings. The underlying belief is that if they act on their own behalf, they will be abandoned" (p. 10).

Terri poignantly articulated borderline separation sensitivity: "I can't stand to be alone. So I've gone from one relationship to another. And I've never broken up with anyone until there was somebody else there." She experienced separateness as being so painful that she reflexively managed to avoid being without a relationship.

ABANDONMENT DEPRESSION

Masterson (1976, 1981, 2000) gives a name to the terrible feeling that Terri called "I can't stand being alone" and that she tried so hard to avoid: *Abandonment depression* is an underlying complex of the seemingly catastrophic affects that go with abandonment. It is repeatedly triggered by real or imagined separations or by experiences or expressions of the real self that, based on expectations and experience (encoded in the internal relational models), herald disruptions of attachment (Masterson, 1976, 1981).

In the internal world of a child like Terri, expression of the real self results in punishment or the withdrawal of emotional support—in either case, there is a loss of connection to the object. And this loss, without the reliable expectation of repair, is felt as being intolerably painful.

> In the throes of the abandonment depression, a person will feel that part of his very self is lost or cut off from the supplies necessary to sustain life. Many patients describe this in graphic physical terms, such as losing an arm or leg, being deprived of oxygen, or being drained of blood. (Masterson, 1988, p. 62)

Siegel (1999) notes that "these dreaded states are not merely uncomfortable and disliked; they can feel like a black hole, a bottomless pit of despair, in which the self is lost for what seems to be forever" (p. 291).

The abandonment depression is the "underhum" of the borderline child's experience. Such a child or borderline adult already struggles with affect regulation and handles it by whatever means come to hand—usually by maintaining or reestablishing attachment through nonconscious, nonvolitional avoidance of the experience and expression of the real self or, failing at that, by rage and externalization. In fact, the effort to regulate or modulate the intensity of the catastrophic abandonment affects may be enacted as the dominant theme of life.

To casual observation, Terri did not look depressed, but her behavior revealed the underlying abandonment depression. She protected herself from all but the slightest brushes with it, by her driven involvement in one relationship after another. Even a day or two between boyfriends was unusual for Terri, who experienced the 6 days after her separation from Daniel as a noteworthy experience of "living on my own." She always mobilized a connection with a new person immediately following the loss of a relationship, so she very seldom experienced real dysphoria. But on the rare occasions that she could find no one to cling to, she plunged into an awareness of intolerable aloneness and despair and would phone me incessantly looking for the reassurance and help that, she hoped, would soothe her terrifying anguish.

MALADAPTIVE DEFENSES

People with borderline personality disorders have developed, from earliest childhood, a constellation of habitual defenses designed to maintain attachment and thereby ward off abandonment depression. The primary motivation for defense in these people is the maintenance of attachment and affect regulation (avoidance of the abandonment depression), but the defenses that they typically enlist tend to be maladaptive in that they inhibit or disallow the experience or expression of the real self.

According to Masterson (1976, 1981), children exposed to abandonment during the first 3 years of life will do whatever they must to maintain attachment and so protect themselves against the terror of abandonment. These measures depend on the contingencies of their early attachment experiences and may in fact develop and support a false self to ward off the abandonment depression. But they come at the cost of growth and adaptation because the potential capacities of the self are impaired (Masterson, 1988, p. 75).

Some children, for example, become passive, avoiding self-assertion so as not to antagonize the attachment figure. Some learn to comply with the perceived expectations of others at the expense of their own autonomous needs. Some cling dependently or maintain helplessness, if doing so is what the parent requires to keep herself available. In this way, threatened children maintain attachment or solicit it and so cause the dreaded specter of abandonment and its related affects to recede, temporarily at least. But these are defensive postures that require that the child overinvest in the other at the cost of real self-expression and real self-development. They are attachment-driven, nonconscious, avolitional procedures that preclude the possibility of real-self development and so destine the child to a life with limited prospects for meaning and enrichment.

Early in her treatment, Terri expressed what she saw as a dilemma: "If I tell Daniel that I need him to get a job, I'll be alone for sure. What would I do then?" The terrifying angst that followed that thought drove her to suppress the self-assertive idea of learning to support herself: "When Daniel loves me, it's because I do whatever he wants," she said on another occasion. "I know that, but I do it anyway. What's wrong with me?"

What was "wrong" with her was that she had learned that it was clinging and compliant relationships that best protected her from abandonment and her underlying abandonment depression, and she applied that expectation to her relationships with men. But the price that she paid for this false sense of security was high, because her natural and necessary capacity for assertion had to be suppressed, which undermined her real self.

THE TRIAD OF THE DISORDERS OF THE SELF

The fundamental dynamic of borderline personality disorder, as Masterson (1981, 1993) sees it, is the "disorders of the self triad." Any experience or expression of the real self—including initiative, perseverance, sticking up for one's self in a conflict, and even participation in therapy—will evoke separation anxiety or an abandonment depression; the experience is followed by defenses that mute the misery of the ensuing depression and anxiety. Succinctly stated, self-activation leads to an abandonment experience, which leads to defense. This sequence can be seen repeatedly in the treatment hour, and it haunts the daily lives of borderline patients.

Jenny entered psychotherapy at the age of 28 because of chronic fearfulness. She was the mother of a 7-year-old girl, married, and employed full-time in a clerical position, but her anxieties were increasingly constricting her life. Her agoraphobia was interfering with her job, and she was concerned about her dependence on her husband. As she put it in her first session, "I feel tense almost all the time. But it's worse when I'm alone." Later she added, "I don't think I've ever been happy. I've always been nervous, a worrier. I was reinforced for being this little ball of fluff. I'm tired of being the weak one with all these problems."

One day she talked about some frustrating responsibilities at home and her anxiety about impending changes at work. Then she went on:

> Yesterday I went downtown for my boss and felt fine. And last weekend I ran all kinds of errands all over town and felt comfortable. This was the first time I've forced myself to do that in ages. And last night I took the dog for a long walk and felt good. I'm really doing quite a bit better.

She was able here to reflect on her feelings, describing her efforts to confront her separation fears and acknowledging these efforts realistically. This was an activation of her real self, and for a while, she was able to tolerate it without defense. But her comfort didn't last long.

> But I feel like I've got too much in my head this week with Rob [her husband] so busy with work and getting home later than usual. And there are all these piddly things that have to be done. I feel kind of overwhelmed and depressed about it.

She started to cry as the first wisps of the abandonment depression emerged. She went on,

> I'm really looking forward to this weekend and having Rob home. Last night I heard these sirens just before I went to bed and saw the paramedics drive up to the house across the street. It gave me this creepy feeling, like something bad might happen to me, and only Becky [her daughter] would be here. What would I do?

Here Jenny was still responding to her feelings, but she was no longer reflecting on them in an effort to understand them better and manage them more adaptively—that is, she was no longer self-activating. Instead, she was acting out her feelings of helplessness. She identified defensively with her helpless, passive, dependent self-representation in the implicit hope that this would activate a sympathetic and caretaking response from the therapist.

This is how the triad of the disorders of the self operates. Jenny's confrontation of her fears was an activation of her real self, but this experience evoked depression, against which she defended herself by behaving as if she were helpless. To feel helpless is not in itself defensive, of course, and may be an experience of the real self. But Jenny's effort to solicit caretaking as if she actually were helpless, when in fact she had just demonstrated to herself that she was not, was a defensive avoidance of affect, not an authentic engagement with it.

Of course, such behavior is neither volitional nor conscious; it is a function of implicit relational knowledge, a reflexive and survival-driven effort to regulate affect by maintaining or reestablishing a connection with the object. As we demonstrate later, effective intervention requires that the therapist and patient identify and curtail the maladaptive defenses and recognize the purpose they serve in the context of the triad of the disorders of the self. Ultimately, if all goes well, the patient will achieve more adaptive means of managing unpleasant feeling states than through this sequence of autonomy, depression, and defense.

SPLIT OBJECT RELATIONS UNITS AND SPLITTING

According to Masterson (1976, 1981, 2000), a personality-disordered individual operates not with the integrated internal model of relationships characteristic of other intrapsychic organizations but with two distinct models. These reflect the experiences of attachment and disrupted attachment that the person has internalized. Psychologically healthy people have internal models of relationships that are procedural encodings of a self and an object representation in interaction, along with the affective tone that characterizes the interactional experience. This is true for borderline-disordered people as well. But because their experiences of attachment—specifically, its lack thereof—have not been securely integrated by the reliable alternation of disruption and repair, two separate models are internalized—one of self and other in attachment and one of self and other when attachment is disrupted—each with its own distinctive affective tone. Kernberg (1976), describing this phenomenon from an object relations point of view, refers to

the buildup of dyadic or bipolar intrapsychic representations (self- and object-images) as reflections of the original infant-mother relationship. . . . What is important is the essentially dyadic or bipolar nature of the internalization within which each unit of self- and object-image is established in a particular affective context. (p. 57)

Masterson (1976, 1981, 1993, 2000) calls these unintegrated represen- tational models of relationships *split object relations units*. Masterson's elaboration of the split object relations units in the borderline personality disorders articulates the connection between attachment disturbance and relational phenomena. He calls one part of the split the *rewarding object re- lations unit*. This includes (a) a self-representation that is good, dependent, and compliant and (b) a representation of a powerful object that rewards and supports clinging, dependent, regressive behavior; these are linked by the pleasant affects of feeling good and loved and being taken care. The corresponding *withdrawing object relations unit* includes (a) an object representation that withholds emotional support or attacks in response to separation or real self-expression and (b) a self-representation that is inadequate, bad, and repellent; these are linked by an affective connection of anger, frustration, and worthlessness.

These split object relations units are the poles of an absolute duality, and Masterson (1976, 2000) has suggested that borderline personality disorder patients oscillate, both in everyday life and in psychotherapy relationships, between the experience of the rewarding and withdrawing object relations units; of necessity, they relate to others on the basis of one or the other of these models of attachment. The rewarding internal object is not sort of good or mostly good but completely, absolutely, perfectly good. The withdrawing object is more than sometimes bad or even pri- marily bad; it is absolutely bad—evil. So at any given time, the borderline patient experiences the object as either totally good or totally bad, as an angel or a devil. Whereas most people have a complex combination of qualities both satisfying and unsatisfying, for the personality-disordered individual, there is no integration of the gratifying and frustrating attri- butes of others. And the self-experience is likewise either entirely positive or totally negative.

Although borderline patients are sometimes aware of these two states, they do not recognize them as being mutually exclusive, nor do they at- tempt to modulate or amalgamate them. This dynamic is seen frequently in the psychotherapy setting—for instance, when the patient makes a wrathful attack on the therapist in one session but returns to the next one acting as if that same therapist can do no wrong—with no appar- ent awareness of the remarkable discontinuity in one's own behavior. In Kernberg's words (1976),

the patients were conscious of the severe contradiction in their behavior; yet they would alternate between opposite strivings with a bland denial of the implications of this contradiction and showed what appeared to be a striking lack of concern over this "compartmentalization" of their mind. (p. 20)

This is the defense mechanism called *splitting*, which keeps these polarized experiences of self and other, sometimes remarkably, from being connected or related to each other in the experience of borderline patients. As Masterson (2000) puts it, splitting "keeps mutually contradictory affective states separated from each other; they remain conscious, but they do not influence one another. It also keeps separate the self and object representations associated with these states" (p. 69). So, perceptions and expectations derived from each relationship model color interactions.

> It is as if the patient has but two alternatives, viz., either to feel bad and abandoned (the withdrawing . . . unit), or to feel good (the rewarding . . . unit) at the cost of denial of reality and the acting out of self-destructive behavior. (Masterson, 1976, p. 63)

The splitting is displayed when the borderline person alternately projects self and object representations of the two object relations units onto others, without any apparent consciousness of their contradictory and unintegrated perceptions. According to Siegel (1999), these split experiences of object and self are wired neurobiologically over time; the Hebbian notion (Hebb, 1949) that what fires together, wires together, forms this split procedure.

Terri's description of her relationships demonstrated this kind of oscillation between clinging compliance (the rewarding object relations unit) and a rageful creation of crises (the withdrawing object relations unit). In her treatment, she began to think about why she repeatedly capitulated to the sexual demands of the men in her life: "I give sex for the temporary feeling of being loved. And I think I believe that they'll leave me if I don't." When the rewarding attachment unit was activated, she would cling obediently to the object, the man with whom she was trying to preserve a connection, and so avoid the experience of abandonment. As her internal templates of attachment to her primary objects played out in her adult relationships, this resulted in a temporary sense of personal value and a view of her partner as a caring, loving man who would take care of her.

But the slightest hint of rejection or abandonment in her relationships evoked in Terri a sense of terrible loss and personal worthlessness, against which she defended with rage and acting out. She would verbally and sometimes physically attack the man whom she perceived as rejecting her. Occasionally, this reached the point where outside intervention was needed—for example, when Terri's raging destruction of property and her threats against her partner frightened her neighbors into calling the police. When perceived rejection and the agony of abandonment activated the withdrawing object relations unit for Terri, she blamed the pain on the disappointing other, never connecting the pain with her early experience with the significant people in her life. (Or, she took the alternative option of reactivating the positive object relations unit in an attempt to coerce someone to take care of her and thereby reestablish attachment.) That is, by identifying and attacking a particular person as the cause of her excruciating feelings, she avoided experiencing the helplessness, fear, anxiety, depression, and rage that derived from her early family history and from the resultant internal world of rejecting and punitive objects.

Not surprisingly, these split relationship templates significantly affect the therapy relationship as well as everyday relationships.

> The transference which the borderline develops results from the operation of the split object relations unit—the rewarding . . . unit and the withdrawing . . . unit—each of which the patient proceeds alternatively to project onto the therapist. During those periods in which the patient projects the withdrawing . . . unit (with its . . . object representation of the withdrawing mother) onto the therapist, he perceives therapy as necessarily leading to feelings of abandonment, denies the reality of therapeutic benefit and activates the rewarding . . . unit . . . as a resistance. When projecting the rewarding . . . unit . . . onto the therapist, the patient "feels good" but . . . is usually found to be acting in a self-destructive manner. (Masterson, 1976, p. 63)

For example, in the early stages of therapy, Martha appeared to be quite meek and compliant. And she clearly respected and appreciated me, often expressing her gratitude for my "helping" her so much. However, as time went by and as I focused my confrontations on her difficulties with self-activation and her failure to take control of her life, I noticed that she occasionally seemed to flare at me, almost imperceptibly at first. Then one day, between sessions, I returned a phone call from her. She reported that she was feeling depressed and that she needed to talk to me. But because of time constraints, the conversation was brief, and I told her that we could talk further about her depression during her session scheduled later that week. The following day, I was in my office between sessions when I became aware of a commotion in our waiting room. Momentarily, the door from the reception area to the hall leading to my office was flung open and slammed shut. I rose from my chair to investigate but was met by an enraged Martha. She shrieked obscenities at me, berated me for cutting short our telephone conversation, and threw a five-dollar bill on the floor, shouting, "That should cover those f—ing five minutes on the phone yesterday!" And she exited, slamming doors and screaming as she did so.

I must admit that I dreaded the next session with her. But to my astonishment (and relief, I confess), she arrived for the session as if nothing had happened. She was her shy, demure self and was pleasant, agreeable, and compliant in response to my confrontations, and she was seemingly appreciative, even when I took up with her outrageous acting out just 2 days earlier. I shouldn't have been surprised, because an awareness of splitting, split object relations units, and the triad of the disorders of the self would predict the very thing that happened. My failure to resonate with Martha's rewarding unit projection by limiting our phone conversation was likely to be experienced as a breach in the relationship, stimulating abandonment feelings and activating the withdrawing unit as a defense against the resultant affective storm. But nevertheless, such experiences are often dysregulating for therapists, and I was no exception in this instance.

THE FALSE DEFENSIVE SELF

In his autobiographical *Telling Secrets*, Frederick Buechner (1991) says,

> There is the self we are born with, and then of course the world does its work. . . . The world sets in to making us into what the world would like us to be, and because we have to survive after all, we try to make our selves into something that we hope the world will like better than it apparently did the selves we originally were. That is the story of all our lives, needless to say, and in the process of living out that story, the original, shimmering self gets buried so deep that most of us end up hardly living out of it at all. (p. 45)

The infant who is becoming borderline disordered is predisposed, both by experience and by the neurological results of experience, to expect that emotional absence will follow investment in the self rather than in the caretaking other. As the child grows, new procedural systems evolve to strengthen the child's chance to maintain attachment and avoid abandonment or to react to the lost connection when it occurs. Instead of a self-system that actualizes the child's real self, a false defensive self develops whose implicit relational procedures actualize ways of keeping the dreaded abandonment depression at bay. Evolutionarily wired to go where there is connection and safety, the baby destined for borderline personality disorder is enabled to survive in this way.

Klein (1998) calls this kind of false defensive self a *magical attachment* because the implicit procedures that maintain attachment, formed prerationally and preconsciously, are based more on fantasy than on reality. At best, they provide an illusory, second-rate sense of well-being based on neglect and suppression of the real self.

When this illusion fails, an alternative set of defenses—the other half of the split object relations units—is called into play, and the implicit rageful procedures of nonattachment are enacted. The more alone, inadequate, and frightened the child feels, the more imperative it becomes to establish a connection or reconnection, and the only conceivable means for doing so is activation of the rewarding object relations unit or the withdrawing unit.

A depressed, helpless, clingy presentation is characteristic of the borderline patient who uses the rewarding object relations unit as a defense against the abandonment depression. Self-activation and separation strivings are terminated, and regressive and self-suppressing defenses are deployed. The patient is relieved of the separation anxiety and abandonment depression, at enormous cost to the development of the real self. Terri's predominant defensive self was an activated rewarding object relations unit, with an avoidance of self-initiative and compliant adaptation to the wishes of others.

But the withdrawing object relations unit is also available for defensive purposes. In fact, for many borderline patients, the withdrawing unit is "home." The success of these patients in using others for attachment purposes has been so limited and their experience of positive internal objects so meager that they live in a near-constant state of anticipated abandonment. They respond to perceived separations or even minor misattunements with punitive, aggressive, rejecting, and otherwise provocative defenses against the full experience of the abandonment depression; they externalize the source of their anguish by attributing it to someone else rather than to an intrapsychic condition. Reliance on the withdrawing internal model of relationships is another way of dealing with the underlying abandonment depression and separation anxiety.

Many of the adolescents in the residential treatment center where we work operate like this. Anticipated home visits, progress in therapy, limit setting by staff, and the prospect of discharge from the facility are just a few of the events that evoke intense separation anxiety and abandonment fears. In response, these youngsters typically become enraged, oppositional, or combative with the staff, projecting their withdrawing object representations onto them and seeing them as the source of anticipated pain. This temporarily relieves the kids by locating the source of their discomfort in the imagined malignancy of other individuals instead of within themselves, but again, authentic expression of the self is disallowed, contributing to its further impairment. Of course, the experience of rage may well be an authentic expression of a threatened self. But when acted out, based on the projection of the withdrawing object onto another person, it mollifies the abandonment experience of the real self and, in that way, is defensive.

Of course, borderline people can and usually do resort to both of these defenses. When the desired caretaking is not forthcoming in exchange for dependence, compliance, and helplessness, the withdrawing object relations constellation is likely to be experienced and then enacted in anger, devaluation, and aggression. A particularly memorable example occurred with Terri, whose boyfriend bought her an expensive leather jacket with the proceeds of an especially successful drug sale. Several days later, he accused her of sitting around the apartment on her "fat ass" and not helping, and then he stormed out. When he got back, Terri was gone—and her new leather jacket was in shreds. Once the withdrawing unit was activated, Terri expressed her rage by shredding the jacket that she had been given and by leaving (an angry reaction destructive to herself—and to her jacket!).

When the withdrawing unit is activated in relationships outside of the psychotherapy arena, it is relatively easy for the therapist to manage during the treatment hour. But it's a real challenge when the withdrawing relational model intrudes into the therapeutic relationship—which it does. Being the object of a borderline patient's rage can evoke any number of countertherapeutic feelings and, sometimes, behaviors.

Terri had her share of provocative outbursts with me. Early in treatment especially, she responded ferociously to my expectation that she behave responsibly, variously berating me, accusing me of malevolent motivations, and threatening to leave and never come back (a thought that at times didn't sound all bad).

But we want to emphasize that although it is tempting to perceive a conscious intentionality in the trying behaviors of the borderline patient, it is important to remember that these defensive constellations are neither volitional nor even conscious. An infant has only one attachment option—to develop whatever attachment system she or he has available. And once that infant is grown up, she or he has only one option—to live out the only attachment system she or he knows, which involves false-self procedures. For the infant who grows up to have a borderline personality disorder, this is an enactment of helplessness, clinging, and compliance or, when a connection cannot be created, an acting out of the withdrawing model of object relationships, with its expectation that both the self and the other are bad. Options for a more integrated and modulated view of the self and others are not available. This is the person whom we meet in the office.

IMPAIRED SELF FUNCTIONS

When severely insecure attachment compromises the growth of the autonomous self, the development of adaptive self-functions also suffers. Reality perception, for instance, is impaired by the oscillating operation of split object relations units and the resulting divided perception of self and others. Terri did not recognize other people as complex beings who were sometimes gratifying and at other times frustrating; at any given time, she could experience them as either one or the other. Her perceptions of others were incomplete and distorted. And her desperate need to feel connected to someone prevented her from seeing another reality—the self-destructiveness of her clinging and compliant relationship behaviors.

Because insecure attachment is often accompanied by a history of inadequate affect attunement, autonomous affect regulation is typically underdeveloped in these individuals. Children whose mothers cannot focus adequately on them have little opportunity to learn to focus on themselves and make sense of their feelings. The development of self-soothing and affect-modulating techniques is compromised, and the result is a disconcerting lability of mood. Related capacities for frustration tolerance and impulse control are frequently impoverished as well. Consequently, the behavior of these patients is often characterized by histrionic, erratic, impulsive, and sometimes inexplicable acting out.

Terri's capacity to contain unpleasant affect was so limited that she was consistently reactive, constantly acting out her feelings. She could not "sit with them" long enough to reflect on them and learn to understand them better. She seemed to be utterly incapable of regulating affect on her own, so she repeatedly turned to the men in her life to do it for her. This only perpetuated her failure to develop reliable means of managing affect for herself, a failure of which she was unaware because no one had ever modeled self-management for her or, more important, provided a consistently soothing experience that she could internalize and use on her own behalf. This is the task of and an opportunity for the therapist.

The borderline impairment in reflective function (Bleiberg, 2004; Fonagy, 1991, 1995, 2000, 2001a) interferes with reality perception through related deficits in sociocognitive skills. According to Bleiberg (2004), underdeveloped or inhibited reflective function results in "difficulties in processing social information," including

1. encoding deficits, that is, a failure to pay attention to some social cues while being hypervigilant to others;
2. attributional bias, which consists of frequently assigning hostile intention to others' behavior;
3. misinterpretation of social cues, particularly misjudging other peoples' affect; and
4. social problem-solving deficits, that is, a limited capacity to generate effective and adaptive solutions to interpersonal conflict, and a preference for aggressive solutions. (p. 115)

Especially under conditions of threat, loneliness, vulnerability, or helplessness, people with borderline personality disorders may see and experience others in a rigid and one-dimensional way, with little or no awareness that other interpretations of their thoughts, feelings, and intentions might be possible (Fonagy, 1999). According to Bateman and Fonagy

(2004), "there is something like 'an interpersonal perception deficit' in [borderline personality disorder] patients leading such patients to be poor in judgments of personality and interpersonal situations" (p. 93). Reality perception is skewed further by the borderline individual's extensive dependence on projection and fantasy that encourage reactive functioning over reflective functioning.

This, too, could be seen in Terri. By her own admission, she did not know how to focus thoughtfully on her experience of herself, let alone how to reflect on it. Instead, she reacted to experience, acting out in self-defeating ways. For example, in the early weeks of her enrollment in vocational school, Terri skipped a lot of classes, and her caseworker questioned her about this. Terri told me later that she experienced this mild confrontation as criticism and rejection and as a likely precursor to withdrawal of support and help by the caseworker. But at the time, she was too frightened by the idea of impending abandonment to allow herself to be aware of her feelings and reflect on them, nor could she consider any other possible interpretations of the caseworker's question. She could only project the abandoning object representation onto the person who had been her most loyal advocate and thus assail her. She reacted to the only experience that she knew, and her reaction was based not on reality but on projection.

Impaired reflective functioning makes for tumult in psychotherapy, too. When I noted to Terri that she seemed to be allowing her relationships with men to sabotage her efforts to stabilize herself, she reacted to me, instead of reflecting on her experience; she adamantly insisted that I didn't like her and that I actually wanted her to fail. Her inability to see beyond her feelings and speculate about what other meanings might have lain behind my comments—that is, her lack of capacity to separate me from her projections—resulted in her relating to me as if I really were her projection.

Impaired reflective function can reveal itself in a lack of concern for others' feelings. Oblivious to the other person's separate "mind," a borderline-disordered person lacks empathy and its moderating influence on aggression and may even become violent and cruel. When Terri's withdrawing unit was activated, she was caustic and apparently unconcerned about the effects of her rageful, sadistic attacks on others, typically, the men with whom she was involved.

Finally, the inability to reflect makes it hard for borderline patients to recognize and identify their own affects, in a pattern akin to alexithymia, a condition in which feelings cannot be put into words. Terri insisted at first that she didn't know what she was feeling or why she did something. It really did seem a mystery to her. So she was ill-equipped to understand her own experience, affects, and motivations and to make reflective choices about how to manage them. This, again, is the relational terrain of the therapy of a borderline patient.

To summarize, in our attachment–object relations model, the presence of the following vulnerabilities suggests a borderline personality disorder:

1. Insecure attachment
2. Separation sensitivity
3. Abandonment depression
4. Maladaptive defenses
5. Triad of disorders of the self
6. Split object relations units
7. False defensive self
8. Impaired self-capacities

I increasingly suspected the presence of a borderline personality disorder in Terri as our early work progressed. She was severely separation-sensitive, probably because of an attachment history that, by her report, was highly conditional upon her refraining from genuinely individuating experiences and autonomous efforts. Defensive strategies for maintaining connection to others and thereby avoiding the dysphoric abandonment experience had evolved into implicit relational procedures for clinging and compliant relationships, avoidance of self-expression and self-support, and rageful acting out. All of these functioned self-protectively in the sense that they maintained interpersonal connections or externalized the source of her intrapsychic pain, thereby muting her experience of it. But attachment-oriented defenses had coalesced into a false defensive self designed to maintain connection to the object, and any activation of her real self evoked separation anxiety and abandonment depression. Her defenses were not at all protective of her real self.

Terri's rewarding object relations unit consisted of the representation of an object who was indulgent, succoring, and extravagant in the provision of emotional supplies in response to compliant and clinging behavior. Her representation of herself was of an adored child who was passive and helpless. These two representations were linked with a feeling of being good and intensely loved.

Terri acted out this vision in her relationships with men. As long as they adored her, infantilized her, and offered her help and material goods, she clung to them, complied with their every wish and expectation, and became increasingly passive and helpless. She felt loved and valued, and she could conceive of no happiness that exceeded this. At these times, as brief as they typically were, she came to her therapy sessions with no sense of what she wanted to talk about or to focus on—there *were* no concerns or issues—or she didn't show up at all.

But the other aspect of her internalized model of relationships—the withdrawing object relations unit—was less comfortable. This consisted of a harsh, punitive, and withholding object and a representation of herself as evil and destructive. The predominant affective experiences related to this relational model were rage and despair. This vision was activated when Terri perceived rejection by a man or when he expected her to contribute something to the relationship or to him—by providing sex, selling drugs, supplying money for rent or food. She understood these demands as being sadistically cold, uncaring, and punitive, and she saw herself in this context as being dirty, contaminated, and ugly. Not surprisingly, she presented in therapy at these times as being passively hopeless (the rewarding unit) or as indignant and enraged (the withdrawing unit).

Historically, alternating alliances with—identifications with—these two object relations units had protected Terri against the underlying abandonment depression. Activation of the rewarding unit occurred when an idealized person in her life resonated with Terri's projection of the loving object representation. She would become clinging, compliant, and avoidant of adaptive self-support or any significant activation of her real self. Rejection or emotional withdrawal by a significant person would invariably stimulate the despair and rageful acting out of her negative self-representation and her projection of the rejecting object that she understood to be the cause of her wretched feelings.

To summarize, the borderline personality disorder represents an insecure attachment style derived from unmodulated attachment experiences without opportunity to restore disruptions. One of the results of such experiences is an exquisite vulnerability to separation and abandonment. In addition, without consistent alternation of disruption and repair, the experiences of attachment and disrupted attachment have no chance to become integrated. Two separate internalized models of relationships develop in the crucible of intensely affective engagement. Laid down implicitly and unavailable to reflection, the procedures contained in the rewarding and withholding object relations units are ways of coping with fear; it is implicitly believed that compliance will ensure the availability of the object and that real self behavior will result in abandonment. These fantasies of attachment and loss can be observed operationally in the triad of the disorders of the self. That is, gestures of the real self evoke fears of abandonment, which in turn evoke the habitual maladaptive defenses of compliance or rage. Out of these defenses, a self grows that is alienated from its own needs and impaired in its capacities. A chance to be real has disappeared in an effort to survive.

This is how it was with Terri in the beginning. Our work was at first tumultuous, frustrating, and disheartening. But over the course of our year together, as subsequent chapters show, a productive process developed. Given a second chance, Terri was able to set out once more upon the path of growth.

3

Compassionate Attunement

Igniting the Self

Because a person with a borderline personality disorder has become trapped in a false defensive self, the task of psychotherapy is to provide an experience that will allow for the emergence and practice of the real self. Masterson (1993) poses the challenge succinctly:

> It is important to keep in mind that a therapist cannot direct, suggest, seduce, threaten, attack, or torture a patient to self-activate. If it happens, it will be because the patient does it. The therapist can only create the conditions that make it possible. (p. 67)

Attachment research and theory have both directed our attention to the psychotherapy process and enriched our understanding of the developmental process. Slade (1999) is circumspect but clear in her appreciation of the clinical usefulness of an attachment perspective:

> An understanding of the nature and dynamics of attachment *informs* rather than *defines* intervention and clinical thinking. Attachment theory offers a broad and far-reaching view of human functioning that has the potential to change the way clinicians think about and respond to their patients, and the way they understand the dynamics of the therapeutic relationship. At the same time, an understanding of attachment organization does not define all aspects of human experience. Nor does it substitute for other equally important and equally valid kinds of clinical understanding. (p. 577)

Lyons-Ruth (1998) suggests that "something more" (p. 284) than technical interventions is needed to effect change in psychotherapy. In her view, psychotherapy technique alone cannot achieve alteration of behavior or reduction of symptomatology; a certain quality of relationship is also required. And we agree. This is reminiscent of Rogers (1957), who proposed years ago that conditions provided by the therapist, such as congruence, unconditional positive regard, and empathy, are both "necessary and sufficient" (p. 95) to effect change in therapy. Our attachment–object relations model of psychotherapy shares the belief that relational factors are essential to change in psychotherapy.

ATTITUDE

The therapist's awareness that implicit relational knowing is fundamental to development of the personality is of more than cognitive importance. It is also a corrective to our tendency to attribute consciousness and volition to all interpersonal behavior. However, Lyons-Ruth (1998) says,

> Implicit relational knowing begins to be represented in some yet to be known form long before the availability of language and continues to operate implicitly throughout life. *Implicit relational knowing typically operates outside focal attention and conscious experience, without benefit of translation into language.* (p. 285; emphasis added)

The borderline patient lives with a formidable handicap, in that the characteristic insecure attachment strategy and false defensive self operations are formed preverbally and prerationally and thus remain unconscious and avolitional. Originally driven by adaptive needs, these rigidly maintained behavioral propensities remain resistant to reexamination and reflection, even when they have become self-defeating over time. The borderline person is imprisoned in a severely skewed but resolutely perpetuated and largely unconscious "understanding" of the procedures required to initiate and sustain connections with others.

This view encourages a compassionate and empathic appreciation of the plight of borderline patients. As it is implicitly communicated to the patient in words and emotional tone, a new and revised "way of being with the other" (Stern, 1998)—that is, a new object relations unit—is offered.

One 43-year-old woman, at the end of a long-term treatment, interrupted her session to express her thanks for the therapist's attitude:

> Over and over, I've come in here whining and complaining, or crying, or mad. And I appreciate so much your listening to me without becoming irritated or impatient. That wasn't even a possibility growing up in my family. They were always either annoyed or critical.

This attitude of kindness, understanding, and patience had gradually been incorporated into her new, evolving internal working model of relationships.

Clear understanding of the motivational primacy of attachment strivings, with the knowledge that everyone's repertoire of attachment behaviors is implicitly derived and maintained, demands a genuine respect for the difficult plight of the borderline patient in trying to make the best of a bad deal. Constrained by the limited relational possibilities of their childhoods, these people are destined to continuously reenact the chaos, confusion, frustration, disappointment, pain, and emotional impoverishment of the past. Until a relationship supportive of the real self and secure attachment can be consistently experienced and internalized, their implicit learning blinds them to other options and possibilities. Their efforts to emotionally survive by establishing interpersonal connections in the only ways that they know are almost heroic. Although *heroic* and *borderline* may seem an unlikely combination of descriptives, these patients are certainly worthy of our respect, given their underdeveloped capacities and implicitly limited awareness of possibilities.

Finally, attachment theory encourages an attitude of curiosity and concern toward the struggling self of the person with borderline personality disorder. One notable early intervention program for young mothers and their high-risk infants schedules time for each mother to spend on the floor with her baby, physically accessible to him or her but with no purpose but simply to "watch, wait, and wonder" (Cohen et al., 1999, p. 431) as the infant engages in spontaneous and undirected behavior. Just watching is intended to foster a reflective and observational stance in the mother, from which she can derive insight into the baby's inner world and relational needs and so be able to attune to him or her more sensitively and responsively. Similarly, this kind of attachment-sensitive perspective in the therapist fosters greater sensitivity to the patient's plight and needs.

It also offers an implicit communication to the patient, an invitation expressed not in words but in tone and in affect:

> I honor and respect your real self, which I know to exist, although hidden, disguised, or even disavowed, beneath the painful strategies that evolved to ensure your survival. I know that you once learned to suppress this real self, lest you be subject to the dangers and agonies of abandonment, but what enabled you to survive in the past may no longer be necessary. So I will watch and wait and wonder about who you are. And, I hope, through *my* attention to that elusive self of yours, you will begin to let yourself experience it, too, finding yourself reflected in my eyes.

ATTUNEMENT

Affective attunement is needed for the development of secure attachment bonds, reliable affect regulation, and the consolidation of a coherent self. And the borderline patient needs a consistent experience of this kind in the relationship with the psychotherapist. As the therapist attunes to the moment-to-moment shifts in the patient's affective experience, a mutual and reciprocal communication process is activated between the two of them.

This communication occurs largely in a nonverbal, right-brain-to-right brain mode. Schore (1994) has written, "Right hemisphere-to-right hemisphere affective communications mediate psychotherapeutic transferential transactions" (p. 448). So what does that mean? Put simply, there are moments in which the patient experiences "I think you got it," or "Wow!" or "Aha." These moments can be experienced on either side or on both sides of the dyad, and they are accompanied by a biological, limbic experience of feeling known and felt—and a light turns on.

In Siegel's words (1999),

> a therapist and a patient enter into a resonance of states of mind, which allows for the creation of a co-regulating dyadic system. This system is able to emerge in increasingly complex dyadic states by means of the attunement between the two individuals. The patient's subtle nonverbal expressions of her state of mind are perceived by the therapist and responded to with a shift in the therapist's own state, not just with words. In this way, there is a direct resonance between the primary emotional, psychobiological state of the patient and that of the therapist. These nonverbal expressions are mediated by the right hemisphere of one person and then perceived by the right hemisphere of the other. In this way, the essential nonverbal aspect of psychotherapy, and perhaps all emotional relationships, can be conceived as a right-hemisphere-to-right-hemisphere resonance between two individuals. (p. 298)

Affect attunement, then, affords the patient a "mirroring frame of reference" (Mahler, 1968, p. 19), an opportunity for self-discovery. A fundamental goal of inner psychotherapeutic exploration is "to allow the individual to recognize, understand, and accept one's own 'unknown face'" (Joseph, 1992, as cited in Schore 1994, p. 463). Just as the infant discovers her or his self in the dyadic affect transactions with the mother, the patient may find his or her self reflected in analogous interactions with the therapist, through which both are affected and enlarged.

Support of the Real Self

As reliable affective attunement begins to unmask the patient's underdeveloped real self, it begins to structure it. Masterson (1976, 1981, 2000) says that a borderline personality disorder develops when the primary

who is the real - self ?
underneath defense

caregiver is not available for support of the child's emerging self, when there has been no mutually vital exchange around real-self activity. Clinging, dependence, compliance, and incompetence instead become the conditions of attachment and thus shape the patient's false defensive self.

Psychotherapy with these patients must provide attunement and support of the real self. But to be effective in therapy, attunement must be to the real self of the patient and not to the false self. This is a critical distinction. For example, it may be tempting for a therapist to attune to and mirror a patient's feelings of helplessness and affirm a sense of impotence. But to do so is to confirm the rewarding unit false self and to support and fortify its maladaptive defenses, including the acting out of these feelings in regressive, dependent behavior.

Similarly, the borderline patient might project the withdrawing unit and angrily accuse the therapist of being cold and uncaring or angry and rejecting. The therapist who attunes to this enactment of the false self by mirroring the patient's anger merely supports the defensive externalization. And the experience of the real self is neglected.

Or, the therapist may resonate with such a projection by accepting the misperception as accurate, by believing that the patient is right—that the therapist really is uncaring and rejecting—or by failing to address the patient's response as a projection. In this case, attunement to the false self supports the defensive externalization of the source of the patient's dysphoria. That is, the patient is affirmed in the belief that the problem is the therapist rather than a phenomenon that resides in herself or himself. It is important to help the patient recognize that her or his response is based principally on a projection of one's internal world, that she or he is the source of the feelings. Otherwise, the experience of the real self will continue to be avoided, and use of the false self to defend against the abandonment depression will be reinforced, at the cost of therapeutic movement.

(Of course, there will be times when the therapist will feel cold and uncaring; such feelings are commonly induced in the therapy relationship with borderline patients. In such cases, these feelings may be distortions created by the patient's projections. However, the therapist may really be put off by the patient and, as a consequence, have little empathy for her. In either case, it is necessary for the therapist to recognize these feelings and take care to contain impulses to act on them with the patient. The real self will not be attuned to, nor will any of its capacities be developed, if the therapist does not watch for and refrain from attuning to the false-self procedures.)

Enhancement of Affect Regulation

Accurate attunement to the affective experience of the patient has been demonstrated to enhance affect regulation. In fact, according to Schore

(2001b), "attachment can . . . be defined as the dyadic regulation of emotion" (p. 14). The experience of attunement to the real self that modulates affect is also the mechanism that creates attachment.

The patient's eventual experience of the therapist's attunement is soothing and calming; it occasions a metaphorical, if not a literal, sigh of relief ("My gosh! Something different is happening here!"). In patients with borderline personality disorder, a poorly developed capacity for affect regulation typically foils attempts to modify self-destructive behavior; the abandonment depression and separation anxiety are so intolerable that reliance on self-defeating behaviors such as clinging, compliance, or acting out stubbornly persist. In terms of attachment theory, survival takes precedence over the self; what began as a way of maintaining attachment becomes self-destructive because it doesn't allow for self-activation and self-support. Painful or terrifying affect states must be attenuated through the process of affect attunement by the therapist and so rendered tolerable and amenable to reflection and exploration. In other words, this new relationship with the therapist helps regulate affect by genuine interest in the real self and in why it's so difficult to be experienced and expressed.

One patient began a session with a scathing attack on me (DSR) for not responding with questions or directions to a period of silence in the previous hour. Projecting the withdrawing object on me, she said, "It's irresponsible of you to just sit there when I can't think of anything to say! And then you let me leave without providing some closure! What's your job, anyway?" I described my perception of the process:

> What I saw was that you became very angry at me when I expected you to figure out what was important to you to talk about, and I see that you're still angry. It wasn't my intention to make you angry. I would like to understand better both what you feel and why you feel that way.

The patient relaxed and began to process the feelings evoked by my implication that she would do better to focus on her self for direction, instead of looking to me, the object. My attunement to and acknowledgment of her intense anger (an expression of defense and glimpses of the underlying abandonment depression), along with my genuine interest in understanding her feelings, had an affect-regulating effect that allowed her to resume productive self-reflection for the remainder of the hour. I had invited her anger into the relationship, to be looked at, co-reflected on, and understood, and this was the metaphorical sigh of relief that became the on-ramp for the new attachment with me.

Cultivation of a New Object Relations Unit

Finally, the patient's experience of accurate attunement, of feeling known and understood in the relationship with the therapist, fosters a different kind of attachment relationship, one that can be internalized incrementally over time as a new object relations unit, a new internal working model of relationships. Mutual and reciprocal knowing with the therapist is a corrective experience, an invitation to the real self of the patient to emerge and, perhaps for the first time, remain active. As the patient's intrapsychic world gradually changes, so do the ways that self, others, and relationships are implicitly conceptualized. In the words of Flores (2004), "treatment requires that patients' internal working model be altered in a way that transforms the implicit rules that guide all their intimate relationships" (p. 220).

Such experiences of attunement result in actual alterations of brain morphology and function. According to Siegel (1999),

> whatever tools or techniques are used, the relationship between patient and therapist requires a deep commitment on the therapist's part to understanding and resonating with the patient's experience. The therapist must always keep in mind that interpersonal experience shapes brain structure and function, from which the mind emerges. (p. 300)

Schore (1994) is more explicit:

> Recent neurobiological investigations indicate that adults retain certain capacities for plasticity. . . . Affect regulatory dialogs mediated by a psychotherapist may induce literal structural change in the form of new patterns of growth of cortical-limbic circuitries, especially in the right hemisphere which contains representations of self-and-object images. (p. 468)

When affect attunement is consistently offered in psychotherapy, new experiences of self, other, the conditions of attachment, and the potential affective tenors of relationships are offered as well. Over time these are internalized, both intrapsychically and neurobiologically, as a new object relations unit, neither rewarding nor withdrawing but supportive of the budding real self.

THERAPEUTIC SPACE

Attunement is sometimes equated with mirroring, an active process in which one person monitors and reflects the affective experience of someone else. We suggest that there is a quieter form of attunement as well, one that is sensitive to the other's need for space and separation and does not preempt or impinge on the patient's experience. Winnicott (1965) gave an elegant explication of the infant's need in this regard:

It is only when alone (that is to say, in the presence of someone) that the infant can discover his own personal life. The pathological alternative is a false
life built on reactions to external stimuli. When alone in the sense that I am
using the term, and only when alone, the infant is able to do the equivalent
of what in an adult would be called relaxing. The infant is able to become
unintegrated, to flounder, to be in a state in which there is no orientation, to
be able to exist for a time without being either a reactor to an external im-
pingement or an active person with a direction of interest or movement. . . .
In this setting the sensation or impulse will feel real and be truly a personal
experience. (p. 34)

Winnicott made this statement in the context of his articulation of the
notion of the spontaneous gesture as the manifestation of the true self in
action. This suggests that the emergence and development of the real self,
the spontaneous discovery of the real self, requires repetitive experiences
of aloneness, separation, in the presence of the other. In Winnicott's view,
the false self reflects a failure on the mother's part to attune to the spontaneous gesture of the infant—that which is alive, creative, and real in the
infant's experience. Instead, out of her own attachment style, the mother
responds to feelings that she attributes to the infant. She may think, "Oh,
you can't do that by yourself. You need me to do it for you," or "Oh, you
don't want to do that. You want to be here close to Mommy." Attributions
like these, based on the mother's internal world, evoke the child's compliance. "This compliance on the part of the infant," Winnicott (1965) says,
"is the earliest stage of the False Self, and belongs to the mother's inability
to sense her infant's needs" (p. 145).

It is the mother's support of the child's solitary activity that encourages and allows for real-self experience. By the mother's relaxation with
the child's independent play, she is saying, "It's okay for you to have a
separate experience from me and to enjoy exploring." In a similar way,
the therapist's ease with silence communicates to the patient, "It's okay
for you to have your own separate thoughts in the room—I'll wait." It is
this attitude of patience that provides a safe environment for the silent,
spontaneous, separate self to emerge.

Extrapolating from infancy to psychotherapy, Summers (2001) comments that "creation of a new self-structure requires a relationship that
provides ample room for the emergence of new ways of being and relating" (p. 639). Stern (1998), too, has proposed that effective psychotherapy
requires so-called open spaces, times when the patient can be alone in the
presence of the therapist and focus on his or her real-self experience and
on the exploration of alternative, more authentic ways of being with another person. The therapist must provide space for the patient to be with
himself or herself, leaving room for the spontaneous gesture, the interest,
desire, wish, longing, or feeling—perhaps never before expressed, per-

haps never before experienced in another's presence—that is an expression of the underdeveloped real self.

DISRUPTION–REPAIR VERSUS DISRUPTION–DESPAIR

As discussed in the previous chapter, people with borderline character pathology characteristically display an implicit expectation that a connection will not be restored after a rupture. In effect, a model of disruption and despair has developed, instead of a model of disruption and repair. The opportunity to internalize a more hopeful model is critical for these patients.

In addition to offering an attuned relationship, the therapist helps the borderline patient make good on the missed experience of a reliable disruption–repair cycle. Consistently accurate affect attunement alone, even if it were possible, would not be enough for the evolution of a healthy, autonomous self; repeated disruptions of the attuned relationship, followed by repair, are essential to optimal development (Schore, 1994; Settlage, Bemesderfer, Rosenthal, Afterman, and Speilman, 1991; Siegel, 2001; Tronick, 1989).

Compassionate attunement to the real self is required to ignite the self system but not sufficient to keep the flame burning. The process of repeated disruption and repair is necessary, as well. The flame of the underdeveloped self of the borderline patient is easily extinguished. Only through the repetitive experience of this process of rupture and repair is the self able to find disruption to be tolerable and transient. As Holmes (2001) says,

> alliance rupture and repair are as much a part of the work of psychotherapy as are key changes and harmonic tension and its resolution in music. Only in the context of an object found, lost and refound can a patient begin to develop autonomy—a sense of self to which he can turn in times of stress. (p. 33)

Focusing on neurobiology, Schore (1994) states,

> Dyadic transactions of interactive repair that reduce negative affect, especially after critical moments of shame-induced ruptures of the positive affect bonds of the therapeutic alliance, act as catalytic regulatory mechanisms that facilitate the development of a structural system that can homeostatically maintain positive and recover from negative affective states. (p. 464)

In other words, both attachment (compassionate attunement) and separation (disruption and repair) are essential to psychotherapy as well as to development.

Two levels of relational disruption are common in the course of psycho-analytic psychotherapy. There are intentional misattunements that occur when interventions focused on defenses create a disruption of the patient's false-self relationship to the therapist. For example, bringing to the border-line patient's attention a clinging or helpless attachment style and its effect on the self promotes an experience of separation, a disconnect, that inter-feres with any illusion of attunement to the false defensive self. However, the possibility of repair is afforded by just such moments in the encounter, if the therapist is willing to empathically acknowledge the rupture, attune to the patient's discomfort, and invite conversation about it.

Early in her therapy, Terri was erratic about keeping her scheduled ap-pointments. Her irresponsibility to herself and to me (DDR) and her ex-pectation that I would sanction such self-defeating behavior were clearly a reflection of the felt helplessness of the internalized rewarding object relations unit. After each missed appointment, I addressed, as a central therapeutic issue, her failure to behave in her own best interest. I would say something like

> I understand that you believe that you had important reasons for miss-ing your session last week. But you keep telling me that your number one priority is to learn how to manage your life better—and I really do believe that that is your desire. So I have to wonder why you so often allow these "reasons" to come before your own self-care. It seems to me that through your behavior you are reinforcing your view of yourself as helpless and victimized by life.

"Oh, sure!" Terri would respond derisively. "Like I could have done anything about all that shit! You really don't get it, do you?" I would fol-low up her rejection of my cautious confrontation with further interven-tions directed at the enfeeblement of her real self, questioning both her perpetuation of the incompetence and irresponsibility of her false self and her neglect of her potential real-self capacities. The resistance continued: At first, she experienced a disruption in the relationship with me when I refused to take her defensive self at face value; that is, I intentionally mis-attuned to her false self. But in time, she recognized my efforts to continue to talk to her about it as an effort to restore our relationship. And it was. I intentionally misattuned. I expected that she would experience rupture. I kept watching the process. I offered, by my empathic presence, an in-vitation to talk about our process in a relationship that was safe enough to explore the conflict. These intentional misattunements and ruptures, experienced and processed over time, gave rise to a new relationship and moved her therapy along.

Because these interventions resonated with a fundamental, although long suppressed, need to express her real self, in time she became able to hear them and understand that I was persistently supporting her real-self needs. In time, she became able to integrate them and contain her acting out of helplessness. They contributed to a new internalized model of relational disruption and repair.

Although the patient may experience interventions like these as misattunements, they are in fact deliberate efforts to attune to the real, rather than to the false, self of the patient; they are calculated to discourage defense and support activation of the real self. But the therapist inevitably, often unwittingly, misattunes to the patient's real self at times. This creates a different kind of disconnect, and the qualities of the abandonment depression—pain, terror, frustration, rage—result. The therapist must directly address such misattunements and acknowledge their reality. The therapist must also clarify any misunderstandings or misperceptions and, when appropriate, apologize for the failure in empathy or understanding.

Terri was eventually able to contain her need to avoid the self-activation expected of her in therapy, and she became more consistent in keeping her appointments—but not perfectly consistent. One day, she called to tell me that an unforeseen event had arisen and that she needed to cancel at the last minute. I assumed that she had reverted to her old defenses, and at the outset of the following session, I almost-reflexively challenged her avoidance of the emotional material that had emerged in the previous few sessions. Terri responded with intense anger, as she usually did when I confronted her avoidant defense. But this time, along with the anger, she made clear that she really did have to cancel the session for reasons beyond her control—that is, not for reasons of avoidance—and that my failure to believe her hurt her feelings. Recognizing that I had been insensitive, I acknowledged my error and apologized for my failure to clarify her circumstances before confronting her. Terri appreciated the apology, and yet another repaired rupture was added to her slowly developing new relational model (and, painful to myself, I had shown her how to make mistakes and how to make repair with apology).

Experiences like these allow the therapist to "be with" the patient, explicitly and implicitly, in his or her abandonment depression. As Fosha (2001) has reflected, "re-experiencing pathogenic affect and unbearable states in itself is not therapeutic. It is the experience of not being alone in the process of re-experiencing the affects that creates healing." In the therapeutic relationship, the patient experiences the abandonment depression and separation anxiety in the context of attachment. This renders the painful affective experience tolerable and therefore amenable to working through, and over time, it alters the internal working model of relationships itself, augmenting it with a model of disruption and repair. According to Safran, Crocker, McMain, and Murray (1990),

The successful resolution of an alliance rupture can be a powerful means of disconfirming the client's dysfunctional interpersonal schema. While failure to adequately resolve an alliance rupture is likely to lead to poor outcome in psychotherapy, the successful resolution of an alliance rupture can be one of the more potent means of inducing change. (p. 156)

A REAL RELATIONSHIP

Patients in psychoanalytic psychotherapy sometimes complain that the relationship is not "real." We propose, however, that the therapist working from this theoretical model is offering a relationship that is very real, although partial. The frame of psychotherapy and the necessary neutrality of the therapist impose limiting parameters on the therapeutic relationship, but these do not preclude the active presence of the therapist's real self.

The therapist must be a real object or person, not in the sense of sharing his personal life but rather by manifesting an emotionally warm interest in the patient's problems, sympathizing with his real life defeats and congratulating him on his triumphs, and being empathic about the fact that coping and adaptation are vital to emotional survival. (Masterson, 1985, p. 55)

In other words, the patient is cared about and, ideally, feels cared about. The real self of the therapist in relationship to the real self of the patient ignites the spark that allows a new and healthier attachment experience to be internalized as the fresh way of being with the other that is a new internal object relations unit.

It is the real self of the patient that is sometimes hard to entice into the relationship. The entire therapy enterprise, as formulated from this theoretical perspective, is designed to evoke the experience and expression of the patient's real self, to invite her or his real self into the relationship. When interventions targeting maladaptive defenses of the false self are effective and defenses are contained, real-self affects associated with the abandonment depression will be experienced, and this is extremely alarming until trust develops that they can be expressed and explored in the context of the relationship with the therapist.

Neurological changes in the circuitry of the self often develop in the context of affective arousal. In Siegel's words (1999), "although even one-time occurrences can alter synaptic strengths, repeated experiences and emotionally arousing experiences have the greatest impact on the connections within the brain" (p. 47). Psychotherapy, intended to effect changes in the neural circuitry of the self, requires mutual, reciprocal, co-experienced relational moments of strong feeling.

For the borderline patient, such moments first come up when the dreaded abandonment depression is surfacing to awareness—that is, in those spaces of time and experience when the old relational procedures are momentarily relinquished or otherwise disrupted. When the patient is not focusing compliantly on the object, is acting out helplessness, or is otherwise avoiding self-activation (the manifestations of the rewarding object relations unit), the affects of the abandonment depression are inexorably experienced—likewise, when the projection of the feared object, with its accompanying self-protective behaviors (withdrawing object relations unit) are interrupted. And the therapist eagerly anticipates these slender real-self moments, which often occur immediately after an intervention, because it is in them that the old relational procedures are sufficiently disrupted to allow for a moment of meeting, real self to real self. There may be no more than a quick, nonverbal, almost imperceptible startle, a pregnant pause, or an instant of eye contact. Still, it is precisely at such times that the real relationship is experienced most intensely. And when these moments can eventually be brought to the attention of the patient, a time of co-reflection can ensue.

For instance, if the patients do not talk spontaneously about their difficulty expressing and supporting themselves, either in session or in extra-therapy life, the therapist might comment, "I notice that the last three times I've asked you why you think you don't speak up for yourself, you paused—as if you were feeling something. Do you know what was going on with you then?" Most of these patients have never experienced someone else caring about their processes and how it feels to them; to the contrary, their implicit relational procedures have usually driven them to monitor other people's processes at the expense of their own. This attention from the therapist, this attunement to the slight movements of affect beneath their awareness, invites them to become more cognizant of their real selves in the presence of a benign and interested other. This primes the pump for the real relationship that will, over time, be internalized as a new and more adaptive relational procedure.

Although momentary glimpses of the abandonment depression signal the entrance of the real self into the therapy relationship, interventions focused on defenses open up possibilities for real-self interaction. The borderline patient is likely to experience frustration, rejection, or anger when the therapist fails to collude with a defense calculated to evoke a caretaking response. But the therapist is always offering an implicit—and sometimes explicit—invitation for the patient to share and explore such feelings. In those moments of open exploration, the patient is responding to the therapist with the real self.

Twenty-four-year-old Susan demanded, "How can you say you weren't angry at me yesterday? You wouldn't even remind me of what we were talking about!" My (DSR's) unwillingness to help her in the way that she wanted tipped her out of her cajoling efforts to make me into a proper rewarding object, and suddenly, in an instant, she was experiencing me as the withdrawing object. I said quietly, "I can hear that you think I was angry, yet the opposite is true. I am confident that you can do what you feel you are unable to do." We shared her momentary startle; it was a moment of real-self to real-self connection. I was open to her query regarding any anger I might have felt toward her, but in truth—at that moment—she was the one who was angry, and later she was able to acknowledge it.

As the patient experiences and reflects on these heightened affective moments in the therapy hour, the defensive behavioral constellation of the false self becomes less necessary. Old defenses are allowed to atrophy through lack of use; new relational procedures become stronger with familiarity. The relationship with the therapist is increasingly trusted as an opportunity to be one's self in an authentic, spontaneous, and self-supporting way—in time, it will be internalized as a new, healthier object relations unit, a more self-supportive internal working model of relationships.

As this new relationship template is internalized by the borderline patient, the potency of the earlier pathological attachments and related object relations units is further diluted (Blatt, 1992; Schore, 1994; Watt, 1986). In Masterson's words (1985), "the patient internalizes the therapist as a new, positive object representation along with his positive, supportive attitude to the patient's individuation and self-representation of being adequate, based on self-assertive efforts at adaptation" (p. 61). Or, in attachment theory terms, "the working model of the therapeutic relationship eventually exerts dominance over hurtful experiences and models of the past, countering the patient's image of himself as unlovable and unworthy of secure affectional ties" (Sable, 2000, p. 333).

Because this relational practice with the therapist is experienced as being both surprising and satisfying, it fuels the desire for more real-self relating outside of the therapy relationship. So with a budding new appreciation for real-self attachment experiences, the patient is likely to seek to establish and enjoy more meaningful relationships in everyday life.

4

Stance, Neutrality, and Frame With the Borderline Patient

The psychotherapy process is complex and affected by many variables. One is that of relational factors, as discussed in the previous chapter (attachment and attunement experiences, repetitive experiences of the disruption–repair cycle, therapeutic space), which are certainly influential in effective psychotherapy. But it is misleading to suggest that these relational variables alone are mutative. Gelso (2005) points out that "recent years have witnessed the emergence of two powerful, and seemingly contradictory, visions of what most fundamentally causes change in psychotherapy" (p. 419). He continues with a description of these two points of view, one focusing on the primacy of the relationship between the therapist and the patient and the other on therapeutic technique as the primary determinant of change in psychotherapy. But he concludes that "technical factors and relational factors are indelible elements in each and every psychotherapy encounter" (p. 419).

This is our position, as well. Although the so-called relational factors are instrumental in effective psychotherapy, there are structural and technical factors that are also necessary. For instance, there are three equally critical structural variables—the therapeutic stance, therapeutic neutrality, and the therapeutic frame. The following case makes this point clearly.

It's painful but, for me (DSR) at least, instructive to remember the time that a patient convinced me that affect attunement was not enough, that something else was needed. This was about 25 years ago. I had never before had any difficulty attuning to someone's pain. When this 38-year-old single woman came into my office and poured out her story, I felt it deeply, both with her and for her. In fact, the tale of what she had been through in her life and the agony that she felt were so dense for me in those moments that I told her that I didn't know if I could help her. Diane's history and problems were complex. I was not sure that I was equipped to handle them, especially when she told me that she had been in treatment before, with 10 or so other therapists. But she liked me. She said that she felt that she could trust me, that I was genuinely interested. She was willing to do whatever was needed for me to help her.

Diane had never married. She was the youngest of three children. Her history revealed a moderate capacity for self-functioning; she had been employed, if sporadically, in several secretarial jobs, and she described a social life that seemed superficially unremarkable, except for one thing: Diane's absolute avoidance of close relationships with men. She never had a significant relationship with a man. She was sexually abused by her father between the ages of 4 and 6. Her mother, whose relational style was one of avoidance and denial, ignored the abuse and tended to cling to her children, looking to them for the fulfillment of her emotional needs.

Diane's mother and siblings were still alive, and clarifying and managing relationship issues with them, both past and present, often assumed center stage for Diane in therapy, as did her expressed "need to forgive." She looked to me for insight and comfort. She felt helpless to manage her own feelings or make the necessary decisions in her life. Indeed, by the time that Diane came to me, she was extraordinarily passive and helpless, and she had developed phobias that imprisoned her in fear. She was convinced that she couldn't even drive herself to work or, eventually, to her therapy.

Our three sessions a week, focusing on deep attunement and problem solving, soon expanded into telephone calls before and after office hours, as I "caught," as if it were contagious, Diane's conviction that only I could help her feel better and could take care of her. The anxiety and exhaustion that I finally had to acknowledge made clear to me that something was at fault in my approach to Diane's psychotherapy. I was giving her my therapeutic presence and my psychobiological attunement, but something more was clearly needed. My reading of Masterson's work (1976, 1981) on internalized object relations clarified for me the problems in this misguided therapeutic venture.

In this case, the notion of something more implied the operation of something else. That is, even sensitive, accurate, and consistent attunement to the patient and repeated experiences of the disruption–repair process, are likely not to be enough in the treatment of personality-disordered patients, if offered in the absence of vigilant attention to structural factors and intervention strategies. The therapist's attunement must be to the needs of the real self. Otherwise, the therapist will unwittingly collude with and support defensive procedures that may have been adaptive at one time but have since become self-defeating. Although the patient is likely to feel this collusion as a familiar and gratifying affect, it will not reinforce the growth of the real self.

Fools rush in! Over time, I became aware that I was not only attuned to Diane's experiences of abandonment, abuse, and rejection but was also experiencing them the way that she did—along with her helplessness and the fears that kept her from paying attention to her real self or letting it thrive. In addition, I caught her belief that she needed direction from me to regain her missing self-confidence. In my loss of perspective, I reinforced her implicit learning, colluding with her sense of herself as being helpless and incompetent and resonating with her view of me as a rewarding caretaker.

When Diane related to me in this manner, she felt safe, cared about, and taken care of; her fear subsided, and all seemed to be well. But it was her false self that was being supported and reinforced, not her real self, which remained undeveloped as she became ever more helpless and defended.

Many psychotherapists have learned from experiences similar to these how important it is to keep in mind the critical distinction between the real self and the false self. Again, it is the real self that needs to be attuned to and encouraged in the relationship with the therapist. So, although relational factors are undoubtedly a necessary something more (than structural parameters and intervention strategies), in the psychotherapy formula, they are not sufficient. The structural and technical elements of the psychotherapy venture—which may well be communicated relationally—are necessary, too. It is these that enable the emergence of the patient's real self and, ultimately, the development of a revised internal working model of relationships. Unless these structural and technical elements inform and shape the therapeutic environment, the real self cannot emerge.

THE PSYCHOTHERAPEUTIC STANCE

From our perspective, an effective psychotherapeutic stance with borderline patients must reflect a different expectation from the one that was internalized in childhood (Masterson, 1993). These patients have learned a general posture of dependency, helplessness, and incompetence, which shows in their psychotherapy as passivity, compliance, and an expectation that the therapist will assume responsibility for the treatment process. They may look to the therapist not only to initiate and structure sessions, for example, but also to provide direction, advice, affirmation, and encouragement and take responsibility for the regulation of the patient's feelings and behavior.

To collude with this expectation in therapy, however, is to support the false self's maladaptive defenses and to neglect the potential of the enfeebled real self. The therapist's resonance with the false self is actually a *mis*attunement—the attunement is not to the real self—and a reenactment of the patient's early pathological experience with caregivers. Instead, the therapist must communicate belief in the patient's capacity, albeit underdeveloped, for self-activation, self-assertion, self-initiative, and self-soothing.

From their object relations perspective, Clarkin, Yeomans, and Kernberg (1999) emphasize that

> we view borderline personality disorder (BPD) as a condition where (a) most patients are capable of some level of goal-directed functioning . . . even at the stage of entering treatment, and (b) most patients are capable of making substantial progress and of becoming autonomous and productive. (p. 55)

That is, they assume that the patient can manage his or her own life in a realistic, self-supportive, and adaptive way and can thus take a similar responsibility for the work of therapy.

This is the firm and constructive expectation needed and missed in childhood by borderline patients who received acceptance, affirmation, and approval only at the cost of remaining clingy and needy and looking to the caregiver for help. The therapist's alternative expectation is a communication to the real self of the patient, and it is designed to anticipate and support its emergence. It is based on a belief in the capacity of the real self to grow and change—a belief that could not thrive before but can now be internalized and thus facilitate the development of a more adaptive working model of relationships.

> I did believe that Diane was capable of substantial progress. But I had not realized just how important it was for me to find and maintain a reliable inner stance that would help me hold onto that belief. I hadn't appreciated how easily I could be induced by her fear and desperation into treating her as if she were as incapable as she felt. If I had been able at the time to diagnose her identification with her false self and to point out to her that she was living as if she actually were helpless, rather than just fearing that she was, we would have been able to work on competence, personal power, self-support—a truly therapeutic effort. A response like that would likely have felt like a rupture to Diane at first because she still believed that her emotional survival was imperiled—as it had once been—if she did not cling helplessly. She probably would have responded for a while to my expectation that "you can do this" by seeing me as a harsh, critical, and unavailable figure—as the withdrawing object. But we would have had the opportunity to co-explore why she felt that way.
>
> But that is not how it happened. Without a solid therapeutic stance, I too often forgot to communicate my confidence in her capacities. I colluded in her lack of confidence, and in so doing, I functioned for her, acting out in the countertransference the rewarding unit—that is, her view of relationship as being dependent on compliance and helplessness. Nor did I consistently

enough point out that she was living in a way that was not in her best interest. I was, indeed, reenacting her early pathological experience with caregivers, and in this context, she could not develop new procedures for taking responsibility for herself. Needless to say, therapy without the therapeutic stance is not sufficient.

THERAPEUTIC NEUTRALITY

The therapeutic stance is communicated through an implicit attitude as well as through the structural parameters of the treatment and the therapist's intervention strategy. Therapeutic neutrality is another of these parameters that helps to support the experience of the real self (Masterson, 1976, 1993). But in work with borderline patients, neutrality refers not to the classical neutral stance but to neutrality with regard to the patient's projections of the false defensive self. The therapist must be neutral by making every effort to look for and relate to the real self of the patient and not resonate or collude with false-self projections that defend against the experience of the real self.

> Caroline, a 23-year-old single woman, presented for therapy complaining of general underachievement. She had a history of jobs lost owing to her unreliability, as well as a series of impulsive and self-destructive relationships with men. In the first session, she told the therapist, a supervisee of ours, that she didn't know where to begin and that she would appreciate being told what to talk about. When she pointed out that her former therapist, who had recently retired, "always told me what to talk about," she was acting out her helplessness and demonstrating her tendency to focus on the other instead of herself, a common characteristic of borderline personality disorder.
>
> The therapist, who was relatively inexperienced, felt pulled to oblige her by directing Caroline's explication of herself and her difficulties. But she knew that this would be a resonance with Caroline's projection and thus a loss of therapeutic neutrality. So, she merely wondered aloud why the patient found it so difficult to reflect on her own concerns and describe them. Predictably, Caroline experienced this as an unhelpful and uncaring response. Her expectations—her implicitly learned conditions of attachment—were challenged by the therapist's expectation of self-focus, and when her wishes to be taken care of were frustrated, she experienced the therapist as a cold and withdrawn figure. She got angry at the therapist's expectation of self-initiative and self-exploration. To this projection, the therapist had to respond from a position of neutrality, resonating with neither the dependency nor the anger. She inquired why her question had been so disturbing; she had merely been demonstrating her confidence in Caroline's capacity to think her own thoughts about her own concerns. Neither infantilizing, withholding, nor angry in her response, she communicated as clearly as she could to the patient's impaired real self and its nascent capacities the opportunity to

engage in a process of discovering and articulating her real—though heretofore invisible—self.

Therapeutic neutrality offers patients a fresh understanding and experience of their selves and their vulnerabilities. As they begin to reflect on, rather than react to, their perceptions and feelings, borderline patients often say things like "I don't know why I do that. Nobody ever asked me before." As their own stories are felt and heard, often for the first time, compassion for the self grows; grief is experienced; and difficulties that so far have been inexplicable begin to have meaning.

Neutrality also demonstrates that real-self expression, real-self activation, and real-self attachment are possible, without the consequences that the patient anticipates and dreads. To hear implicitly and explicitly that "You can do it. You can think about it. You can figure it out" is as empowering as it is startling. Self-activation may continue to evoke the abandonment depression, but in the context of therapy, this affective experience is tolerable for the first time because the new relationship allows for the development of more adaptive, self-supportive means of managing painful feelings. Real-self experience and the affective aliveness that comes with it become self-perpetuating through new procedures that promote activation and spontaneity. And it is because of the knowledge and practice of therapeutic neutrality that the probability of real self-relating is enhanced. Therapeutic neutrality is necessary.

THE PSYCHOTHERAPEUTIC FRAME

The frame is a set of policies and procedures that encourages activation of the real self and limits acting out of the false self. It concretizes therapeutic neutrality and the therapeutic stance and provides a specific means whereby the therapist can communicate to the patient's real self the expectation of self-activation and self-responsibility and thereby provide a benchmark for adaptive behavior.

There is enormous pressure on the therapist in work with borderline patients to resonate with the patient's false-self projections and relinquish the neutral position. Feelings and needs are expressed behaviorally, to the exclusion of verbal reflection and expression. The patient may come to sessions late or inconsistently, to keep from activating the real self and the abandonment affects that responsible participation in treatment evokes. Emotionally laden material may be withheld until the last minutes of the hour, with the expectation that the therapist will extend the session. Crises may stimulate requests for after-hours telephone sessions. Gifts may be offered, or hugs requested. The therapeutic frame helps the therapist resist such pressures.

It is helpful to have policies in place to deal with such practical issues as missed appointments, lateness, payment, and so on, all of which invite the patient's expectation that the therapist will behave like the rewarding objects of the past (Masterson, 1981, 1993). Similarly, a frame prohibiting abuse of the therapist and damage to property or persons is required to delimit the patient's enactment of the withdrawing object relations unit. It encourages the verbalization of feelings, instead of acting out, and the containment of destructive defenses. The frame is essential as a set of policies and procedures on which the therapist can fall back when feeling overwhelmed by the experience of pressure to cooperate with the patient's false-self projections.

The borderline patient has been formed not by mutual collaboration in the patient's best interest but by relationships that reward dependence and helplessness or threaten withdrawal and abuse. A frame that resists familiar defenses will be uncomfortable and frightening at first. The frame will therefore be violated, and when it is, the violations are the first order of business. Missed appointments, lateness, lingering at the end of the session, failure to pay, verbal abuse, and any other countertherapeutic acting out must be addressed immediately and consistently. To overlook the behaviors that are critical indicators of the patients' vulnerabilities is to join them in avoidance and, once again, miss the opportunity to make the implicit explicit. When acting out is occurring, it must be talked about.

Masterson (1992) has said that for people with borderline personality disorders, "nothing is ever so bad that it can't get worse." We believe that the same holds true for their therapists—at least in the absence of accurate diagnosis and proper technique. In the case of Diane, it did get worse.

If I had understood Diane's internalized object relations units at the time, I might have been able to remain neutral. I would have known when I was resonating with the rewarding unit or the withdrawing unit when I was re-creating in her psychotherapy the enactment of her old relational procedures. I would not have become knotted up in confusion when her splitting produced sudden incoherent shifts in the ways that she related to me. Perhaps, I might even have been able to recognize when she was projecting the withdrawing object representation onto me, like the time when she threatened to report me to the state licensing board when I had emergency surgery and couldn't return her telephone calls or the time when, in impulsive anger, she threw a coffee cup at me.

If I had known to adhere to a reliable psychotherapeutic frame, I would not have unwittingly steered both of us into a corner where she suddenly felt abandoned and desperate. I accepted too many after-hours phone calls without questioning her helpless and demanding acting out. I didn't systematically take up her late arrivals and payments. Her behavior became steadily less healthy and less responsible, and the more chaotic her life got, the more demanding she became. It became obvious to me that I would have to alter my approach or refer her to a colleague.

I did attempt to facilitate some genuine therapeutic momentum by modifying my approach to her treatment. I began to focus on her underdeveloped real self rather than on her false self; I tried to communicate an expectation that she really was not as helpless as she felt and that, on her own, she was capable of managing her life better; and I attempted to establish a realistic psychotherapeutic frame that limited enactment of her helpless and dependent behavior. But by that time, Diane was so used to my gratifying her regressive needs that she seemed painfully and ragefully unable to make this shift with me.

I referred her to another therapist.

The case of Diane is a vivid example of what happens when a therapist fails to establish a clear and firm frame of psychotherapy. In contrast, Klein (1989b) reports a case in which limit setting became glaringly essential because the frame of therapy was challenged aggressively by a particularly difficult borderline patient. In this instance, however, the therapist was resolute and consistent in his adherence to the frame; his case demonstrates how the frame is a structure that supports the therapist and the patient in the process of psychotherapy.

The patient was a 22-year-old woman who was first referred by her therapist of several months, who conveyed two quite different impressions of the patient when making the referral. While he stated that the patient needed "analysis" and this was the primary reason for the referral, he also stated that the patient was being referred because she had repeatedly damaged his office by throwing things and "the landlord insisted that I get rid of the patient or that I leave."

As soon as she entered my office for her first appointment, the patient stood by the door and declared that she had three needs that had to be met for her to be able to enter into treatment with me: (1) she needed to know that I would still see her even if she broke something in my office, because at times she could not control herself; (2) she needed to know that she could call me anytime day or night and that sessions would not be strictly limited to 50 minutes (in fact, she later told me that her previous therapist had always arranged for her to be his last patient of the day so that she might stay in the waiting room as long as she felt she needed to and then would lock up when she left); and (3) she needed to know that she could walk around my office and did not have to stay seated; she insisted that when seated she became too anxious to talk.

It is important to understand the true meaning of these questions or demands. Put into action, these feelings would be a simple expression of the patient's false defensive self. Put into words, these questions are at one and the same time arising from both the false, defensive self and the impaired real self. Both are asking, "Will you give me what I want and need?" Only one of the selves will be satisfied with the answer. If it is the false self, then the treatment will most likely fail. If it is the impaired real self, then treatment will be possible and the first link in the chain of the therapeutic alliance will have been forged.

[Her] questions were her way of asking if I could set limits, unlike her former therapist (and her parents before that). Could she rely on me to be any different? Also, was I willing to hold her responsible for acting in an appropriate and adaptive manner? Would I respond to her false, defensive self—a helpless, impulsive child who needed to be excused and tolerated because she was basically unable to care for herself? Her stated need to walk around my office, and her refusal to stay seated, can be viewed as an assertion that acting out was her principal means of expressing her feelings. She rationalized this by stating that it enabled her to think better. In general terms, the patient's tests were geared to determine whether I would step into the rewarding unit, dismantle the therapeutic frame, forgo therapeutic neutrality, and conspire with the false, defensive self. (pp. 224–225)

Klein (1989b) clearly describes the crucial distinction between the false defensive self and the real, though impaired, self. To resonate with the patient's projection of the rewarding object representation by providing "understanding" and succor is comfortable at first but supports old implicit relational procedures. However, to attune to the needs and affective experience of the real self would likely trigger the projection of the withdrawing object. Over time, however, this second approach catalyzes new procedures for a more authentic way of establishing and maintaining attachments.

I replied to [her] (who was still standing by the door) in the following manner: First, I, and not the landlord, would not tolerate her breaking things in my office. Further, I could not understand why she would use that method of communication rather than telling me her feelings. Second, although she could call me any time, I would not return calls that I felt could wait until the next session. I emphasized that I did not feel useful therapy could take place over the phone. I further questioned her conviction that her problems, which were longstanding, needed or could be dealt with in such an immediate and erratic fashion. Finally, I remarked that it was unacceptable for her to constantly walk around the office, because this was a way to dispel her anxieties by converting feelings, literally, into "leaps and bounds" rather than by clarifying and understanding these feelings. (pp. 225–226)

Implicit in this vignette is the therapist's belief in the patient's potential for self-control, reflection, and adaptive functioning in general. He communicated this to her explicitly in his adherence to the policies and procedures of the therapeutic frame and in his confrontations, both of which limited the enactment of her false-self procedures and promoted a relational mode of being that could support real-self experience and expression.

The patient responded to the therapist's insistence upon the therapy frame and his explication of the therapeutic stance by reluctantly entering the office, sitting down, and providing "some minimal initial information about her present and past life" (Klein, 1989b, p. 226). However, her internalized procedure for being with others was to act out the helplessness that she thought would procure the aid that she believed she needed, and she soon demanded that the therapist hospitalize her.

> I stated that I saw no reason to do so based on what I now knew of her, and I felt that she could work in treatment as an outpatient. But, I added, if she felt between now and the next session that she needed hospitalization for reasons not at all clear to me she could present herself at any emergency room. In order to emphasize my refusal to conspire with her false, defensive self, I added that she did not need my permission, agreement, or help in order to get hospitalized.
>
> She exploded in anger and insisted that she would not leave my office until I had arranged for hospitalization. I responded that while she seemed to be making quite an effort to convince me that she was out of control, I felt that she could control herself, and I would hold her responsible for her behavior now and throughout the course of her therapy.
>
> She dropped the subject of hospitalization but stated that she needed more time and did not want to leave the office yet. I responded that we could talk about those feelings next time and that the session was over. She responded by stating that she could not and would not leave. I only repeated that the session was over. She repeated that she would not leave. . . .
>
> I . . . arose and stated that I would not conduct therapy in an atmosphere of duress or coercion or emotional blackmail of any sort. If she did not leave immediately, I would be forced to throw her out myself or call the police if necessary. In either case, treatment could not then continue.
>
> She stormed out of my office. I wasn't certain that she would return, but I was certain that I had acted therapeutically. (pp. 227–228)

In fact, Klein's patient did return, and she eventually engaged in an effective therapy experience. This did not happen, however, without further acting out of her false defensive self; she repeatedly resorted to her early helpless and demanding attachment style in a frantic effort to compel the therapist to respond in a complementary manner. But the firm frame, the therapist's clear limit setting, and his steady confrontation of the self-destructiveness of her enactments resulted in the gradual softening of her false defensive self and the development of new procedures, new ways of being with others and with her (real) self.

Refusal to collaborate with the false-self projections that ineluctably occur in work with borderline patients is necessary if old relational procedures are to be reworked and intrapsychic object relations units restructured. Attunement and the consistent repair of disruption experiences are not sufficient by themselves for maximally effective psychotherapeutic treatment. The entire psychotherapy process must be designed and structured in such a way as to support activation of the patient's real self and not the old false defensive one. This requires a therapeutic stance that expects adaptive functioning from the patient and a determined commitment on the therapist's part to therapeutic neutrality. In spite of pressures to let it remain invisible, the therapist must, as consistently as possible, speak always to the patient's real self and thus communicate a belief in its existence and in its nascent capacities. To do so is the most empathic and caring communication possible, even when firm limit setting is the first order of business. It is in this relationship, fueled by attunement but informed by critical structural and technical variables (both necessary and sufficient to effective therapy), that the real self can feel invited to emerge in safety.

5

Listening and Speaking to the Borderline Patient

An Invitation to a Secure Separation

Truth telling is an important part of psychotherapy. All therapy interventions are about telling the truth. We observe a patient's behaviors and feelings and communicate to him or her ideas about their origins and motivations of which the patient is unaware. But how the truth will be received depends to a large extent on how the truth is told.

How do you talk to a patient? What do you say, how do you say it, and when? How do you listen, and what do you listen for? In other words, how do you communicate with the patient's real self? The answer to that question varies across patients; a person's particular vulnerabilities and defensive style determine what verbal interactions will be most useful. Masterson (1976, 1981, 1993) has proposed differential developmental determinants for the borderline, narcissistic, and schizoid personality disorders (see chapter 2) and, with them, diagnosis-specific interventions of choice, interventions that are empathic to the patient's real-self needs. He contends that the characteristic intrapsychic structure and defensive false self of each of these disorders informs the clinician about the most efficacious intervention strategy for each. From her attachment perspective, Slade (1999) thinks similarly: "How therapists talk to patients and what they endeavor to do in their talking and in their listening will vary as a function of the patients' predominant attachment organization" (p. 585).

DIAGNOSIS-SPECIFIC INTERVENTIONS

Masterson (1976, 1993, 2000) proposes that people with narcissistic personality disorders, because of their exquisite esteem sensitivity, are most responsive to interpretations of narcissistic vulnerability, which communicate both an appreciation of that vulnerability and the self-protective function of the defenses against it. For example, a therapist might comment to a narcissistically disordered patient, "Something happens here that I think is painful for you. What I notice is that when you focus on yourself, it is uncomfortable for you. You seem to distance from these feelings, intellectualize, and then criticize me to soothe yourself." Such interpretations typically evoke a feeling that the painful fragility of the impaired self has been understood. However, because of the narcissistic patient's extreme sensitivity to criticism, confrontations are more likely to be experienced as critical and devaluing episodes and thus activate intensified defenses.

Yet, a person with a schizoid personality disorder requires a different approach to communication (Klein, 1995; Masterson 1993, 2000). The schizoid patient is torn between the twin fears of being controlled and being hopelessly isolated; these are the only experiences of relationship that he or she has known, and neither experience feels safe. This is a person who is fundamentally "safety sensitive" (Cooper et al., 2005, p. 2). Interpretations of this "schizoid dilemma" (Klein, 1995) facilitate the patient's eventual acknowledgment and relinquishment of defenses. For instance, an interpretation might be framed,

> I wonder—and, of course, I may well be wrong—but I wonder if, when you share your experience in here, you become afraid of the closeness. So you withdraw in order to feel more safe, but then you feel isolated, and that's scary too. It's like you aren't really comfortable either way—it's either too close or too distant.

For the schizoid patient, interpretations need to be offered tentatively and in the form of wonder so that he or she does not, once again, feel told and controlled.

According to Klein (1995), once therapist and schizoid patient are in agreement about this dilemma, it is time to interpret the various "schizoid compromises" by which the patient regulates distance in relationships. For instance, the therapist might wonder with the patient,

> Is it possible that you're holding back part of yourself in your relationship with your wife, as you've said you sometimes do in here with me? Perhaps this "one foot in and one foot out" approach is the best way you've found to feel both comfortable and safe.

Such interventions speak empathically to the schizoid patient's felt need for interpersonal safety, whereas an interpretation of narcissistic vulnerability is typically experienced as being invasive, too close. Interventions that confront reliance on the distancing more directly are likely to feel coercive and controlling. Whatever the diagnosis, all people need to feel understood and spoken to in a way that honors their particular vulnerabilities and allows such vulnerabilities to be explored. (A thorough explication of the differential developmental deviations of these disorders and the rationale for corresponding differential intervention strategies can be found in works by Masterson [1981, 1992, 1993, 2000].)

Different still is the borderline patient. Interpretive interventions are generally not effective for borderline patients. Interpretations are explanatory links between behaviors and underlying causes and genetic material. As such, they tend to support a borderline patient's "belief" that he or she is incapable of reflecting on one's own experience and trying to understand it and that such a function needs to be provided by the therapist. Interpretations are likely to activate fantasies of being taken care of and to encourage regression in the form of passivity and dependence. Interpretations with borderline patients risk supporting the helplessness of the false defensive self, instead of activating the real self, and they reinforce self-defeating relational procedures as well. Although these patients may well feel better in response to such interpretations, they are not likely to get better because, once again, the interpretation has communicated, "You can't figure this out. I have to do it for you." In response to an interpretive approach to psychotherapy, the borderline patient typically tends to become passive and clinging instead of active and reflective, expecting the therapist to provide executive functions of which the patient is at least minimally capable. A carefully designed confrontative approach, however, expects and supports responsible and adaptive self-initiative, both in therapy and outside it.

Borderline patients also use interpretations in the service of resistance—insight as defense or insight as excuse—to validate the conditions of attachment of the false self and so discourage activation of the real self. A borderline patient who has accrued a substantial "understanding" of her or his difficulties through years of interpretive psychotherapy may not modify her or his behavior accordingly, saying in essence, "I did it because I'm borderline. I can't help it." I once had a patient (Kathy, discussed later in more detail) who had had several brief stints of psychotherapy and who had informed me during her initial visit that she was promiscuous because of her fear of abandonment. She used that insight as a rationale for her behavior, and her acting out and chaotic behavior continued unabated. So, if interpretation is not the intervention of choice for borderline patients, then how do we communicate? How do we as therapists help them to get to their own truths?

CONFRONTATION

Masterson (1976, 1981) and Klein (1989b, 1989d) suggest that the intervention that best addresses the real self of the borderline patient is a form of confrontation that communicates the therapist's understanding and observation of the triad of the disorders of the self. In borderline patients, a poor attachment context gives rise to a compliant and dependent false self, a constellation of defenses that protect against the dreaded experience of the real self.

To the contrary, a psychotherapeutic context built on a firm stance and frame provides a new environment, with an attachment that is secure enough to invite and support real-self experience and exploration. The therapist's expectation that the patient will identify thoughts and feelings, verbalize them in session, and behave in a mature, healthy, and adaptive manner outside of session establishes a benchmark for competent and responsible behavior. But how is this expectation communicated? Masterson (1976, 1981) considers confrontation the intervention of choice for the borderline personality disorder and the most sensitive and empathic way to relate to the needs of the real self.

The notion of confrontation as an intervention in the treatment of the borderline personality disorder is not new (Adler, 1985; Kernberg, Selzer, Koenigsberg, Carr, and Appelbaum, 1989). But Masterson (1976, 1981) offers a distinctive conception of confrontation as a technical intervention. Like others (Adler, 1985; Hamilton, 1988; Kernberg et al., 1989; Clarkin et al., 1999; Rinsley, 1982), he believes that confrontation is a way to call to the patient's attention something that has been kept from awareness. According to Masterson (1976),

> the poor reality perception of the borderline patient, together with the degree to which primitive pathologic defenses—splitting, avoidance, denial, acting out, projection, clinging, projective identification—result in the further obscuring of reality, leaves the borderline patient at a great disadvantage in adapting to reality. . . . The therapeutic confrontations lend to the patient the therapist's reality perception and thereby help him/her to start to repair this defect through identification [with the therapist]. (p. 136)

Specifically, it is confrontation of defenses against the experience and expression of the real self and, ultimately, against the abandonment depression that Masterson considers essential to effective treatment of borderline patients. So, what does such a confrontation look like?

THREE COMPONENTS OF A CONFRONTATION

Confrontations that are useful in the treatment of borderline personality disorder, where defenses are characteristically ego-syntonic, have three components. First, the maladaptive defensive behaviors of the false self and, second, their self-defeating, self-destructive effects must be brought to the patient's attention. Third, the patient is asked to consider why these behaviors are perpetuated. A generic confrontation states, "I've noticed that you . . . , but when you do so, it's not good for you. Why do you think you do that?"

As such, the defense is identified for the patient. When a patient fails to identify feelings and explore them in session, to support oneself in a relationship and when he or she acts out with drugs, alcohol, or sex; avoids self-activation; or otherwise behaves in a nonhealthy, maladaptive, self-irresponsible manner, the behavior is identified, and an expression of concern or surprise is related through the vehicle of confrontation. As Klein (1989b) has stated,

> in working with the borderline patient, the therapist must be prepared to confront the pathological defenses and resistances of the patient as these manifest themselves both outside and within the treatment setting. All of the borderline patient's attempts at reality distortion and maladaptation through flight from responsibility for thoughts, feelings, and actions must be responded to. They represent the activation of and operations of the patient's false, defensive self. This is of crucial importance, because these attempts at defense and resistance hold sway over the borderline patient, who identifies with the false, defensive self and views it as the real self. (pp. 218–219)

In other words, "I've noticed that you . . . "

But identification of the defense alone is insufficient; the self-defeating effects of the defense must be underscored also ("It's not good for you"). Implicitly or explicitly, the confrontation asks why adaptation, initiative, self-support, and self-activation are neglected or why blatantly self-destructive behaviors perpetually repeated ("Why do you think you do that?"). In this way, the therapist challenges not only the defense itself but also the patient's assumption that it is protective. In confrontation, the therapist implicitly suggests that there is a more satisfying way of being with others and with one's self—namely, the experience and expression of the real self. Interventions like this initiate a reproceduring of the borderline person's archaic conditions of attachment and allow for the emergence of a new working model of relationships. They offer hope for the patient, in the form of another chance to be competent.

CASE EXAMPLE

Kathy was 24 and single when her mother suggested that she seek psychotherapy. She had recently lost her job as a hotel housekeeper after making persistent sexual overtures to a fellow male employee. She had a several-year history of addictive, promiscuous, and self-demeaning sexual liaisons, and she believed that she couldn't control her sexual impulses. She also felt helpless about managing her moderate obesity. She began an early session like this:

KATHY: I'm still back in the old habit of going to the Internet and getting together with men.

THERAPIST (DDR): What I'm noticing is that you talk about sex and eating as if you're at the mercy of your appetites—like you don't have any control of yourself. Are you aware of that? [*I'm noting the defensive acting out of her helplessness and calling it to her attention.*] And that just leaves you feeling even worse about yourself. [*Here I address the self-destructiveness of the defense.*]

KATHY: Yeah. I am pretty impulsive.

She responded to the intervention in an almost-reflexive, compliant, and nonreflective manner. Further confrontation is indicated.

THERAPIST: You do seem to be pretty impulsive, but you also behave as if you have almost no control over your behavior, as if you're a victim of your feelings and impulses. Do you think that is true? [*Again, I address the way that she acts out helplessness as a defense against self-support, and then I allow her a moment to reflect on my intervention. But she remains silent, so I go on to raise for her a question that I'm pretty sure she's never asked herself.*] Have you ever thought that you might be selling yourself short when you buy into that way of thinking?

KATHY: You're probably right. [*There's a sigh and a long pause, then tears.*] But when I think of not having sex, I get this ache inside, like if I don't give them sex, no man will ever want me.

The mere thought of containing her defensive acting out is sufficient activation of Kathy's real self to stimulate the underlying abandonment depression—the ache inside—against which Kathy's promiscuity is supposed to defend her (an example of the triad of self-activation → abandonment depression → defense). The self-activation is short-lived—this was early in her therapy—and repeated confrontations of her denial and acting out of helplessness were necessary before she began to support herself in a consistent manner.

In another session, Kathy tried to justify her persistence in pursuing her sexual affairs.

KATHY: Sex makes me feel better about myself. It helps my self-esteem. These men think I'm attractive if they want to have sex with me.

THERAPIST: Now, I want to be sure I'm understanding you. You're telling me that your self-esteem is actually *better* after you have sex with one of these strangers whom you will never see again?

KATHY: Yes. [*A long pause.*] But it doesn't last. It's like after you have a double latte—you feel good and then later you feel down. [*Another pause.*] But it's better than nothing.

Again, she skirts the abandonment depression and returns to her defense, so I challenge her once more.

THERAPIST: I'm not so sure it is. You know, I read a poem recently about someone who went to the hardware store every day to buy a quart of milk, in spite of being reminded daily that hardware stores don't sell milk. You remind me of him. You talk about wanting a relationship with a man in which you feel valued for who you are, yet you settle for fleeting sexual encounters with nameless men who verbally abuse you. And while you long for self-esteem, you make choices that doom you to feeling bad about yourself. Are you aware of this?

KATHY: I sometimes wonder if I don't confuse abuse and love. It seems like that was how my mom loved me.

This time, Kathy apparently does integrate the confrontation. There is at least a momentary containment of defense and evoked associations and memories. She allows herself a moment of reflection on meaningful genetic material, with deepened affect. A new object relations unit, a new internal working model of relationships, is beginning to emerge; the old relational procedures of compliance and deference to the other person are beginning to give way to the reproceduring of self-awareness, self-support, and self-assertion.

Although each confrontation comprises these three components, the content of each confrontation and case may be different, but the process is the same. As such, we watch for process—the triad of the disorders of the self—and respond with a confrontation. What do we hope to accomplish?

THE GOALS OF CONFRONTATION

A confrontation has four goals. First, the confrontation is intended to bring to the patient's awareness the operation of defensive thoughts and behaviors that interfere with the experience, expression, and growth of the real self. Second, it is calculated to render the identified defense ego-alien. Third, the confrontation is designed to encourage the containment of the defense, to allow for the emergence, experience, and activation of the real self. Fourth, the confrontational process is intended to let the patient experience and observe the operation of the borderline triad and wonder about its genetic roots.

A successful series of confrontations therefore results in the patients' awareness of what we see: their habitual thoughts and behaviors (defenses) that interfere with the growth of their real selves, a growing sense of its ego-alien quality, and efforts to contain these chronic practices. In other words, the patients will stop doing what they have been doing that has prevented activation of the real self. As the containment of defense frees dreaded feelings to emerge for expression and exploration, there will be a deepening of affect. (At this point the patients will either talk about the feelings—*with* feeling—and continue with self-reflection or will activate a new defense against that affective experience. This would then require further confrontation.) Ideally, when the patients are finally able to reflect on the depth of their feelings, they will be able to make sense of why they feel this way and thereby make a link between their defensive habits and the affects that such habits have protected them from. In short, the patients will become aware of the operation of the borderline triad: Self-activation results in abandonment depression, which results in defense.

THE NECESSITY OF CONFRONTATION

Why are confrontations necessary? Confrontive interventions are particularly necessary with borderline-disordered patients because their habitual ways of managing their lives are not related to reality. As Masterson (1976, 1981) says, these people have no awareness or a very limited awareness that their alternating projections of the rewarding and withdrawing object representations are not necessarily reflections of reality. Borderline patients are seeking a relationship with a therapist who supports dependence, irresponsibility, incompetence, and regression. This is predictable from the implicit relational procedures that borderline people internalize early on as conditions of attachment. If the therapist resonates with this projection of the rewarding object—by sanctioning irresponsibility in the form of missed appointments and payments, by providing explanations for the patient's behavior, by offering direction in sessions, by accepting requests for regular telephone contact, or by any other way of taking over for the patient—the patients will most likely feel good. But there will be no accessing the real self. In other words, there will be no therapy. The patients experience these self-protective scenarios as ego-syntonic episodes; they are not conflicted about their maladaptive defenses, because they consider them to be "normal." It is the therapeutic frame that provides the foundation for the first order of confrontations that open the eyes of the patients to what is real. In other words, therapy will ask them to assume responsibility for themselves; the therapist is not going to do for them what they are capable of doing themselves.

However, if the therapist does not collude with the patient's projections of the rewarding object and confronts them instead, wisps of the abandonment depression will probably be tapped. In accord with the triad of the disorders of the self, the borderline patient is then likely to shift to projecting the withdrawing object and attribute the source of the painful abandonment feelings to the therapist rather than to an intrapsychic experience.

The task for the therapist, then, is to intervene in such a way as to call into question the usefulness of the patient's defensive reality distortions and expectations and to foster internal conflict as to the "normalcy" of behaviors that are in fact self-defeating. As such, confrontations are the necessary means to alter the borderline patient's distortions of reality. Furthermore, the confrontations will necessarily and alternately focus on the rewarding unit and the withdrawing unit distortions, and they will result in disruptions in the relationship with the therapist.

A CASE EXAMPLE

Mary was 36 years old and single. She had accumulated an extensive treatment history with multiple therapists by the time she came to me (DDR) for treatment. She told me that she had been diagnosed with a borderline personality disorder, and she expressed the hope that a new approach to therapy would be more helpful than her previous treatment experiences had been. The following excerpt is taken from a session early in her work with me:

> MARY: Well, I didn't sleep very well last night, so I've been really tired today, and I just really feel on edge—kind of crabby and irritable—just too many feelings coming up with this therapy, and I don't know what to do with them. [*Pause.*] I'm still not sure about how this therapy works, like what I should talk about. I got the feeling that talking like I did in the last session—getting all upset and crying—is being discouraged.
>
> THERAPIST: You did? Hmm. [*Thoughtfully.*] I don't remember saying anything like that. Why do you suppose you think I'm discouraging your expressing your feelings in here?

Apparently in response to my therapeutic neutrality and my failure to provide direction and thereby resonate with the projection of the rewarding object, the patient is projecting and enacting the withdrawing object relations unit. That is, she is projecting onto me (as far as I am aware) her conviction that I disapproved of an activation of her real self in the previous session—an affectively lively replay of her experiences in her early years with her mother. I confront this defense, her projection, by asking her the reason for her misperception of me.

MARY: Well, when you ask questions about what I'm feeling, I feel like you're telling me I shouldn't be feeling whatever it is that I'm feeling. And, I've been thinking about it, and I'm afraid that I'm just "acting out," and I'm not supposed to be doing that in this kind of therapy.

My confrontation has been ineffectual. Mary continues to defend against focusing on herself and her experience. She persists in her struggle to discern my expectations so that she can comply with them—a predominant aspect of her implicitly procedured attachment style. This defense, too, requires confrontation.

THERAPIST: You know, it sounds to me like you've got a lot of ideas about what this therapy should look like or what I expect from you. Rather than trying to figure out what's important to you to talk about, you're trying to plug yourself into some picture of what I think you should be doing in here. But that takes you away from yourself and your experience. Have you noticed that? [*Pause.*] Do you have any idea about why you might be doing that?

MARY: [*Pause.*] Well, in here I start to feel really little—and afraid—afraid I'll say the wrong thing. I don't know what to say. [*She pauses again, in tears.*] Another thing—I really appreciate your finding this time for me to come in; it works a lot better for me with my job.

This time, the intervention is apparently integrated because she does refocus briefly on her self-experience, and her tears seem to signal some deepening of affect. But almost immediately, she shifts her focus away from herself and back to me, a renewal of her characteristic defense. This is how the triad works: Activation of the real self stimulates the abandonment depression, which stimulates defense. I track this sequence for her as a prelude to a new confrontation, and I watch to see if she begins to watch her process with me.

THERAPIST: What I noticed is that you began to describe some feelings about why it's so difficult for you to know what to talk about in here. Then you quickly shifted the focus from you and your feelings to me. What do you think happened?

MARY: [*Crying.*] Well, like I said, I just start to feel really little, and then I freeze. I'm afraid I'll say the wrong thing. I don't know. And I feel kind of confused about what direction I should take. I'm aware of this part of me that feels really little and like I want to cry, but I don't know what I'm supposed to do.

Again, she responds to the confrontation by containing defense long enough for affect to emerge and for a moment of self-reflection. But she quickly defends again with efforts at compliance to feel reconnected to me.

THERAPIST: Now, did you notice how you started to feel some real feelings—about the experience of feeling very little—and then stopped yourself by questioning whether you should feel them? When you do that, of course, it is hard for both you and me to listen to your self and your experience.

MARY: [*Crying.*] I guess I really don't know what's okay. [Pause.] I kind of feel mad and little! [*Pause.*] It reminds me of feeling little and panicky and afraid and like I'm supposed to be quiet, but I can't be quiet because I'm crying. [*She sobs, and then there's a long pause.*] I don't know. I feel like I probably shouldn't be talking like this—going over and over this stuff—like I'm probably acting out or something. I don't know what I'm supposed to do.

Her resumption of focus on herself results in the emergence of feelings and associations. But again, her firmly procedured attachment strategy of compliance with the object, acting out of helplessness, and intellectualization replaces the incipient real-self procedure.

THERAPIST: It seems like you're doing it again. You started talking about your feelings, then questioned whether you should be having those feelings, and then dismissed them with a theoretical label. Can you see how, in doing this, you keep removing yourself, one step at a time, from your self and your feelings?

MARY: I just feel so young and like there's nowhere to go with my feelings. I can't remember much of anything about my relationship to my parents when I was young. I remember more here today, just talking about these feelings, than I've remembered before. I guess it's just a really early lifetime feeling of what I felt as a young child, like scared and mad, and like my mom's gone and I don't know what to do. [*She sobs deeply and then goes on slowly.*] I guess it just reminds me of that feeling, of being afraid and alone. [*Pause.*] You're right. My tendency now is to think about all of this theoretically, like I can face the feelings only for so long.

This time, the defenses are contained sufficiently to allow for the emergence of real-self experience, affect, and at least glimpses of memories. In addition, there is the beginning of an awareness of the link between the activation of her real self (her focus on herself), her abandonment depression, and defense. As such, she did begin to watch her process, but persistent confrontations of Mary's oscillating projections were necessary for her to accomplish this.

Unfortunately, in this session, Mary is not yet beginning to see who I am, a therapist who is there to provide support for her to listen to herself, someone in this world who is really interested in her. This is a reality that she has never known. Instead, she is imprisoned in the projection that I am critical and withdrawing, unless she complies with what she thinks I expect of her.

CONFRONTATION AS ATTUNEMENT

Although confrontation is necessary to the treatment of these patients, its effectiveness is due to the therapist's compassionate attunement to them. However, some have cautioned that confrontation can be misused with patients with borderline personality disorder (Adler, 1985); others (Rowe and MacIsaac, 1989) insist that confrontations must be avoided altogether, on the grounds that they disrupt the empathic bond between the patient and the therapist. We contend (to the contrary and perhaps counterintuitively) that confrontation of maladaptive defenses offers a pointed, sensitively attuned communication to the underdeveloped and impaired real self of the borderline-disordered person. Interpretation risks collusion with the patients' projection of the rewarding object, who will gratify their dependency and passivity by doing for them what they need to do for themselves. Confrontation, however, makes clear that the patients are expected to discover their own interpretation of their behavior, as they become more familiar with the operation of the triad of the disorders of the self. In doing so, they begin to find their own stories.

Hahn (2004) and Masterson (1976, 1981) maintain that the pairing of the defense with its destructiveness to the self-experience resonates with a fundamental developmental need of the real but impaired self of the patient. That is, confrontations communicate a confidence in the underdeveloped real self's latent need and capacity for activation and expression. This conveys, in a profound way, the therapist's empathic understanding of and attunement to the patient. In fact, the patients can experience the truths about themselves and their stories in an altogether new way. The borderline patient has never had a relationship that consistently communicated,

> You don't have to fear reality or responsibility. I believe that you can deal with it. You can feel and think and talk about your feelings and thoughts and discover what they mean. When you don't, you deprive yourself of the chance to improve your lot and experience your competence.

These individuals have never had anyone confident enough in their potential and dogged enough in expressing it for that confidence to be internalized. The therapist is the patient's first persistent champion of the real self and, in fact, offers the patient an amazing new opportunity.

> Mary's developmentally derived deficits were profound, her projections insistent, and her acting out intense. Not only did she present herself as being sad and hopeless, but over and over, she returned to whiny and, at times, demanding insistence that she was unable to reflect on her own experience, that I was her only hope of salvation, and that she desperately needed my direction or, lacking that direction, needed to discern my covert expecta-

tions for her. As you might imagine, empathic attunement was not always my natural response to her plight; my primary countertransference reaction was irritation and impatience. However, my theoretical foundation gave me a reliable awareness of her vulnerability and desperation. This fueled the needed compassion. Mary's understanding of others and her ways of relating had created a prison out of which there was no escape—except possibly through a corrective relational experience that would enable a revision of her now-destructive implicit relational procedures.

When Mary came into her sessions, she projected onto me the rewarding object representation that supports regression and dependence, and she accepted the accompanying belief that I wanted to be depended on. She enacted in the therapy relationship her implicit memory that the price of emotional survival is helplessness and her conviction that I believed this, too. Therefore, she imagined that the executive functions of directing, guiding, and thinking were necessarily my business. Her assumption that the work of therapy is the therapist's is expressed in her statement "I don't have any answers. I don't even know what my problem is, and that is why I have come to you."

Yet, when I failed to respond as she had wanted me to, Mary projected the withholding aspect of her split experience and expected me to be depriving, emotionally withdrawing, or punitive. She actually believed, in a mildly paranoid way, that I was intentionally scheming to make her life miserable. Early in her treatment, she would, in furious rages, accuse me of trying to destroy her or see her suffer. Remember, when the withdrawing object relations unit is activated, the self-representation is "bad"—worthless, ugly, and despicable; the patient may express this "badness" in self-criticism and self-harm, as well as in the acting out of anger or resistance.

Whichever side of her split experience was active, however, Mary, like other individuals with borderline personality disorder, really did not know how to feel or think for herself. If she needed help, maybe someone would be there for her; experience had taught her that, at least some of the time, someone would come if she asked for help. But if she were spontaneous in her expression of herself, any supportive emotional connection would be destroyed; this would activate angry acting out and devaluation, but at least it was a connection, albeit an unpleasant one. So, as a bee goes to honey, she sought the complementary affects that, to her, meant connection—support in response to her helplessness or struggle in response to her rage.

When she first came to my office, Mary didn't know any different way of being herself with someone else. It was my job to remember that fact, to remind myself that her alternating projections were not a function of the will, and to provide a new kind of relationship that acknowledged and supported Mary's real and spontaneous self. It was my business to interrupt the cycling of and need for her split false-self relating. This meant inviting her into an alliance in which she could learn to watch and wonder about herself and her process and to practice thinking about her thoughts, feelings, and behaviors—all in the presence of a genuinely interested other. It is this attunement to the person's real self that vitalizes the therapist's confrontational approach.

Most borderline-disordered individuals are not only unaware of their feelings, however; they are also resistant to facing them, because they have long been accustomed to fending off the haunting affects—mostly, dark and helpless ones—of the abandonment depression. This avoidance further neglects and suppresses the real self. This understanding of their despairing histories provides the technical and emotional framework for the therapy of borderline patients, which is based on a compassionate confrontation of defenses. Only when defenses are disrupted can feelings be experienced and eventually put into words. As the therapist points out the self-destructiveness of the patient's false self and wonders about it, he or she is inviting the patient's real self into the relationship and watching for a moment of real-self experience or expression. It is this resonance with borderline patients' underlying real needs that enables them to accept and integrate therapeutic confrontations. Shared moments of real awareness—of knowing and feeling known—are the building blocks of the real self's growing freedom to be.

CONFRONTATION AND EMPATHY

The concept of empathy is important to this discussion of confrontation as a therapeutic intervention, in two ways. First, confrontational interventions are commonly considered to be *un*empathic. But to really be effective, they must be empathic. Confrontations of borderline patients are meant to address the deepest needs of the struggling real self. Because the real self cannot be forced, directed, manipulated, seduced, coerced, or bullied into activation, confrontations must not be offered in aggressive, harsh, forceful, coercive, emotionally detached, or otherwise misattuned ways. To the contrary, if they are to be received, they must be communicated as empathically as any other psychotherapeutic intervention; this, of course, requires affective attunement to the real self of the patient.

> The therapist must be able to be "really there," empathic and "tuned in" to the patient's feeling state in order for the confrontation to work. The confrontation must be faithfully wedded to the content of the patient's associations and the patient's feeling state. It must be clearly in the patient's best interest. If it is not, the authority inherent in the dynamic theme itself is replaced by the therapist's authority. (Masterson, 1976, p. 101)

What are the differences between empathy and attunement? As we understand it, attunement is the resonating search for the nascent real self that we believe is there. Empathy is a fruit of the therapist's attunement to the tragic plight of the borderline patient, and it is born of the resulting awareness of the painfully despairing experience of the patient's under-developed real self. Imprisoned by once-necessary but now destructive early implicit relational procedures, borderline individuals despair of finding satisfaction, freedom of expression, or personal competence. The empathic response to this impaired real self is communicated through confrontation: "I know you're in there. Let's stop and think about who you are and what you want. I'm ready to listen."

Second, when confrontations speak to the needs of the real self, they are eventually experienced as empathy by borderline patients. All patients need to feel seen, known, and understood, and for the borderline, the experience of being known results from the therapist's empathic communication through confrontation that she or he understands the enfeeblement of the patient's real self yet still believes in its latent capacities. Of course, confrontations may not initially be experienced as empathic exchanges. But with repetitive experiences of the disruption–repair cycle, the patient will come to accept them as expressions of the therapist's genuine interest in supporting the real self.

Of course, it is not just the words of the confrontation that communicate to the patient. The therapist's actions and prosody speak as loudly as her or his interventions. The consistent confidence and firmness communicated through confrontations make possible a relationship safe enough for experience and exploration of the real self. At the same time, the therapist offers a demonstration of how to really be present to another person, by persisting in the relationship in spite of disruptions. Even firm limit setting by the therapist will be experienced at some level as a recognition of the patient's need for restraint and an understanding of an underdeveloped capacity to provide it for oneself.

As Cassidy (2001) has said, "a hard truth in a difficult time is a safe haven." For borderline people, because of how they live their lives, all times are difficult times. But the truth communicated through confrontation or limit setting provides a context of safety for the negotiation of a secure separation.

The therapist's tone may be concerned, interested, quizzical, confused, startled, or even shocked; what matters is that the real impaired self, however feeble it may be, is addressed with empathy in an effort to support its emergence and free it for growth. New conditions of attachment based on real-self relating are introduced. This is why, in the context of therapeutic neutrality and the psychotherapy frame and when offered with an eye for the nearly invisible real self of the patient, confrontations are like tuning forks: They set up an interactive affective resonance between the patient and the therapist. These are the "now moments" of which Stern (1998) speaks, "a point in ongoing process where change can occur between the two participants" (p. 304). Real-self feelings are "jump-started," perhaps for the first time. And there is a life-imparting, vivifying, collaborative communication that says, "There you are! I see you! I feel distressed with you, but I believe in you. Can you see that?" The excitement of feeling known invites the repetition of new procedures of being.

Stated simply, the truth of confrontation will speak for itself; it requires no coercion or control. If laid out thoughtfully, with empathy, kind intent, and sensitive attunement to the real self, the confrontation will make sense at a deep level by virtue of its call to dignity, the dignity of choice.

CONFRONTATION AND STRUGGLE

A caveat is warranted at this point. The process of confrontation and response described here probably sounds clean, orderly, and comfortably coordinated. However, the reality is that the interplay between therapist and patient, when confrontation is involved, is often, if not usually, conflicted, miscoordinated, and sloppy, particularly in the early stages of the treatment (Bruschweiler-Stern et al., 2005). The typical borderline patient is implicitly loathe to let go of defenses that have more or less successfully protected him or her from the experience of feelings related to separation and abandonment. When the therapist repeatedly brings to his or her attention the implication that there is a need for the relinquishment of these behaviors, the patient and the therapist are at cross-purposes—a metaphorical "stick in the spokes" is created.

Intrinsic to any technical stance or strategy—and, certainly, including this one—is the moment-to-moment grappling within a dyad about the direction that the therapy process will take. Intense negotiations are ongoing for both parties: "Are you willing to make this leap to try to find yourself? to explore deeply your experience of yourself? to put words on it, as fuzzy as it is?" And it does not feel good; it feels more like scuffling—and not just for the patient. Such times are often deeply disturbing and disorganizing for the therapist as well. Questions of intrinsic truth addressed to the patient result in a cliff-hanger experience as the therapist waits and watches to see if the disturbing invitation is received rather than angrily rejected. These moments can be intense and disordered. But they are also the moments that produce the elements of amazement and anguish that can build onto the sloppy therapy process to create a shared new direction that spontaneously produces a co-created relationship in which the patient's real self can be tried on. This is the poignant and deeply human nature of confrontation.

COUNTERTRANSFERENCE

Countertransference poses a formidable obstacle to therapeutic neutrality in work with borderline patients. One reason for this is the apparent willfulness of the patient's defensive behaviors, which in fact are implicit relational procedures that are neither conscious nor willed. It is important to keep in mind that the patients cannot help themselves; it is not that they have determined to assume their provocative stance but that they do not yet know how to do otherwise. They believe that you, the therapist, want them to be and act as if they were helpless and that you want to be the one with all the answers. They believe that they are helpless. They do not know how to think for themselves about their feelings and thoughts. And they are not likely to discover otherwise until the therapist first communicates to them the strong expectation that they can learn to do it and then waits and watches patiently while they do so. Sometimes, the only hope that the patients have is the therapist's confidence in them.

If negative countertransference reactions are enacted in session so that confrontations become angry, critical, or argumentative, interventions will resonate not with the patient's real self but with the projection of the withdrawing object relations unit. Aggressive or otherwise resistant defenses are likely to intensify in response to an experience of the therapist as a punitive or emotionally withdrawing figure. According to Masterson (1976),

> the therapist must be able to confront quietly, firmly and consistently without being angry or contentious. He must be able to disagree without being disagreeable. If the patient senses that the therapist is angry he will use the anger to avoid the validity of the confrontation—i.e., the therapist is saying it because he's angry, not because it is true. (p. 101)

Schore (1999b) amplifies this point. Applying implications from infant research to the psychotherapy relationship, he suggests that there must be

> a dyadic mechanism that in the short term disconfirms the patient's pathogenic transferential expectations that underlie defensive avoidance, and in the long-term allows for the emergence of a psychic structural system that more effectively regulates negative affect. How the therapist tolerates the negative affect is a critical factor determining the range and types of emotion that are explored or disavowed in the transference-countertransference relationship. (p. 3)

That is, if confrontations are enacted in resonance with the projections of the withdrawing, punitive internal object, then defense is reinforced. However, neutrality with respect to these projections allows the focus to remain on the real self of the patient, with corresponding encouragement of its free and spontaneous experience in the treatment hour. The therapist may feel provoked but must reflectively confront rather than reactively respond.

Confrontations in the psychotherapy of borderline patients are designed to bring maladaptive defenses to the patient's attention and thereby raise questions about why adaptation, self-activation, and self-support are being neglected. When confrontations are integrated by the patient, defenses will be contained, and more adaptive, self-supportive means of managing emerging dysphoric affects will be considered and perhaps implemented. The patient, who previously did not know that other ways of managing were possible, begins to develop needed self-procedures in a relationship that encourages them.

However, therapists who are beginning to apply this model of treatment are sometimes discouraged when a patient continues to use a defense, despite well-crafted confrontations. But it is not a given that any particular confrontation will be received and integrated. Especially early in treatment, similar confrontations of the same defense may be repeatedly required until the patient is able to contain the defense. For the therapist, this redundant process can be tedious and, understandably, quite discouraging—an "Oh, no! Here we go again!" experience. So, it is important to remind one's self that this model of psychotherapy clearly predicts the tenacity of the patient's defenses and the need for the therapist's equally tenacious hope for the patient, enacted in relentless confrontations.

> When Mary had been in treatment for about 9 months, she began to press me about my plans for an upcoming summer vacation. She said that she was quite certain that she would not be able to tolerate my absence for 2 weeks and that she was planning to arrange consultations with a "substitute therapist." She requested a referral for this purpose. I understood this to be acting out her helplessness in defense against her abandonment depression, and I began to ask why she felt that she couldn't manage her feelings for 2 weeks without a therapist: "I understand that you are really anxious about my going away on vacation. But I'm also perplexed about why you feel you can't cope, without seeing a 'substitute therapist' for those 2 weeks. Doesn't that just reinforce your picture of yourself as weak, needy, and helpless?"
>
> I intended to convey to Mary my belief that she could manage without therapy. But my confrontational queries were met consistently with incredulity, anger, and accusations that I was cold, uncaring, and sadistic. Allegations of unethical practice were leveled, along with the accusation that I desired to see her suffer. In the course of this phase of the therapy, I felt misunderstood and unfairly maligned, and it was distressing to me. Each time she directed one of these charges at me, I took a few minutes before I responded, realizing that this was her habitual response to the expectation that she could take care of herself. I reminded myself that even though this was 9 months into her therapy, defensive repetitions and recurrences persisted. She had not yet begun to believe that I really was for her, that I was her advocate, and that she could be for herself.

Mary's withdrawing object relations unit had been activated. Feeling mistreated and bad, she saw me as a cold, punitive, and uncaring figure and, therefore, the cause of her discomfort. Informed by the knowledge of the necessity of her repetitive defenses and my repetitive confrontations, I responded, "I can see that you're very angry at me, and I'd like to understand this better. Why do you think you feel so misunderstood, so mistreated, and so deserted by my confidence that you can manage yourself in my absence?"

Interventions like these typically triggered a reactivation of the rewarding object relations unit, with pleas for "understanding" and support of her wish for a "safety net" while I was gone. I must admit that Mary's desperate pleas for help in my absence caused me to wonder if she would be able to tolerate the disruption of her therapy. Worse, I even thought of other therapists that I could refer her to. But I reminded myself that I must be committed to believing in her capacity to manage the break in therapy; I determined to stay the course by continuing to confront her acting out of helplessness.

In the weeks approaching my vacation, I took up these oscillating projections with Mary over and over again, with what felt like incredible persistence. Session after session was focused on my plan to "abandon" her for 2 weeks, and it required no mean effort on my part to manage my increasing annoyance and maintain therapeutic neutrality as I anticipated each session. But in time, she became able to integrate the confrontations, forego her attacks and her demands, and assume responsibility for exploring more self-supportive means of managing her anxiety in my absence. She made plans to spend more time with friends while I was gone, and she scheduled regular pleasurable activities ahead of time. She coped successfully with my vacation break. I breathed a temporary sigh of relief, both for her finally supporting herself and for my managing her provocation and my discouragement sufficiently enough to persist in my commitment to her real self.

CONFRONTATION AND A SECURE SEPARATION

It is only in the context of a more secure attachment relationship with the therapist that secure separation becomes a possibility. It is within a secure-enough attachment that repetitive confrontations, faithful to a commitment to the patient's real self, are effective. Incrementally, rupture by rupture, negotiation by negotiation, moment by moment, a model of disruption–despair morphs into one of disruption–repair, and a capacity for tolerance of separation and autonomy grows. New object relations units are forged, reflecting a gradual shift from "I trust you" to "I trust myself." This trust is earned by patient and therapist in watchful relating around differences. It is here, over time, that a secure separation is realized, and the real self is born out of the secure separation that is lived out within this relationship.

In summary, this model of treatment suggests that it is necessary to disrupt old, maladaptive attachment strategies to allow for the development of more self-supportive internal working models of relationships. When the defensive habits of helpless compliance or rageful badness block the experience of the real self, confrontative interventions are required to interrupt and contain them. Because of the tenacity of the implicitly procedured false defensive self, confrontations, especially early in treatment, need to be offered repeatedly and consistently before the targeted defenses begin to become ego-alien, and their containment motivated.

In effect, we midwife a process. When we intervene with perseverance, we are relating to the patient's latent real self and its capacities. This opens the way for a new kind of attachment experience to be internalized with a new object relations unit, one that supports an experience and expression of the self that is real, rather than one that is counterfeit and defensive. With an attitude of persistent commitment, we bring to the patient a relationship offer that may be a "last chance," as Klein (1998) told us once in group supervision many years ago. We may, in fact, become the patient's first chance to discover his or her real self. But first or last, through an earned secure attachment and an earned secure separation, it is at least the chance that the patient needs in order to be real.

6

Psychotherapy

Another Chance to Be Real

In our work with borderline personality disordered patients, we use a combination of relational, structural, and technical elements. We want to support the unfolding of the kind of relationship between patient and therapist that can encourage the development of the patient's real self; more specific goals include the attenuation of separation sensitivity and the development of new and more adaptive procedures for being and relating. But work with these patients is not smooth; obstacles are inevitably encountered, and these must be identified and addressed if the real self is to have another chance.

GOALS OF PSYCHOTHERAPY

From our perspective, the optimal outcome for borderline patients involves a working through of the underlying painful real-self experience—the abandonment depression—and, with it, the development of a capacity for whole (not split) object relations. This accomplished, there is no further need for primitive defensive operations, and the real self is freed for full experience and expression. But the acquisition of new procedures takes time and patience, and so does the necessary mourning for lost time and opportunities as old maladaptive attachment strategies—namely, the false self and its implicit relational procedures—are relinquished. Psychoanalytic psychotherapy aimed at working through the abandonment depression typically requires an intensive schedule of three times a week or more and, often, for several years.

A less ambitious but nonetheless significant goal involves partial attenuation of the abandonment depression and the improved ego functioning that goes with it: stronger boundaries; greater reflectiveness; and better reality perception, impulse control, frustration tolerance, and affect regulation. This makes for generally improved functioning and fewer symptoms because management of the underlying separation sensitivity is more adaptive. Ego-repair treatment can usually be accomplished in a regimen of weekly sessions for anywhere from 40 weeks to several years. The case of Terri, whose therapy we present in detail in chapter 7, illustrates this shorter-term ego-repair approach.

In both scenarios—ego repair treatment and an intensive psychoanalytic approach—these broad goals can be broken down into specific ones. Klein (1989d), in his formulation of a shorter-term approach to the treatment of the borderline personality disorder, identified three: containment, learning, and adaptation.

Containment

The borderline patient has to learn to recognize and contain the acting out of maladaptive defenses—that is, to abstain from the enactment of old, self-destructive relational procedures. It is in the patient's best interest to relinquish self-defeating behaviors, if only because they have such adverse effects on his or her life. But it is only through the control of these defenses that the abandonment depression can emerge into awareness and eventually be understood as the basis of the patient's self-destructive patterns. The triad of the disorders of the self and its effects can be experienced in awareness only when there is a cessation of defense so that the patient can really see the link between the dark feelings and the self-defeating, false-self behavior. For this reason, it is imperative for the therapist to diligently track the operation of the triad, as it is observed in session and as out-of-session instances are reported. If the patient is self-activating through the experience and expression of the real self, there is no need for intervention on the part of the therapist. However, when the patient reverts to defense, the therapist must then confront the defense in an effort to encourage its containment.

> Richard, a 38-year-old borderline patient well into his therapy, was telling his therapist (a supervisee) that his girlfriend had decided to visit her family in a neighboring state instead of spending the weekend with him. Then, he asked abruptly, "What do you think is going on with her? Do you think she's trying to tell me something?"
>
> The therapist pointed out that he shifted his attention away from his experience of this disturbing event to her, the therapist, and to her assessment of his girlfriend's behavior. She wondered aloud why he would do that if he

were really trying to understand better his reactions in relationships with women. Richard thought about this and then said, "I think it's because I get so scared if I think that she might be dumping me." When Richard, with his therapist's help, was able to refrain from shifting his focus onto her and instead continue to explore his own experience, he became more aware of how his abandonment fears were permeating his relationship with his girlfriend. He was able to see his process and go back to work on himself.

Learning

The patient must develop some insight into why he or she relies so on defenses that are clearly self-destructive. That is, the patient must learn something about how the triad of the disorders of the self operates in one's life—how the abandonment depression comes up when it is not being held at bay by habitual but obsolete ways of being and relating. The therapist must watch for the triad and track it consistently for the patient, making its activity clear. As the therapist's interventions are integrated, the patient begins to recognize its dynamics, too. Then, defense is slowly contained; old self-defeating ways are reconsidered; and long-suppressed affects and memories emerge. This link between affect and defense is a necessary insight for the patient.

> Toward the end of his therapy, Richard began to be able to see and track his own triad process and note how he shifted away from uncomfortable affect. "I just did it again," he said one day to his therapist. "I was talking about how difficult my relationship with my father has been, and then I began to talk about him, trying to understand him. I'm noticing lately how I do that a lot, move away from difficult feelings by focusing on someone else. It's pretty scary to realize that I've been doing this my whole life and never even realized it."

Adaptation

Borderline patients cling hard to their early-procedured attachment strategies and affect-regulation schemas. They are under a great deal of internal pressure to avoid the abandonment depression. But the only means that they know for doing this—regression to a false-self defensive system—create sadly chaotic and self-damaging lives. The psychotherapist must therefore be resolutely dedicated to support of the real self and to constructive adaptation.

A central focus of this type of treatment is how patients manage (or mismanage) their lives—that is, how they begin to activate and support themselves in healthy and realistic ways or how they forego their efforts to express themselves assertively and autonomously; how they maintain

appropriate boundaries in their relationships or how they cling dependently to others, disallowing any sense of an autonomous self; how they
communicate their feelings, desires, and needs or how they act out self-
destructively. In short, we watch and we help our patients watch so that
they learn to distinguish between obsolete and self-defeating ways of
regulating affect and ways that are consistent with mature, responsible,
effective functioning. We must help them learn the value and techniques
of self-confrontation ("Wait a minute! What am I doing?") and choose
adaptive options of managing their lives rather than the old habits that
create so many problems.

> Shortly before the conclusion of his therapy, Richard reported that his girl-
> friend had unexpectedly gone out for drinks with some coworkers one eve-
> ning after work. In the past, this would have stimulated intense fear and anxi-
> ety in him, as well as persistent ruminations about whether she was losing
> interest in him and maybe even being unfaithful. These worries would have
> set off an accusatory, inflammatory, and altogether destructive confrontation
> with her—that is, an enactment of the withdrawing object relations unit, in
> which the withdrawing object was projected onto the girlfriend and identified
> as the source of Richard's painful fears. Less abstractly, these fights were a
> way of focusing on the other as a distraction from the dread of being alone.
>
> In this instance, however, Richard reported that although he could feel the
> old abandonment fears emerging, he could also see that they were driving
> his impulse to criticize his girlfriend and that they were not very realistic. So,
> he restrained his impulse to attack and simply told her his fears, maintaining
> his focus on his own experience and acknowledging that the fears were prob-
> ably unreasonable. His girlfriend, not having to defend herself from attack,
> was able to respond with understanding and reassurance. He was learning
> adaptive behavior.

Reproceduring

An additional goal of treatment involves a reproceduring of the real self;
indeed, in some ways, it is the fundamental and primary goal of treatment. The false defensive self of the borderline personality disorder is a
manifestation of implicit procedural schemas about how to be and how to
relate. Although internal working models of relationships tend to endure
across the life span, they are not altogether immutable. Berlin and Cassidy
(1999) suggest,

> Although working models created within early attachments are expected to
> exert far-reaching effects, changes in working models can occur and can dis-
> rupt the influence of early experiences. Moreover, according to the theory, if
> there is discontinuity between early and later working models of attachment,
> current relationships can reflect current as well as former models. (p. 694)

In fact, there is evidence that later experiences, including psychotherapy, can result in an "earned secure attachment" (Pearson, Cohn, Cowan, and Cowan, 1994; Phelps, Belsky, and Crnic, 1998). An early-formed insecure attachment style can be replaced by a new internal working model based on a secure attachment, presumably as a function of a later, more adequate experience.

Successful psychotherapy enables the development of new procedures, implicit and explicit, that facilitate the experience and expression of the real self. Working models of relationships, the object relations units of intrapsychic structure, are reprocedured in the relationship with the therapist. Because this is a relationship that supports real-self development and expression, the need for the false defensive self subsides. Old procedures, now obsolete, are modified and eventually relinquished in the new and trusting relationship with the therapist; new procedures replace the old.

Lyons-Ruth (2001) extrapolates from research on early infant development and suggests that this is a nonlinear process that is neither systematic nor symbolic and is accomplished in the relationship itself. In infancy,

> enactive or procedural knowing regarding how to do things with others develops and changes by processes that are intrinsic to an enactive system of representation and that do not rely on translation of "procedures for being with" into reflective (symbolized) knowledge. (p. 16)

In other words, working models of relationships are internalized presymbolically and demonstrated preconsciously in behavior. The reproceduring of internal object relations units at this implicit level is relatively independent of interpretation, insight, verbalization, or technical intervention strategies. As Lyons-Ruth says, "the emphasis here is on the *process* of communication rather than on the content of the communication. . . . Process leads content" (p. 15). In her view, it is not "knowing that" or "showing that" that is important in psychotherapy but the therapist's nonverbal "knowing how" and "showing how." It is the relationship with the therapist, not technique or information for the patient, that is decisive for change in therapy.

We agree with Lyons-Ruth (2001) and Lyons-Ruth et al. (1998) that changes occur implicitly, but we add that psychotherapy that is aimed at altering internalized object relations involves both relational and technical factors (see chapter 4). For instance, Holmes (2001) emphasizes the role of the relationship in the psychotherapy process from an attachment theory perspective but states that "within the context of a secure base, the therapist's task is to challenge habitual assumptions and relationship patterns and create sufficient turbulence for new structures to emerge. Interpretation, confrontation and clarification are all technical means to achieve this end" (p. 17).

Masterson (1976, 1981, 1985), who acknowledges the mutative significance of the implicit real relationship in therapy, strongly proposes that
technical factors involving symbolization and verbalization—for instance,
the diagnosis-specific intervention strategies mentioned in the previous
chapter—are necessary for the explicit modification of internal object
relations and the related emergence of the real self. Although empathic
attunement to the real self of the patient is crucial to the reproceduring
of the internal self and object representations, so is the tracking of old,
maladaptive procedures and the interventions directed at their disruption
(Masterson, 1976, 1981).

These technical elements of the psychotherapy communicate, implicitly
and explicitly,

> You can feel. You can think and talk about what you feel. You can learn to
> watch and to correct what you do instead of merely act on your feelings. You
> can reject your destructive habits once you see them. You have choices. You
> can change.

In effect, these communications show what in the context of how. In
other words, the attitude of the therapist shows how, and the verbal communication shows what. The content is embedded in the process. It's the
attitude of the therapist that demonstrates and offers the invitation for the
borderline patient to try.

THE PROCESS OF PSYCHOTHERAPY

The achievement of these goals is not an easy or linear process; in fact, it
is usually an arduous, complex, and circuitous one. The following case
example illustrates one of the more challenging aspects of effective psychotherapy with borderline patients.

> Sally, a 38-year-old married woman with two daughters in early adolescence,
> entered treatment, ostensibly because of chronic depression, anxiety, and low
> self-esteem. However, she revealed that for 2 years, she had been intensely
> enamored of a midmanagement coworker in the department store where
> she worked as a clerk. Her "friend" had become uncomfortable with her
> emotional dependence on him and had discussed this with her in an effort
> to limit their interaction. Sally felt abandoned by her esteemed friend and
> confidant and so plunged into a deep depression.
>
> By the close of the intake session, it was apparent that Sally had almost
> instantly made a positive emotional connection with her male therapist (a
> relatively inexperienced clinician whom I (DDR) was supervising). In fact,
> the therapist's process notes indicate a discernible and surprising lifting of
> her depression, just over the course of that first 50-minute session. As the

therapist continued over the next several weeks to investigate her personal history and formulate a diagnosis and treatment plan, Sally became noticeably more bright in her affect and increasingly appreciative of him: "I'm so grateful to have a doctor like you," she would say, or "You're the only person I've ever been able to trust to take care of me." She told him that no one else had been able to help her, that she felt safe with him, that he was like the mother she had always wanted. The therapist relished her appreciation. He enjoyed her gratitude and felt gratified by her quite surprising positive response to his efforts to be helpful to her. And she repeatedly reported that she had never felt better.

But over time (here's where the scuffle starts), Sally seemed less certain about his trustworthiness. Was he really concerned? Did he really care? Were they really friends, or was this only a doctor–patient relationship? She made escalating demands on the therapist to reassure her that she was a valued person and that he would never abandon her.

In response to this pressure and with the encouragement of his supervisor, the therapist began to take a more neutral stance with Sally. He became less active, less directive, and more firm about her responsibility for the work of her therapy. This shift in therapeutic stance evoked angry and critical responses from the patient. Now she was saying things like "You're an awfully expensive friend!" "All I know is that you're cold, cruel, uncaring, and just in this for the money!" and "Why don't you tell me what to do? What am I paying you for anyway?" She revealed fantasies of slashing his tires, burning down his house, and even murdering him. The criticism and threats were unrelenting. In Sally's view, the withdrawing object had replaced the rewarding one; her splitting had taken over—the savior had become a sadist. (Needless to say, this therapist was by now thinking that finding a second career was appealing. But he resisted this impulse and, in desperation, sought supervision.)

OBSTACLES TO TREATMENT

Transference Acting Out Versus Transference

The case of Sally and her therapist illustrates a phenomenon common among personality-disordered patients who are early in treatment: transference acting out. Masterson (1976, 1981, 1990, 1993) makes a critical distinction between transference and transference acting out, which is essential to an understanding of borderline functioning and effective treatment of these patients. In transference, the patient has some awareness that there is a difference between the reality of the therapist and the fantasies and feelings that the patient projects onto him or her; that is, the patient is able to recognize the independent reality of the therapist. This requires the capacity for reflective function.

In transference acting out, however, the patient's awareness of the difference between projective colorations and the reality of the therapist is much more limited. Kernberg (1984) puts it this way: "Patients confuse transference and reality and fail to differentiate the therapist from the transference object" (p. 105); the therapist *is* the projection. The projections of borderline individuals may originate in the rewarding object relations unit or the withdrawing unit or both in alternation (Masterson, 1976, 1981). This oscillation may be bewildering to the therapist (and to the patients) until it is considered in the context of these patients' split intrapsychic structure.

A genuine therapeutic alliance—a "real object relationship which is conscious and within which both patient and therapist agree to work together to help the patient improve through better understanding and control" (Masterson, 1990, p. 182)—is impossible as long as transference acting out of the pathological object relations units persists. As such, one goal of treatment is the conversion of transference acting out into transference and therapeutic alliance. This conversion is effected through empathic confrontation and facilitation of the patient's capacity for self-experience, self-expression, self-focus, and self-support. Over time, transference acting out gives way to transference and therapeutic alliance wherein the characteristic borderline defenses are acknowledged and relinquished and their nature and genesis explored. According to Masterson (1990),

> as the therapist confronts, lending his reality perception to the patient, the latter integrates the confrontation, controlling his maladaptive defensive behavior and thereby interrupting his defense against his abandonment depression. The depression surfaces and, following the borderline triad, the patient defends again, and the therapist confronts again. This circular sequence eventually results in the patient overcoming defense and containing the depression. (p. 185)

At first, Sally clearly demonstrated transference acting out of the rewarding object relations unit, manifested in clinging and protestations of helplessness. At the same time, she projected her rewarding object expectation that the therapist would resonate with this attribution of enabling and caretaking behavior, that he would be supportive of her dependency and felt incompetence—and he did.

But Sally's identification with the withdrawing unit was equally powerful. The more the therapist failed to resonate with her projections of the rewarding unit, the more she acted out a "bad," despised, withdrawing self-representation in anger, aggression, and criticism. She projected her perception of her own withdrawing object representation onto him, viewing him as a punitive and emotionally distant figure. If he confronted her or just did not respond as she had hoped, she saw him as a cold and uncaring being.

For Sally, the splitting between these two polarized projections was absolute for a long time. She would walk out of sessions early, so engaged was she in her sense of herself as "bad" and so enraged at the therapist for his refusal to take care of her. But she would return for her next session with the rewarding object relations unit activated again. Helpless and compliant, she would thank him for his kindness and helpfulness; there was no apparent emotional residue from the previous session. It was as if nothing of note had occurred. Once again, she was reenacting the old relational procedure of helplessness for connection. But Sally's alternating projections of the rewarding and withdrawing units were not recognized by her as projections, as would occur with transference. In her transference acting out, she believed that these disparate perceptions really reflected who the therapist was. Again, and not surprisingly, this was a jarring experience for him, and he often came out of these sessions feeling emotionally pummeled.

The nonlinear nature of the psychotherapy process with Sally was evident in the necessity of dealing with, not one, but two self-presentations. The shift from one object relations unit to the other was typically abrupt and stunning to the therapist. Although predictions could be made as to which she would be projecting, there was never a certainty about which to expect—or about what would trigger a shift to the other side of the split intrapsychic structure. Also, defenses once controlled repeatedly reemerged, again requiring confrontation and the patience and persistence of the therapist. This is characteristic of work with borderline patients, and the process does not begin to become more linear until transference acting out is contained and a therapeutic alliance begins to form.

This transference acting out can be seen in another case, this time, a 24-year-old woman with a relatively higher-level borderline personality disorder. At the beginning of each session, Sarah would sit silently for 10 or 15 minutes. She seemed to be at a loss about how to start, how to focus on herself. I (DSR) would wait, wondering out loud about the silence, particularly in light of the considerable depression that Sarah had displayed during the intake session. But, typically, Sarah only said that she felt "uncomfortable."

When I asked her why self-reflection was so difficult, she commented, "I think—I *am* thinking. Even when I'm alone and think, it gives me a headache. And then I worry that I'll get a headache, so I can't think. Because I'll think about anxiety-producing stuff . . . like if I'll get a headache . . . or about work . . . or about moving out of my parents' house. But, I feel selfish about wanting to move out. I work for my uncle. But I'd be better not to be there. I know everything about his business. But he gets bad moods. But if I go to work somewhere else, I'll be afraid of how he'll deal with it—if he'll cut off the relationship."

Sarah appeared to be inert, but it was obvious that she had been thinking. Her fear of focusing on herself and her own experience kept her from thinking about the goals or even the wishes of her real self—in this instance, her desire to get another job. Because of her fear of being "selfish" and risking the painful experience of abandonment, she avoided asserting herself with her uncle. And these same fears blocked her self-expression in session, leaving her efforts to be reflective not very coherent.

"I do feel selfish—even here," she continued. "This is so unnatural. I always focus on other people. My focus on me means I can't be with Mom as much, and it makes me sad." Sarah's mother was quite dependent on her daughter's attention. "It makes me feel bad that if I make myself feel better, I'll make her feel worse. So I don't do that. I don't take the time to think about what I want. Instead, I focus on someone else's needs." *I* was getting a headache just trying to stay with her in her line of thinking. At this point, I suggested, "It's no wonder you have headaches," pointing out the self-destructive consequences of not listening to herself, of not even thinking about herself.

Sarah's primary in-session transference acting out, her procedural reenactment, showed in her compliant focus on the object and her related unwillingness to talk or even think about her own experience. The pathological ego that supported these behaviors locked her into a preoccupation with others so that as long as she focused on other people, she didn't feel "selfish" and therefore likely to be rejected or abandoned. Of course, she couldn't not focus on me, unless she was willing to risk being seen by me as a selfish person and then rejected. She really did believe that rejection would follow if she paid attention to her own experience. It was not until Sarah recognized the consequences of her unwillingness to reflect, to watch what she felt, and to think about it that she began to work on talking more openly in session. She then began to discover what she felt, thought, and wanted; her compliant and clinging internal working model began to be reprocedured in accordance with an activated real self.

It didn't surprise me to learn that transference acting out of the rewarding object relations unit wasn't Sarah's only experience in treatment. The process of her therapy was punctuated by transference acting out of the withdrawing unit as well. At those times, she perceived me as a withholding or punitive figure and herself as a despised and deprived person. "Are you deliberately not telling me the answers?!" she would ask furiously. I always felt disorganized by that sudden split perception of me, but it made sense when I considered it with eyes toward her split procedures.

When the patient expresses anger and criticism toward the therapist, it is with the largely unconscious hope that the therapist will resume a caretaking and enabling stance in the treatment to feel less guilty or clinically inept. But the therapist who holds to a neutral stance will be less susceptible to such dynamics.

Alternately, fearing the loss of the object, the patient may direct her anger at herself, protecting the other from her destructive impulses and so preserving her connection to the object. This dynamic can be seen in suicidal, self-mutilating, or otherwise self-destructive behaviors, as we detail in this chapter and in chapters 9 and 10.

An example of this sort of overtly self-destructive transference acting out was demonstrated by Anna, who had been hospitalized twice for suicidal thoughts and impulses by the time she was 17. She had had multiple admissions to residential treatment settings earlier in her adolescence, and I (DDR) met her when she was admitted to an inpatient facility where I consulted. Anna's initial reluctance to participate in treatment soon developed into a compliant and clinging relationship with her female therapist. But in time, the therapist had to point out that Anna was not taking responsibility for her behavior and that she was undermining her stated goal of assuming control of her life. These confrontations frustrated Anna's desire to be taken care of; it activated projections of the withdrawing unit; and it precipitated escalating anger. Anna's dramatic shift in perception of her therapist, from trusted confidant to malevolent tormentor, was striking.

After one especially intense session, Anna went on an afternoon pass with her mother (possibly, her original withdrawing object) only to return to the unit with blood running down her arms from self-inflicted cuts. The withdrawing object relations unit had been activated, but she turned her anger on herself, rather than on her mother, as an unconscious attempt to restore a helpless and dependent relationship and so maintain a connection with her.

These scenarios of transference acting out serve to regulate affect and preserve attachment. They are neither volitional nor conscious; they are reflexively activated. As maladaptive as they appear, these are procedures that have been encoded in implicit relational memory, and they represent the only reactive options of which the borderline disordered person is aware. But they are costly in that they prohibit or compromise the experience and expression of the real self and encourage the activation of a false defensive self.

Therefore, transference acting out is at cross-purposes to effective psychotherapy: It repeats old imprisoning procedures; it perpetuates a reliance on self-defeating behaviors; and it disallows activation of the real self. According to Masterson (1981),

> the initial objective of the therapist is to render the functioning of [transference acting out] ego-alien by confronting its destructiveness, either the denied, destructive behavior of the RORU [rewarding object relations unit] alliance or the distorted attitudes of the WORU [withdrawing object relations unit] alliance. (p. 150)

That is why these entrenched implicit procedures for regulating affect (for avoiding the experience of the abandonment depression), along with their destructive effects on quality of life, must be brought to the borderline person's attention through patient, consistent confrontation. Again, the focus must be on watching his or her process and bringing it to his or her attention—with the goal of co-watching in mind. This is how transference acting out is converted to transference and therapeutic alliance, bearing in mind that each of these confrontations also holds the possibility of an open space, a moment of meeting, to implicitly reprocedure the patient.

Ego-Syntonic Defenses

One obstacle to the conversion of transference acting out into transference is the fact that borderline patients typically experience their defensive operations as ego-syntonic, so there is little motivation to contain or relinquish them (Masterson, 1976). Patients must learn that these defenses are in fact ultimately self-defeating and in opposition to their most important personal goals—they promote the dependency and incompetence of the false defensive self and thereby nullify an individual's efforts to achieve a genuine sense of personal potency and autonomy. Again, learning is a goal of psychotherapy, and this learning occurs as the patient feels both known and shown, even with the distress that comes with the recognition of the effects and consequences of old behaviors.

When the therapist aligns with and attunes to the healthy ego of the patient, repeatedly pointing out the self-destructive quality of the defenses, old defenses gradually become ego-alien, and new motivation develops to contain and relinquish maladaptive procedures.

> Confrontation . . . throws a monkey wrench in the patient's defense system by introducing conflict where there previously had been none. The patient had been regulating his internal equilibrium or making himself feel good by acting out in ways that were harmful, but because he denied the harmfulness he felt no conflict. When the therapist points out the harm the patient can no longer act out without recognizing the harm. Therefore conflict and tension are created. The patient can no longer act out freely without conflict. He has to recognize the cost of "feeling good." (Masterson, 1976, pp. 100–101)

Reaction Rather Than Reflection

Another impediment to the treatment of borderline personality disorders is the tendency of these patients to react to, rather than reflect on, dysphoric affect (Masterson, 1976). The conversion of transference acting out into transference is made more difficult by underdeveloped capacities for affect regulation, frustration tolerance, and impulse control. When affects are discharged defensively, they are no longer available for the affective experience that is so critical to the psychotherapeutic process. The patient must learn that the distressing affects that emerge with the containment of defense must be experienced, identified, verbalized, clarified, and explored in therapy rather than enacted in or out of treatment (Klein, 1989b, 1989d). It is through such experience and exploration of these feelings, when defensive operations are contained, that the nascent real self realizes the potential for replacing old false-self procedures with new real-self ones. And the vehicle for this is conscious learning through co-reflection.

Unawareness of the Abandonment Depression

A related complicating factor is that most borderline disordered individuals, especially early in treatment, are unaware of the depression and anxiety that underlie their maladaptive functioning. Longstanding defensive responses are evoked so reflexively that even hints of the dysphoric core around which life has become organized are disallowed. If, however, the therapist can bring this dynamic sensitively, consistently, and persistently to the patient's attention, self-defeating defenses can gradually be contained, and the painful affects against which they defend will emerge. The patient can then become aware of the centrality of the underlying abandonment depression in the organization of his or her approach to life. As Sarah said, "if I think about myself and what I want, I'm afraid that I might hurt other people and that they might leave. And then I get headaches and get depressed. So I don't think." She was beginning to see the link between her depression and self-activation.

Effective confrontations will eventually begin to be internalized, and control of habitual defensive operations will increase; the defensive procedures can be noticed and overridden. As defenses are contained, feelings of abandonment emerge and predictably evoke the need for further defense. A circular process, rather than a linear one, is initiated (an important process for the patient to see), whereby defense leads to confrontation, which leads to lessened defense and then to abandonment feelings, more defense, further confrontation, more abandonment depression, and so on (Masterson, 1981). Still, over time, there is a gradual giving up of transference acting out, and a therapeutic alliance and a true transference become increasingly available, as old relational procedures are replaced by new, real, and vitalizing ones.

Fritts (1989) reports a case that illustrates this process.

Mrs. S., a 45-year-old white woman, was referred by a psychologist who had seen her approximately six years earlier for a period of one year. Her previous therapy had been precipitated by a major loss causing unmanageable separation anxiety. . . . Her husband had left her, complaining of her helpless, overly dependent behavior. She described the months after the marriage ended as the worst time in her life. "I felt like I was going to die. I walked around like a zombie for months. I cried endlessly. I could not think straight. I did not know how to cope. Parts of me felt like they were missing. I was becoming confused and panicky. One day I fell apart; something snapped inside of me." She then sought treatment for the first time.

Her reasons for returning to therapy six years later were vague. She complained of depression, a lack of vitality and commitment to life, of floating through life without a purpose. . . . She went on to describe herself as lacking self-assertion; she felt compelled to please and adapt to others' opinions and ideas in order to ensure their approval. . . . She complained of having a difficult time making decisions. She turned to others to help her decide what to wear, what to eat, and what to do with her leisure time.

From the very beginning of therapy, Mrs. S. waited for me to direct her sessions. When I sat quietly, she asked me many questions and looked frightened when she was unable to "read me." When I didn't respond to her questions directly but, rather, investigated the meaning of her questions, she would almost always say, "I just don't know." She continued by asking whether I knew what was wrong. I was supposed to ask the questions and supply the answers. (pp. 251, 252, 256)

As we have noted, the borderline patient typically enters treatment projecting the rewarding object—that is, looking to the therapist with the implicit hope that emotional supplies will be forthcoming in return for helplessness, incompetence, and regression. Clearly, this patient's approach to therapy conforms to that picture; she presented herself as helpless, with the hope or expectation that the therapist would respond complementarily and assume the self-functions that she had abdicated. If the therapist had colluded with this projection, the patient would have felt gratified but at the cost of a reinforcement of the false defensive self and collusion against real-self experience.

I wondered whether or not she was, in fact, through her helpless behavior with me summarizing the real issues in her life. (p. 256)

This patient was certainly demonstrating early learned procedures for evoking attachment in caretakers by her helplessness. She was also communicating to her therapist, in the only way available to her at the time, what she had learned about how to establish and maintain a relationship.

She seemed determined to look to others around her to direct and choreograph her life, rather than using her capacities to do that for herself. If she felt as if she could not run her own life, then *that* seemed to warrant investigation. (p. 256)

Such observations and reflections on the part of the therapist are signal wonderings to be raised and wondered about with the patient.

My silences early in the therapy were always seen and felt as a withdrawal, similar to her mother's. My support and persistence in encouraging her own investigation by confronting her projections helped her to differentiate the therapeutic process from her mother's behavior. (p. 256)

The therapist's failure to resonate with the patient's projection of the rewarding object elicited the withdrawing object projection. That is, the therapist was now experienced as an emotionally detached and uncaring figure. However, the content of the therapist's interventions and her confidence in the patient's real-self capacities appeared, in our terminology, to be vitalizing a previously underdeveloped self-system. A process of reproceduring of the real self had begun.

Theoretically, the patient can at this point do one of three things. She can contain the identified defense—the acting out of the projection of the withdrawing object—and express her real self by focusing on and reflecting on her experience. She can revert to the projection of the rewarding object in a renewed effort to elicit caretaking from the therapist and so feel better. Finally, she can continue to externalize onto the therapist the source of her dysphoria. This last option is precisely what Fritts's patient (1989) did.

> She continued to accuse me of not caring about her because I was not, in fact, taking over for her. I repeatedly confronted this by wondering why she would want me to do for her what she could do so well for herself. Her response was, "I can't." The investigations that ensued concerning my quiet listening and her feelings of helplessness gave way to small steps toward defining her thoughts and putting them into language. (p. 256)

The therapist's refusal to support the patient's acting out of helplessness resulted in further activation of the withdrawing object relations unit. But in time, the therapist's sensitive and accurate attunement to the needs of the Mrs. S.'s real self communicated to her a patient, persistent belief in her capacity to look within herself rather than to others. This allowed something that had previously been diffuse and primitive to begin, in the company of a concerned and understanding other, to take form and be verbalized. Containment of defense was realized, for a while; at least temporarily, the patient stopped acting out her early attachment procedures. The therapist's empathic confrontations had opened the door to verbalization of internal experience and allowed for the emergence of new implicit procedures and alterations of the intrapsychic experience of the self in relationship with others. It was now possible, in those moments at least, for the patient to reflect in the presence of another and for them to wonder together.

Several months into her therapy, Fritts (1989) reports, Mrs. S. responded to countertransference lapses (in which the therapist succumbed to the patient's projected need for suggestions and directions) by returning to passivity and helplessness. Wishing to be taken care of, pulling to reactivate old relational procedures, she canceled a session with insufficient notice and expected the fee to be forgiven, despite the therapist's clearly communicated policy. When the therapist told her that she would still be financially responsible for the session, Mrs. S. became furious and said that she would be looking for another therapist. The therapist asked her why, and Mrs. S. replied, "Because you're not nurturing, not sweet enough, and if you were an 'understanding' human being, you would not charge me." According to Fritts,

> Mrs. S. was requesting more than understanding. She was, in fact, demanding that I take care of her and the situation. I disagreed with her and said, "Why would you want me to take the responsibility for your decision?" I continued by wondering why she was confusing being responsible with the emotional component of caring. "Why would you be angry at me for expecting you to be responsible by keeping our initial agreement?"
>
> For the moment she ignored my confrontation and continued to attack me. She had heard that other therapists held, cuddled, and hugged their patients. At the very least, they asked lots of questions and provided many answers. She wondered whether she would be better off finding such a therapist.
>
> I responded, "I suppose you can do that if you want to, but I think your wish to be cuddled and 'made to feel better' has stood in the way of your growth and development. Why would you want to continue to find people who will 'take away' your feelings and take care of you in ways that undermine your own ability to think and feel?" (p. 258)

For this patient the implicitly procedured conditions of attachment—helplessness and clinging—had clearly been maladaptive. But at the same time, they had been ego-syntonic. Through confrontation, the therapist was clarifying the self-defeating quality of these behavioral habits, in the hope that, in time, they would become ego-alien.

> I added that I did not see that as my role; rather, I saw therapy as a partnership (therapeutic alliance) to assist her in better understanding herself and her life. She calmed down a bit and started to speculate about her relationships with other people. Again, there was temporary containment of defense.
>
> She hesitantly agreed that most of her relationships were based on the quality and quantity of caretaking that she could extract from them. (p. 259)

The patient's calming was evidence of a confrontation accepted and the consequent regulation of affect experienced in the real relationship between her and her therapist; that is, attunement to the real self often results in soothing and affective down regulation. In addition, a moment of shared awareness is feasible at these times, a shared recognition that allows for "feeling felt"; this, too, allows for the possibility of self-reflection. So, the patient was able to shift her focus from the other to herself and to reflect on her experience rather than merely react to the therapist through transference acting out.

I also wondered why she was so quick to leave therapy rather than stay and work this out. When faced with her own self-expression, which at the moment was anger, she was eager to run. Rather than to feel, express, and work these issues out in her treatment, her impulse was to trade one therapeutic relationship for another. She was looking for a quick fix—this time a "sweeter" therapist.

That confrontation with Mrs. S. hit a nerve. She connected "our fight," as she called it, to old patterns and feelings. Her anger or strong feelings have frequently been followed by running from the situation or replacing people. Tears followed as she said, with sadness in her voice, "I can't even imagine how many times I have run away from myself and my feelings, never giving myself the opportunity to work this out." The session ended by her saying that leaving therapy was obviously not the solution. (p. 259)

Here, too, sensitively conceived confrontations helped to render ego-alien the patient's maladaptive defenses and hence effectively disrupted the operation of the triad. This allowed for productive self-reflection, enhanced insight, and an opening of the door for adaptation and learning. A successful series of confrontations, patiently wedded to deep attunement and an implicit invitation to the self to show up, effects changes in the patient. With Mrs. S., there was a gradual shift from transference acting out of the oscillating projections of the rewarding and withdrawing units to transference and a therapeutic alliance. Instead of acting out her expectations, Mrs. S. increasingly began to wonder about her demands to be taken care of and, in the attuning presence of her therapist, explored the origins of her difficulties. Her own story, her narrative, spoke for itself.

"When people don't take care of me the way I want them to, I notice that I feel angry. I then want to get even, so I become more demanding. I want it all done for me. . . . I feel helpless, yet I encourage others to keep me that way." She was realizing the extent to which she had colluded with her own problems. "Under all this mess, I have no idea who I am. I am a shiny, well-polished robot; a furious robot, mother's robot." (p. 260)

The fruit of this reproceduring was that Mrs. S. could remember with feeling the reasons why she denied herself, why she could not get to and express her own truth. So the goal of "learning" was being realized.

"To be held, to be loved, to be touched. I've felt like I would die without it. I've been willing to do almost anything for it. I am starting to see how much I've done that has hurt me. I was 'starved' and betrayed by my mother. Then I betrayed myself. What I did to myself to get those crumbs." (p. 261)

Mrs. S.'s therapy was certainly far from linear in its progression; enhanced experiences of self-focus, self-experience, and self-expression were predictably followed by regression, clinging, and acting out of helplessness. But over time, the intense turbulence in her life gradually gave way to a more consistent experience of herself as being empowered and capable of managing her life and her friendships in a mature, assertive, adult, adaptive manner. Her "triumphant reunion with herself" (p. 262) impelled her to continue her quest to consolidate these significant therapeutic gains. She had found another chance to be herself.

Interestingly, but characteristically for the borderline patient, as Mrs. S.'s ability to contain her defenses increased, the therapist's required level of activity diminished. This is consistent with the premise of this approach to psychotherapy that the patient, not the therapist, is responsible for the work of therapy—the therapist is merely a servant of the process. Certainly, the patient who is engaged in self-defeating defenses—avoiding real-self activation, acting out helplessness, denying self-destructiveness, being enmeshed in projection or projective identification—is in need of confrontation. But confrontation is necessary only if the patient is in defense. When the patient becomes able to focus on her or his real-self experience, reflect on it with feeling in the session, and activate the real self in everyday life, she or he may need no more from the therapist than quiet interest. This is so because the therapist's silence at those times reflects an advocacy of the patient's real self and supports its experience and expression. Although we say that for borderline patients, confrontations are experienced as empathic episodes, silence is sometimes the therapist's most empathic response.

In this regard, we once read a review of a concert—Zubin Mehta conducting the New York Philharmonic with Isaac Stern, Pinchas Zuckerman, and Itzhak Perlman in, if we remember accurately, a Vivaldi triple concerto. The reviewer recalled an unexpected moment when Mehta lowered his arms to his sides and stood motionless. Later, when asked about this, he replied, "There are times when the best thing a conductor can do is to stop conducting." Likewise, there are times when the best thing that a therapist can do is to be still and allow the patient to experience and explore the real self.

We all would probably like to witness our patients doing their work in therapy so that we can sit back and silently applaud their real-self expression. But getting from here to there is a long, winding road with circuitous detours and periodic dead ends. Throughout therapy, it is easy to be detoured by getting caught up in the chaotic and often intriguing stories and ways of relating that these people bring to us. But the therapist's foremost attention must be given to the process of relating, a process that is invisible to the patient. We must watch for these relational procedures, which are living them, imprisoning them in self-destructive lives. We must see these habits that have brought them to the very therapeutic hours in which we sit with them.

For change to happen, our patients must begin to see their own relational habits, the implicit processes and procedures that, in fact, go on without them. And so, as therapists, we watch and we wait and we wonder to ourselves and then wonder in words with them. We bring to the patients' awareness the habits of relating of which they are unaware. We point them out carefully in the transference and in their everyday lives so that they, too, can see what we see.

It is process, not content, that we look for. Of course, we listen to understand the content of what they offer us, but it is their process, with the added dimension of our presence, that we must focus on. Process, process, process. We watch for which side of the split relational strategy they bring to us in therapy. We watch for any real-self experience or real-self activation that stimulates glimpses of the abandonment depression. Then we look for the defense or attachment procedure that follows. Are they looking for a rewarding object, or are they suddenly splitting to react to a withdrawing object (their triad)? We watch for our reactions (we discuss this point further in chapter 10). We attend to therapeutic neutrality and watch their process, what they are doing. We offer our best confrontations. Then we wait to see if they seem to be reflecting on them, metabolizing them, and continuing with self-reflection or if they shift back into defense. And then we wait and we watch again. We watch and give our eyes to the patients through compassionate confrontation. It is not possible for them to watch themselves, unless we watch first. Then we communicate to them what we see, within a relationship where trust is foundational. This is the prime mover of psychotherapy. (This may be the most important paragraph in the book.)

As the therapy continues, patients learn to watch their own triads. Because of the faithfulness of the therapist to not take offense at the split procedures but to reflect back the steps in this process and to invite conversation about these steps, the patients are freed from fear in this relational experience to look at themselves, and something new happens.

When in the context of empathic attunement the therapist watches for process and brings it to the patient's awareness over and over, the patient begins to see and wonder about his or her own habits. It is then, with seeing and recognizing one's own triad, that one can choose to be oneself—because psychotherapy offers, incrementally, another chance to be real.

7

Terri

Destitute and Desperate for Help

Terri, as you will recall, had been my (DDR's) patient briefly at the end of her senior year in high school. She came back to see me again at 22. She had returned to her hometown after a 4-year interlude of drugs, homelessness, and serial relationships with opportunistic, predatory, and emotionally abusive men. It was easy for me to see her desperation; the truth of her circumstances was quite obvious. Her internal crisis had come about as a result of her external crises. She was desperate because she was destitute. But this would give us the opportunity to explore together how she had contributed to her present, wretched state—and when she understood that, she might then have other options.

Now the single mother of two young children, Terri described a frantic need to be in a relationship with a man at all times and at any costs. At the same time, she knew that she had enormous difficulties with assertiveness, self-discipline, and standing up for herself in relationships and that she didn't really know who she was.

Terri's treatment was unusual in that it was time limited from the beginning. Our work together was funded by the state for a maximum of 42 sessions. Still, it well illustrates many of the concepts developed in the preceding chapters. We decided that we would schedule weekly meetings and that we would focus narrowly on two things: her wish to strengthen her sense of herself and her need to achieve economic independence. During this time, Terri worked with a state caseworker on learning more about her work aptitudes and finding the necessary training and motivation to use them. She eventually enrolled in a business school. We did not have to address the chemical dependency issue, because Terri had been abstinent for several months before we began working together. Her parents were understandably delighted that she had returned to her hometown, and they were supportive of her efforts to redirect the course of her life. But they could not accept her lifestyle, particularly, her relationships with men. Consequently, with the exception of their generous provision of child care, they maintained a cautious distance from active involvement in her life.

Unless treatment is initiated under duress, most borderline patients enter psychotherapy projecting the rewarding object relations unit—that is, expecting that compliance and dependency will ensure love and protection. And they anticipate that the therapist will support and sympathize with their passive and helpless behavior.

Terri's circumstances "forced" her into therapy, but there was no sense of duress about it: She knew that she needed help, and she was eager for it. In fact, it soon became apparent that the few telephone calls that she had made to me during her years away had confirmed her projection of me as someone who was willing, if not actively wanting, to rescue her and relieve her of responsibility for her problems. In her previous clinical experience with me, she had not entered into a real therapeutic alliance; she had not perceived her projections well enough to recognize me as a person independent of them. Now, she was transference acting out the rewarding unit and relating to me as if I were in fact the embodiment of her projections; I was her "white knight."

Terri succumbed quickly to her habitual relationship procedures. Her passivity and nonchalance about responsibility were expressed most conspicuously in frequent missed appointments. Of course, no therapy was possible without her presence, so confrontations in the initial phase of treatment focused primarily on her failure to act in her own best interest. I was aware that there was a potential problem in the fact that the state was paying for Terri's therapy; she felt taken care of, and I didn't have the structural lever of requiring payment from her for missed appointments. Nevertheless, I carefully tracked for her the way that she acted out helplessness and the way that she relied on excuses to avoid anything that might be considered self-assertive, or even self-supportive, behavior. I consistently reminded her of how this avoidance reinforced her picture of herself as a weak and dependent person with no power to alter her life.

In taking this stance, I affirmed her capacity for self-activation and made clear my belief that she could manage her life in a responsible and adaptive way—if she chose to. I did my best to speak to her real but impaired self. To do so, I had to navigate between two opposing dangers: I didn't want to collude with her belief that relationships and responsibility are incompatible, by ignoring or accepting her failure to be responsible to her therapy, nor did I want to provoke her rageful sense of herself as "bad," via an impatient or critical stance. I tried to communicate my belief in her capacities, underdeveloped as they were, through adherence to the psychotherapy frame, using its demands to help her define what it might mean to be responsible to herself and to her therapy. I confronted her self-defeating defenses to call her attention to the way that she undermined her efforts to improve her living and her life.

For example, at the beginning of one session, I said to her,

> That was the third session in a row that you've missed. First, you forgot, then the car wasn't available, and then you were late picking up the kids. You say that you want so badly to get your life together, so I wonder why you don't plan ahead so you can be here regularly to work on yourself. You don't seem to take yourself very seriously.

Interventions such as these targeted Terri's avoidance defense and her fundamental neglect of adaptive functioning. In a short time, she had contained this defense and started to consistently come to her sessions. In fact, as we began to wind down her therapy, Terri told me that, at the time, she had not really been aware of the truths that my confrontations communicated. But, they helped her feel understood in a new way—and they helped her to understand herself in a new way—and to understand that confrontational relating could be an expression of support.

At the time, however, it wasn't all smooth sailing. Sometimes, my focus on Terri's need to learn to take care of herself resulted in an intensification of her passive acquiescence. She would compliantly acknowledge the accuracy of my observations and deferentially assure me of her intention to assume greater control of her life and become more goal directed. But her behavior outside of therapy didn't change, and there was no discernible deepening of affect in session. My recognition that her behavior was not matching her words helped me distinguish between the times when she was really living out of her growing sense of her real self and the times when she was defensively complying with what she perceived to be my expectations. I tracked the former for her appreciatively and confronted her on the others: "Sometimes, it looks like you are really making an effort and, at other times, like you are just saying that you are, but I see no follow-through." And I pointed out how this was just potentiating her view of herself as an incompetent person. In time, Terri became able to recognize when she was responding compliantly to my interventions; she also became aware of her underlying anxiety about displeasing me and, ultimately, her fear of being abandoned by me.

Of course, it was not only the rewarding object relations unit that was acted out in our work together. Especially in the early stages of treatment and occasionally thereafter as well, my confrontations were just as likely to activate the withdrawing unit as a defense against the emerging abandonment depression. The fragile therapeutic alliance was repeatedly disrupted with furious accusations that I was cold, critical, unsympathetic, and uncaring. I was berated, vilified, and devalued. The split could appear in an instant, and even though I expected it, it always disrupted my equilibrium. I was never entirely comfortable with these radical shifts in her perceptions of me. But I kept her implicit relational models in mind for structure and to support my neutrality. I was usually able to regain my balance and counter her rage by asking why my belief that she could assume more positive control of her life should cause her to perceive me as anything but supportive of her best interests. I tried to show her that her projected view of me as an attacking figure was, in fact, a projection and that it was a response to her own experiences and fears, not to my behavior. When Terri could accept and integrate these interventions, they affected a repair of the connectional rupture. I began to see that she was getting to know who I was, separate from her reactive projections. And over time, she became able to contain this externalizing defense and get back to her exploration of her painfully impaired self.

This oscillation of the rewarding and withdrawing object representations could be seen throughout the entire span of treatment, although its frequency and intensity decreased over time. Characteristically spasmodic and tumultuous, the psychotherapy process was regularly punctuated by flagrant acting out of one or the other of these two views of relationship, both in and out of session. With each disruption of the delicate therapeutic alliance, I had to deal with my own "Here we go again"; remind myself of her reactive habits; and once again find a firm and neutral stance from which to make my confrontational interventions, facilitate containment of defenses, and repair and reestablish the working alliance—Terri's real attachment to me. Some defenses, contained for a while, would reemerge as obstacles to the attainment of Terri's therapeutic goals. They would then need to be confronted again. At times, it seemed like a long, difficult road.

As we went on, it became apparent how her overcompliance and self-destructive accommodation to the desires of the men in her life had been interfering with her achievement of economic self-reliance. One day, I asked her why she remained with him—given that we both agreed that Daniel's emotional abuse of her was detrimental to the development of a positive sense of self-worth.

"Because after all this time, he finally told me all the things I'd been waiting to hear—that he loves me and wants to take care of me," Terri responded. "But," she went on, showing her new and clearer perspective, "that stopped as soon as my money ran out." There then was a sadness in her eyes. Although she could not yet verbalize it, there seemed to be a shifting inside of her at the admission of this truth. I felt sad with her but also hopeful for her.

I continued to confront her clinging and her avoidance of realistic self-support in her relationship to Daniel and to target it as being contradictory to her best interests. One day, when she was bemoaning her mistreatment by him, I said,

> You act as if you are at the mercy of the relationship, as if you're helpless in his presence. You criticize him to me, but I don't hear you supporting yourself with him. I wonder why you aren't telling him what you want from him. You act as if you must accept whatever he gives you, as though you are of little value.

Then I watched to see if there might be a moment of reflection or a change in behavior. This would be evidence of the effectiveness of the confrontation.

As Terri began to integrate these interventions, containing her defensive compliance and supporting herself more adaptively, her abandonment fears surfaced, and the cycle began again. Fearing that consistent and realistic self-support in her relationship with Daniel would result in rejection and loss, she intensified her clinging and compliance, and we had to look again at her deference to others and its self-defeating effects. Knowing that we would not have enough time in this limited therapy for a definitive attenuation of the abandonment depression, I did not encourage exploration of Terri's abandonment fears in a systematic way. I maintained my focus on adaptation and on management of her fears in the present, rather than on investigating their roots in the past. So, when she turned to self-destructive relationships with men in an effort to soothe her abandonment fears, I confronted her; I also acknowledged her progress when she chose a more adaptive defense—for instance, reaching out to supportive female friends when she felt needy.

In time, Terri began to absorb the viewpoint that I was trying to convey. I was always pleased and a bit surprised when she demonstrated that she was getting it. She was able to extricate herself from the relationship with Daniel, and she announced to me, with obvious pride at the beginning of a session, that she had been able to persuade him to move out of her apartment. "Well, after the last session, I went home and we really got into it. Finally, Daniel left—and he broke all the windows in my car on his way out." I had just enough time for a brief, silent sigh of relief before Terri went on: "And Bill [the father of her first child] has been with me since." "Here we go again," I said to myself.

The cycle began again. Terri was still in the grip of her unwitting dedication to regression, and I had to resume my confrontation of her compliance and denial, trying to reawaken her awareness of how self-defeating her behavior was and demonstrate yet again my unswerving belief that she could do better. As time went on, her clinging defense became increasingly ego-alien, and she was able to exercise greater control over dependent relating. Her ambivalence about the relationship with Bill was enormous, but her need to support herself with him gradually took precedence over her longing to feel taken care of. She reported one day,

> I have been able to tell Bill that he'll never again be the center of my universe like he wants. No man ever will. And I am trying to work through things. Lots of times I'll think, what would Dr. Roberts ask me? Because it's usually not what you tell me. It's what you ask. Because that forces me to do the thinking and make the decisions.

Terri paused. "Of course, just because I see these things doesn't necessarily mean I'm not going to revert back to my old behaviors." She stopped to think again. "But I did stop myself with Bill. I could see that going back to him would just sabotage myself. And I wasn't impulsive. I'm getting somewhere." It really did appear that she was getting it.

Of course, as predicted, she did periodically revert to her old defensive behavior, clinging helplessly to Bill and failing to rebuff his emotional abuse of her. But her support of herself in the relationship became more and more consistent. This nudged her into a growing awareness of her fear of separation and functioning on her own; glimpses of the underlying abandonment depression came up. But because of our time constraints, we kept the focus on adaptive management of the feelings, not on a systematic exploration and elaboration of the depression. Still, the more control Terri exercised over her clinging and compliance and the more she focused on herself rather than on the object, the more aware she became of her fears and anxieties evoked by separation stresses and her nearly reflexive tendency to defend by engaging dependently in a relationship. That is, she began to observe the operation of the triad of the disorders of the self in her own life.

As Terri got better at containing the acting out of her clinging defense and realistically supporting herself in her relationships, Bill opted to move on. Reflecting on his departure, she said, "I seem to have this intense need to feel loved, and I'll do almost anything to get that feeling. But I think for the first time in my life, I've started to feel of some worth for something other than sex or as a mother."

Predictably, regular school attendance and punctuality with class work were real problems early in Terri's treatment. Here again, I concentrated on repetitive confrontations of gradually escalating intensity. I persistently questioned her self-sabotaging behavior in the light of her own insistence that her primary goal in therapy was to secure employment and become financially independent. Eventually, she overcame her regressive inclination to miss classes and procrastinate about completing assignments. Characteristically, as she contained the acting out of her avoidant defenses, she became able to activate herself in her own best interests.

After nearly a year of treatment, Terri was living alone with her children. She was more consistent in her parenting role. She reestablished reasonably comfortable relationships with her parents and siblings. She completed a clerical course and was employed part-time. She learned to recognize some of her self-destructive patterns and their relationship to the underlying abandonment depression. She controlled her tendency to resort to self-defeating defenses, and she managed in far more adaptive ways the affective storms that shook her during times of separation or increased autonomy.

We had realized the treatment goals of containing self-destructive defenses, learning with regard to the operation of the dynamic of the triad of the disorders of the self, and better adaptation. Her life and self-esteem had improved significantly, but because of the limited number of sessions, the underlying abandonment depression remained relatively unaltered, leaving Terri still vulnerable in the face of separation stresses and individuative urges. Would the changes endure?

About a year and a half after the end of her treatment, Terri called me to arrange for a "tune-up." She told me that she was employed, although she had lost two jobs in the interim, partially out of inexperience and partially out of irresponsibility. She had arranged on her own to get some remedial job training and now felt that her competence was no longer an issue. But she did acknowledge that there were still times when either inertia or emotional chaos kept her from getting herself to work on time.

She had begun another destructive relationship with a man, but this time she recognized the pattern and ended the relationship within 2 months. Now, however, she was once again becoming involved with a man who was exploiting her, so she contacted me for an appointment. She was lonely enough that she felt vulnerable to settle for such a relationship, but she was determined not "to throw myself at the first man to come by." Clearly, she had made great strides, but I still had to watch to see if her actions were supporting her determination not to settle for another self-destructive relationship.

For this round of sessions, Terri and I met five times over a period of 2 months, during which she was able to disengage from this latest relationship. Part of what struck me about this brief series of sessions was the way that Terri used our time together to recapture the learning from her earlier therapy experience, providing many of her own confrontations and problem solving her continued struggles about being on her own and pursuing the goals in her life. By the time the 2 months were up, she decided to actively nurture a couple of relationships with female friends, in the hope that this would be at least a partial solution to her aloneness, to her abandonment depression. I have not heard from her since.

Terri's outcome falls short of the ideal therapeutic goal of working through the abandonment depression and consolidating a stable and cohesive real self. Nevertheless, the results are striking and significant. As Klein (1989d) has concluded with respect to such work,

> when short-term therapy enables a nonfunctional patient to function, or improves a patient's overall capacity to work and to love, or assists a patient in attaining his or her own goals or ideals, the experienced therapist knows that these are difficult feats and is able to feel, along with the patient, a sense of accomplishment. (p. 109)

8

Susan

Immobilized, Helpless, and Hopeless

T his is an extended case study of the patient who may have taught me (DSR) the most about effective treatment of the borderline personality disorder. After Diane (in chapter 3) taught me what not to do with borderline patients, I vowed that I would never again, if possible, be caught uneducated regarding diagnosis and treatment. Susan proved to be such a complex case that I continued my education in the form of excellent supervision throughout the course of treatment.

I write this chapter as a retrospective. It may seem disjointed in formulation and presentation, but it reflects my experience in trying to put together who Susan was and who she became. She kept herself so defended and hidden away that her real self did not come out of hiding until, after long testing, she learned to trust me. But this may be the story of all patients.

PRESENTING COMPLAINT

Susan had just come back to college following a 5-year hiatus. Two and a half of those years had been spent mostly in psychiatric hospitals. She had seen 11 other therapists before coming to me.

When Susan and I first met, she was 24 years old and a full-time university student. She was significantly overweight, had curly blonde hair, and drove a pickup truck. She dressed plainly, always in pants and sweaters, and was sometimes even a little disheveled. In the early sessions, her affect was fairly flat. She was referred to me by a counselor at the student health center, who specified three concerns. First, Susan lacked motivation to do her schoolwork. Academics had always come easily to her; in fact, they had served as an effective defense against her periodic episodes of depression and impaired self-esteem. But now she was having difficulty following through in her courses. Second, Susan had been avoiding her feelings for years, but they had finally caught up with her, and she was now drowning in them. Third, Susan was concerned about her lithium level.

During Susan's third hospitalization, she was diagnosed with bipolar disorder as well as borderline personality disorder. Lithium seemed to help stabilize her mood. Her prescribing psychiatrist had encouraged her to notice her experience. As such, if Susan's lithium levels were too high, the drug caused headaches; if they were too low, the drug didn't help with mood regulation. When Susan came to see me, she was concerned that her levels were too low, and she was afraid of another manic episode. She had learned during that third hospitalization that the biological dys-regulation of her manic states powered uncontrollable rages. (These were not her words but mine in an effort to make explicit what she had learned about her problem.) For this reason, her first requirement for self-care was to manage her medication, and it appeared from her history that Susan was compliant and responsible about her lithium. She hoped that I would be one to help her with her other issues.

For 4 years, I saw Susan three times, sometimes four times, a week. During the first several sessions, she was more than cooperative in sup-plying diagnostic and past treatment information. Of course, by then, she had plenty of experience being a patient. She was able to tell me that she was sexually molested by her brother but that her parents hadn't been paying enough attention to know what was going on. It seemed that she was more than willing to work to figure out her problems until I refused to do the work for her or give her direction to start her sessions. It was then that I saw how profound Susan's sense of helplessness was. Instead of dealing with the continuity of her presenting concerns, she would be-come passive, helpless, hopeless, and desperate in her looking to me to supply her with answers and motivation.

Susan told me that her resumption of her college studies in the North-west had been difficult. She was taking an anti-inflammatory medication for rheumatoid arthritis, as well as the lithium. No one had told her that she must also medicate for the gastrointestinal side effects of these drugs; she had been rushed to the hospital in her first year back in school, after she passed out in her dorm room with a bleeding ulcer. Furthermore, her beloved grandfather had died a few months earlier, and then Susan her-self was diagnosed with thyroid cancer.

It seemed likely that Susan had never dealt with these traumatic events, let alone grieved them. But why were they keeping her from her academic efforts? Why did she feel paralyzed and act paralyzed? Where to begin?

Once we completed an initial history, the question became "What do you think is the problem?" When I put this question to Susan, she didn't really respond; there was neither answer nor affect. She seemed stuck in cement, in inertia, in a nebulous and diffuse state. "Was that not a good question?" I asked myself, confused. I often felt with Susan that I was in a room padded with absorbent sponges, into which my words just disappeared. How could this bright young woman, so relational and capable throughout her elementary and high school years, have come to this point? She seemed not to have a clue about what her problem was or why she was so inert that she didn't respond, even with frustration, to my query. She didn't even say, "You tell me, you're the expert." Not then, that is.

Session after session, she sat in silence. I knew that there was meaning behind her silence but also that if I did the work and talked for her, we would never find out why. So my work lay in waiting for her to decide to talk. Was she angry? If so, at whom? Was she overmedicated? Did she really not know how to explore her self and her feelings? Susan's nonresponse to my expectation that she start her sessions exposed a procedural counterexpectation—that someone else would do the thinking for her. When she finally began to get the drift that starting for herself was where her therapy must begin, she talked about recurring dreams—she was in a foxhole, in a battle zone, with bombs and death and skeletons and screaming babies. Sometimes, she would stare at the pictures on my walls and free-associate—but was it free association or compliance? Sometimes, she would say that she could get to nothing except the voices screaming in her head. I knew that these verbalizations were related to her self, but how? Sometimes, she would revert to silence. Again.

> Susan sits in silence for 25 minutes, unengaged with me. She averts her eyes and stares at a picture on the wall, at the rug, at the corners of the room. There are no words. I sit quietly and wait with her. I have to battle with myself to be patient, to remember that my attitude and presentation in the room are as important as my words. Finally, her frustrations escalate to the point where she speaks out angrily.

> SUSAN: Well, we aren't getting anywhere.

> THERAPIST: I noticed that. Did you not want to work on your concerns?

> SUSAN: That's for you to tell me. You people have the answers.

Her eyes are still averted, and she's apparently angry—passively angry—at me for not giving her guidance. I'm not doing what she has come to expect people to do for her, and she is seeing me as the withdrawing object, a model of her early relational procedures. I know that beneath the acting out is a possibility of a real self and a real relationship, so this is fine with me. I firmly remind myself that my job is not to let myself be inducted into her procedures, and I decide to wait. But I make myself available.

THERAPIST: I would be glad to follow you, once you begin.

SUSAN: I wouldn't know where to begin. I don't know what is wrong. That's why I come to you.

I believe her. She certainly does not behave as if she knows what's wrong. So helpless does she seem that if I had the answers and if I believed that quick fixes do it for anyone, I'd be tempted to give them to her. But I don't, and I don't. So this is not a serious temptation. I have to clarify the problem with her, but it must come from her. I know that my interest will eventually model for her how to do this for herself.

THERAPIST: You know, I've noticed in the last few sessions that you've spent much of the time sitting quietly. I know that you must have a reason for that. But whatever your reason for not trying to explore your thoughts and feelings with me, it goes against your goals here. What I do know is that you will not get better unless you look at your life and allow me to look with you. Your not talking about your thoughts and feelings means that we will get nowhere. This may be part of your problem.

Susan remains silent. She has projected the withdrawing object representation onto me. She sees my failure to bail her out of her helplessness as an act of uncaring, and she is angry and refusing to speak. Over the months, I repeatedly point out how destructive this tactic is to her therapy goals, and she begins to think tentatively about her refusal to explore her own confused and diffuse self. Acknowledging her desire to get better, I say to her, "I believe that you want to change, or you would not be here. So why do you not talk?" And I watch for the moment when she will focus on herself sufficiently, with enough aggression, to articulate her reasons for silence and passivity. And, eventually, she does.

One day, she arrives on time and sits in silence for 10 minutes. But then she speaks.

SUSAN: I don't know how to start the session. I can't. I don't know what my problem is. I'm borderline. I can't.

"What?!" I'm thinking. "She has to be kidding." Yet, I see that her pathological ego really does not believe that she can think for herself, and the hospital experiences in which the staff related to her as if she were disabled rather than capable of change seem to support this belief.

therapist: You may have been diagnosed borderline and think that you are helpless, but whether you focus on yourself and try to help yourself is up to you.

SUSAN: That's not what I heard at the hospital. They told me what a borderline is.

THERAPIST: What did they tell you? Did they tell you that you are help-less? [*Susan doesn't answer, so I go on.*]

THERAPIST: You may feel that you're helpless, but guess what? Whether you actually live that way is up to you. It's your choice. Did you know that? [*I was still feeling astonished. Was compliance with the diagnosis a learned role, a learned relational procedure to ensure connection?*]

She remains silent for several minutes, but then she resumes.

SUSAN: So why can't I get to class?

At first, I don't answer. She not only feels but also believes that, on her own, she can't get herself to class regularly, that because she is borderline, she is unable to consistently attend class. She insists that none of it makes sense to her, that she doesn't know why she can't discipline herself to be responsible about class attendance. Unless someone is beside her, inspiring her activity and telling her what to do, she would like us both to believe that she is inert. I feel frustrated, and I work to use my frustration to light a fire through more confrontation.

THERAPIST: Why do you not get up and get going? It's your choice, you know. Why do you treat yourself like you can't do anything different? Why do you relate to yourself as though you're impotent?

SUSAN: You don't get it.

Relational procedures of this kind are new to Susan. Never before had anyone expected—not explicitly, implicitly, or consistently—that she was capable of experiencing feelings and thinking about them (to say nothing of getting out of bed and going to class), even if she felt that she could not. Nor had anyone imposed the notion that she could look to herself for the answers to her questions and decide what to do. She was not a victim of her helpless feelings if she had a choice.

Relational procedures of this kind are new to me as well. It takes constant vigilance on my part to maintain this new type of relationship because Susan, passively or actively and depending on her mood, puts a lot of pressure on me to revert to her expectations to take care of her or become critical or abusive. It feels like gridlock, where every possible gain is met by another roadblock. I have to keep reminding myself of my therapeutic stance: the expectation of self-focus, self-support, and adaptive management of feelings. I have to keep my attention on my working hypotheses about her internal world. In addition, I have to try to convey a kindness toward her, give her a sense that although I insist on remaining therapeutically neutral, I am still present to her with openness and good will. (To myself, though, I admit that she is incredibly frustrating.)

Eventually Susan stops her passive "sit-down strike," as we came to call it, acting out the self of the withdrawing unit. She forces herself to talk. But for a long time, she continues to insist that she does not know what to focus on.

> SUSAN: Okay, you start the session today. I've told you enough now. I don't know what else to say.

"Here we go again!" I think.

> SUSAN: Give me a hint.

"Is she kidding?" I ask myself again. But all I say is this:

> THERAPIST: The hints will all have to come from you. [*I track her process for her.*] What I notice is that when you need to focus on your thoughts and feelings, wishes or wants, goals or dreams, you look to me instead, as if I might read your mind or tell you this important information that only you have access to—if you would pay attention. When you look to me instead of to yourself, as if I am the expert, you miss the very thoughts and feelings in you that could inform us both. You will always be the only expert on your thoughts and feelings. I have to wait on you, or it would be destructive to you and to our relationship.

This is a confrontation that links her need for self-focus with her defense against it (looking to me) and the destructiveness of this defense relative to her own goals. Susan doesn't say anything, but she makes eye contact with a sudden momentary sparkle, a flash of reciprocal knowing and feeling. She sits quietly for a while, and I can almost hear her inner computer clicking. "Will she accept and integrate this confrontation?" I wonder to myself. In the past, she has not. Next session, we will see.

> SUSAN: I'm tired. Up with a stomachache all night. I don't know what to talk about. Any ideas?
>
> THERAPIST: What do you think?
>
> SUSAN: I keep hoping you'll say, yeh, but you won't.

Progress, I think. At least, this time she expected that I would not tell her what to talk about.

THERAPIST: It confuses me. You would pay money to listen to me talk or tell you what is important? Where did you get that? [*This is a question intended to invite reflection.*]

SUSAN: Other therapists did. One used to say things as if it were me saying it and then make me say it. Some therapists never said anything. . . . My foxhole is empty.

She has suddenly changed the subject. She's quiet and then yawns, looks sleepy. In previous sessions, she has talked about her dreams of being in a foxhole where she can hide and stay safe from the war. But why this change of focus now?

THERAPIST: What does that mean?

SUSAN: I don't feel like there's anybody with me.

She is silent, sleepy-looking. It seems that unless I tell her what she feels, she feels alone in the room. Or is she just changing the subject?

SUSAN: So where is God when I need him? These are some of the things on my mind. What do you make of these things?

Another change of focus. Wow, is this disjointed! I knew that Susan didn't know or see the process that I was watching. She was used to looking to someone else to tell her what she was feeling, to direct her. I tried not to do that, but all these changes of subject. . . . They seemed to be an effort to throw me off the track and, probably, herself as well. It would have been easy just to make interpretations and do for her what others had, except that we would have gotten nowhere, other than to have her become dependent on me. The previous session, she had talked about how much she hated her father but that she "had to relate to him and say nothing in order to keep his money coming in." I had wondered out loud about the effect of this on herself and her self-esteem. Now I was remembering this intensely felt comment of the day before. It was dog-eared in my memory and notes. Was it in hers? Maybe, but that was not how she started this session. How was it that she could act as if she did not remember it and say that she had nothing to talk about? This lack of continuity of focus was apparent. I decided to take it up with her.

THERAPIST: What I make of these things is that yesterday you seemed to have many feelings about your father and about how the relationship with him affects you. But today you say you have nothing to talk about.

SUSAN: I don't. It doesn't affect my self-esteem. It doesn't make it better or worse. I'm not me around him and don't deal with him.

THERAPIST: Then you go home and are up all night with an upset stomach. [*I make this connection, tracking her process, because she does not yet link any of the events, thoughts, or feelings of her life to any of the others.*]

SUSAN: I don't know. I could have just had too much beer. But I doubt it.

Again, I feel compelled to track her process. I want her to pay attention, not so much to the content of what she is saying as much as to the relational procedures that she has been using and does not yet see.

THERAPIST: This is like déjà vu. You have feelings; I question what they are; you deny them; you change the subject; I point them out again; you change the subject again; then you blow them off.

SUSAN: It's changed over the years. He used to affect me more. He's not human. [*Now she's back to the topic.*]

THERAPIST: He is, and you are, and the relationship has consequences, and when you're not around him, you still feel you're in a battle zone. Is this what the foxhole is about?

Having made the connection for her, I have to wait to see if it helped or hindered. Susan is silent for a short time.

SUSAN: Mom and I went over finances. I can't do anything different until after Christmas. I hate it. But I use the money I get from him to pay you. It drives him nuts, and I win the battle. It's the only way I know how to play. Dirty. Behind his back. [*She smiles.*] I always thought it would be fun to get drunk and tell Dad off.

Susan yawns. "I'm sleepy," she says, confirming my suspicion that at least some of her silences are medication related. "Last night I took four milligrams of Haldol. I usually take two."

My attention to her process and my reflecting it back to her got her back to real feelings and the way that she manages her anger with her father. Now she is making more sense—and she is not as helpless in her thinking as she has led me to believe. She is withholding her self from me, as she has from her father. She "worked" him, and she felt vengeful. But staying in a relationship where she accepts his disregard to gain his money seems to compromise her self-development. He treats her as being sick, and she accepts this to get his money, she tells me, but what I have seen in these few months is that, with me, she is the one who treats herself as being sick. It is not just her father who relates to her as if she is infirm but also she herself, when she looks to me to take charge. She has developed implicit relational procedures that are manifest not only in her relationship with her father but with the world as well; she presents herself as if she were sick and disabled, and these procedures express themselves with me, in the form of passivity and helplessness. As we begin to grapple with these questions, Susan's temporary silences in sessions become more obvious. Is she testing me to see if I will keep tracking her? Are her medications causing trouble? Is she unwilling to look at her continued acting out with her father? Is she angry at me, and is she expressing her anger passively? Hmm.

Two or three months into our work, it seemed advisable to find a local psychiatrist to evaluate Susan and prescribe and monitor her medications. Up until now, the psychiatrist from her third hospitalization had been prescribing long distance. I could see that it would be easier for me to make sense of her silences and sleepiness in sessions if I could regularly discuss Susan's case with a local consultant. I was receiving weekly supervision from Dr. Ralph Klein, the clinical director for the Masterson Institute. Now Dr. David Grubb, also a graduate of the Masterson Institute and whose practice was in our city, took over the medication collaboration.

We went back to some old questions in a new context. What was Susan's history? What were the attachment experiences that had contributed to this young woman's difficult life? And if the medication could control her mood disorder, what therapeutic tack would give her a new relational experience to correct the disordered development? I felt like a detective looking for hidden clues—and it wouldn't be until I could find them myself, over time, that I would be able to help Susan see them as well.

FAMILY HISTORY

Susan was born and raised in an affluent suburb. She had thought that her parents enjoyed a good, satisfying marriage, so she was shocked when they told her, during her first year in college, that they were getting a divorce. Still, she described her father as being extremely narcissistic, demanding of perfection and perfect mirroring by his family. He came from a wealthy family, and many of the problems among the extended circle of relatives seemed to revolve around who controlled the wealth and what was to become of the inheritance. In fact, as we have said, Susan understood that one condition of attachment to her father was that she had to accept his harsh treatment, lest she lose access to his money.

Susan described her mother as a kind and caring woman who idealized her husband and tended to defer to him; she married him, Susan thought, because "she knew he was going somewhere." Notably, Susan felt that her mother savored Susan's dependence and helpless behavior and that she encouraged Susan to turn to her for direction, advice, and decision making. Susan's relationship with her mother was her predominant source of comfort and soothing. Susan was protective of her mother, and she phoned her almost daily. It took a long time into her therapy before I learned the conditions of her attachment to her mother, the attachment that formed her false, defensive, helpless self. But Susan eventually realized, she told me, that she had always been a bother to her mother ("Don't hang on me. I'm tired"). Only when Susan came to her for advice, which made her mother feel close and needed and which relieved her mother of her headaches, did Susan feel connected. Then, Susan noted, when her mother felt better and calmed down, she did too. This was a strikingly perceptive understanding. Susan thought that she had to comply with her mother's wishes that she be a good student and a good girl. She never believed that she could really share anything with her mother—she would not be heard. Therefore, in withholding from her mother, Susan protected both of them—her mother and herself. That was the best way to handle things. Susan insisted that she felt close to her mother, who was "the only person who stuck by me" through the hospitalizations. But in reality, they discussed only superficial issues—daily activities, health matters, the family. They rarely talked about feelings, and when they did, they used humor to diffuse any intensity and to protect their sense of connection. It was only much later that enormous angers could be expressed between them.

Susan described her brother as a person who combined great self-absorption and an inability to manage his life adaptively. Three years older than she, he abused drugs, stole and sold household goods to support his habit, and was generally irresponsible, oppositional, and rageful. When Susan was 7, he initiated a sexual relationship with her that endured until she was 12. She emphatically insisted that she did not feel victimized, because she believed that she was as responsible as he was, and she denied anger at him until much later in treatment. She had witnessed the emotional and physical abuse to which he had been subjected by their father, and she felt guilty at having watched in terror the father's unpredictable expressions of rage.

HISTORY OF TREATMENT

Susan first sought treatment while in high school, when she found herself feeling hopeless and preoccupied with suicide. Until then, she told me, she lived a dual life. She tried to live up to her mother's expectations by being a good girl—always helping, never being a problem of any kind—but always hiding within herself the relationship with her brother. When she finally could do this no longer, she confided in a friend. The friend encouraged her to tell the school counselor, and Susan later entered psychotherapy with a woman in private practice, who treated her after her hospitalizations. This treatment was arranged by her parents. Having someone to talk to and having less to hide gave Susan some relief: She graduated from high school, worked through the following summer, and then moved across the country to go to college. It was in that freshman year that her life caved in on her.

Susan's first hospitalization occurred when she learned of her parents' plan to divorce. This was upsetting to her—so upsetting that she could not tolerate the feelings, so she overdosed on Valium and beer in an effort to "numb out." She was found in her dorm room and taken to the student health center, to the college infirmary, and then to a nearby short-term-only psychiatric hospital, where she remained for the maximum stay of 4 months. Because she seemed grossly disorganized, had periods of apparent catatonia, and reported hearing voices, she was diagnosed with schizophrenia and medicated with Thorazine and Haldol. She was subsequently transferred to another local psychiatric hospital, where she was in treatment for 14 months. During this second hospitalization, she was diagnosed with a mixed-type schizoaffective–bipolar disorder.

Her treatment there was privately paid for by the family, so Susan's parents, by then separated, arranged for Susan to be admitted to a private psychiatric hospital closer to home, on the West Coast. This was her third hospitalization—the one that she thought was most helpful to her. There, she was diagnosed with bipolar disorder and borderline personality disorder. She was weaned off the antipsychotic medications and started on lithium. She reported that the psychiatrist there helped her and that she appreciated the therapy she received. She was in treatment for 3.5 months and discharged with doctor's orders to enter a nearby halfway house.

However, her depression soon intensified, as did her passive and helpless behavior. Once again, she was admitted to a medical center, a different one because it was less costly, and her inheritance was rapidly being depleted. This time, she was in the hospital for several months. "It was hell," Susan said of this experience. There was, by her account, no therapy, only medication, and indeed, she remembers little except being overmedicated with Thorazine and Haldol. Soon, her mother worked with physicians at this medical center to allow her to be discharged home. Susan began to meet again with her first psychotherapist, the one whom she had seen in high school, three times a week. There was some relief from her depression, and Susan became a little more mobilized. Eventually, she was able to take on a part-time job doing limited clerical work.

During the second and longest hospitalization, Susan felt taken care of as she never had before. She felt better, but she didn't get better. In all of her hospital experiences, she believed that she was treated as if she were a helpless victim of her family experience. By her account, she was treated as though she were incapable of managing her life adaptively—no one expected her to assume any responsibility for her treatment or her life. For a while, probably because of her winsome personality, she became a favorite patient on the ward of her second hospital. She recalled the staff's coddling her, dismissing her occasional tirades, and doing the work for her by putting her feelings into words.

Over time, Susan's acting out of her sense of helplessness intensified. With it came gradually escalating demands for more attention, more indulgence, and more succor; it was as if any cooperation with her experience of helplessness only intensified her desire to be treated like an infant. When the treatment staff responded impatiently to her growing demands, Susan began to respond with verbal and physical rage. She became so irrationally aggressive that, many times, five or six attendants would have to race down the hall to restrain her, take her to seclusion, and wrap her in cold sheet packs for hours or sedate her with major tranquilizers. She did not think that she had received much help in this second facility, but there were several people, a few nurses and a janitor, whom she liked and remembered.

When she returned to her parents' home after her fourth hospitalization (at the medical center), she stabilized somewhat, with the help of regular therapy and her mother's efforts. Then, almost 3 years later, she moved away from home once more, to try college again. Again, a series of traumas disrupted her plans; her grandfather died, and she was diagnosed, first, with the bleeding ulcer and then with cancer. Another episode of depression followed. She began to suffer from lethargy, hypersomnia, and feelings of hopelessness. She started skipping classes and depending inordinately on the encouragement of two professors. They felt pressured by her neediness, and they wanted her to get some help so that she could regain her functioning. They referred her to the counselor at the student health center. This is when she was referred to me. After her report of 11 other therapists, 10 of whom she had seen during the different hospitalizations, I wondered with some apprehension what I would see and how I would make sense of it.

There were no known biological antecedents of psychiatric or medical illnesses in Susan's family. What became apparent to us was that Susan had a long history of reluctance to speak for or about herself, a passive resistance to engaging in conflict, and an apparent inability even to feel her feelings. It was obvious that nothing could proceed unless she would talk. She needed access to her anger to clarify her internal perspective, and she needed to understand the meaning of her "voices." Were they really auditory hallucinations or perhaps expressions of her disavowed self?

When Susan finally began talking, we slowly pieced together her internal world. It appeared that she had internalized two models of relationships. The rewarding object relations model promised her relational survival for complying with her parents' expectations for her: being a good girl, a capable student, a high achiever, an accomplished singer, a comedienne, and, especially, a helpless and dependent person. At first, I found this confusing—how could they expect her to be a high achiever and be helpless and dependent? Later, however, it became clear that being good, doing well in school, performing, being needy and dependent were all ways of accommodating to her mother's needs and expectations;

they were all false-self expressions of compliance and not reflective of her real self. By focusing first on her mother and on her mother's need to be soothed by Susan's reliance and compliance, Susan could relax and feel attached.

The attachment came at the cost of helplessness, however, and any expression of her real self was unacceptable. This relationally wired her to focus on others first and follow their lead because the other half of Susan's relational experience, the withdrawing model, expected that any self-expressive urges would be met with punishment. Her parents, especially her father, were experienced as critical, unpredictably explosive people, as if in a war zone, intolerant of any expressions of spontaneity, emotional separation, or autonomous activity. Her consequent terror was so intense—like being in a foxhole on a battlefield—that she numbed out her feelings and any experience of her real self. So unaccustomed was Susan to authentic ways of being that she did not even allow herself to experience her fear, hurt, and anger. In fact, she disavowed these feelings.

It seemed clear that Susan was heavily invested in her own emotional survival and that she had done a creative job of constructing a character that helped her to do just that—survive—until she was out in a world where her defensive false self of illness and helplessness was ineffectual. This was a formula that had helped her feel attached to her mother and even her father, but it left her incompetent in the real world and unsupported, unless she could coerce others into the expected caretaking role. Over her second, long hospitalization, her old role was successful at first because she let the staff identify her feelings and interpret her behavior for her. But when they became impatient with her, she experienced herself as a bad and unlovable person; it enacted an angry, unlovable self, which often ended up with her subsequent punishment and isolation. In object relations terms, when her withdrawing self was activated, she projected the withdrawing object representation onto the staff, railing at them for their failure to provide her with the regressive support that she so desperately desired. Somatic complaints or reports of auditory hallucinations were sometimes enlisted to coerce others to assume more responsibility for her.

But Susan's false-self adaptation was slowly cracking, and she knew it. In high school, she felt isolated as her friends became interested in boys, an interest that she could not share, haunted as she was by her relationship with her brother. In college, the implicit bargain that she made with her parents for care and safety was threatened by distance and the impending divorce. Susan had no robust sense of self to guide her to constructive ways of coping with the world and with relationships, and under stress, she retreated to the habit that she had developed early on—she became increasingly helpless, in an effort to persuade others to take care of her.

Typical of people who learn to rely on helplessness and passivity to secure attachment, these defenses were ego-syntonic for Susan. Her hospitalizations reinforced her tendency to relinquish responsibility for her behavior; she accepted the fact that she was "ill"—a perfect example of insight as excuse—and she refused to consider the possibility that she had choices. What efforts she did make availed her little. Activation of her real self was considerably impaired, and she could not initiate or complete the projects that might have increased her sense of solidity and worth. Her family relationships were limited to "close" but superficial ones in which neither genuine intimacy nor realistic self-assertion was possible. These could not help her out of her shadow world, and Susan was left to constantly search for someone to tell her what to do and, often, for someone to do it for her. Some people cooperated with this wish at first, but in time they came to feel burdened by her dependence and would thereby withdraw in impatience or anger. She would react with rage, but her capacity for self-soothing, for the down regulation of affect, was impaired, too; ultimately, all she knew was to escalate her demands to be taken care of, and the cycle repeated.

Susan told me the story of her life easily enough, but her capacity for reflection was limited. She was able to wonder with uncertainty who this person was that she had become, but she was neither willing nor able to focus on her concerns and keep trying to figure out what she could do differently. When she finally began to talk in session, we repeatedly ended up in that avoidant process that we came to call déjà vu—talking about anything but Susan's thoughts and feelings. We had no therapeutic alliance, and she certainly did not relate to me in my role—there to help her untangle whatever she was tangled in. But as I talked about her denial regarding the self-defeating effects of these processes, she began, over time, to return to the subject at hand, whether it was her insistence that she could not get to class because it was too hard or her accepting her father's devaluations because she was unwilling to stick with her feelings about them and him and thus come up with some possibilities of self-support.

The issue of her auditory hallucinations came up in the context of her relentless focus on me to fill her sessions with content. She would come in and complain that the voices were so loud that she could not sleep at night, let alone focus on anything else. She was victim to these loud voices, she told me, and could thus move no further. But was she really subject to psychotic hallucinations, or was this just the next line of defense, another distraction from her experience of her feelings?

Dr. Klein, my supervisor, suggested that I take up the voices as just that, a possible distraction from her real feelings. If they were genuinely psychotic, they would not disappear. If the voices were part of her unwitting defensive structure, however, then they were also signals from her real self, and they would be absorbed back into herself once they had given her the access that she needed to what she felt.

So, we looked at these voices, which Susan described as being loud and consuming, especially after a few sessions of emerging anger at her father: "Kill him!" "You're bad!" "Run!" "It's all your fault!" they said, in addition to "the loud crying of a baby." But after I suggested that, perhaps, they were not inhabiting her but were part of her, they disappeared within two sessions. Susan began to see that "Kill him!" expressed her anger toward her father, that "It's all your fault!" was all her own guilt, and the baby crying was herself in mourning. She was stunned to recognize that the voices were telling her who she was.

With vigilance on both our parts, we began to have a real relationship. As Susan accumulated moments of giving up her defenses, the therapeutic alliance was forged. How different this was from the texture of earlier sessions. She worked to focus on herself; I listened; and it was genuine. Not that she didn't test me regularly. She would still come in and ask me to start the session for her, but now, with a smile and a twinkle, she would proceed herself. And she was getting to class, although this was a stop-and-go business. She would get to class, feel paralyzed, and act paralyzed. I would confront her, and she would get to class again, feel paralyzed again, and so it went.

But each time that she reengaged around her real concerns and stuck with her focus there, I saw incremental gains. A new, healthier ego began to form around her being able to think about and identify what had been important in the previous session—to remind herself, with feeling, "Yes. This is how I feel." These tiny, almost imperceptible expressions of Susan's real self were what I came to see as "possibility moments," microscopic glimpses of her potential to live her life differently, to relate to herself and to others in ways that she could respect. Sometimes, she seemed secretly surprised and pleased with herself. I watched these accomplishments in awe, and she watched me watching her. Underneath all of her acting out, there was someone in hiding, waiting to see if I would look for her, and while I practiced managing my countertransference, I was able and gratified to do just that.

Susan was in her fourth year of college and her third year of treatment when she met a very charismatic nurse practitioner who represented herself as an expert in treating borderline personality disorders. In her classes and psychoeducational sessions, Ms. Smith used brain scans of borderline patients to demonstrate the "neurological foundation" of this disorder and, therefore, the inevitability and intractability of borderline symptoms. She also claimed to be able to make medication decisions based on each patient's neurobiology. Ms. Smith had a burgeoning practice, and she taught classes in the community that were impressively well attended by patients and mental health clinicians.

While Susan was still seeing me, she began attending these classes faithfully. I was interested and open to the possibilities for her. I especially wanted to see if she could keep her own perspective on her life and experience while she looked at this biological information. Could she hold onto herself? In time, she reported that she had become Ms. Smith's star student. She began to express the hope of eventually co-teaching with her, and she decided, without discussing it with me, that she would terminate her relationship with Dr. Grubb and transfer responsibilities for her medication to Ms. Smith. Dr. Grubb's working relationship with her had been to listen carefully to her experience and to provide prescriptions for her lithium, as well as her Thorazine and Haldol as needed—that is, if she feared manic symptoms. He also prescribed Susan's thyroid medication and Benadryl for dealing with potential extrapyramidal symptoms. He regularly sent me progress reports on his appointments with her, along notice of any medication changes, and he was available for regular consultation.

When Susan asked me to send Ms. Smith information on her treatment, I did. Ms. Smith began seeing Susan twice weekly to monitor her medication changes and to teach her about what to expect biologically. Ms. Smith wanted Susan to be informed about her condition. In the following months, Susan reported serial medication trials. This attention and direction were comforting to Susan, but they seemed to set up clinging and compliance in her relationship with Ms. Smith. The red flags went up for me. Furthermore, Ms. Smith emphasized to Susan that she was a "hardwired borderline" and that people with her illness can hope only for a limited management of symptoms with appropriate medications. Over time, on the grounds that Susan was severely disabled, Ms. Smith encouraged Susan to apply for social security disability insurance rather than look for a job. She made no effort to help Susan manage her anxiety and lack of self-confidence as she sought employment. In short, this relationship was entirely at cross-purposes to Susan's treatment with me and, more important, to Susan's working through her issues. It activated her rewarding unit, and, predictably, with it came regression. Also predictably, Susan's therapy stalled out.

Until that time, Susan had been activating herself, albeit with difficulty. She had maintained her studies, graduated from college, successfully taken on positions as teachers' assistants, and maintained some important friendships at school, as well as several relationships with some older women whom she had trusted for years. She submitted applications for jobs in the community, taught an interactive Bible study at her church, and had been asked to speak to several groups of psychiatrically impaired people and their families. She believed that this was a genuine expression of herself and how she could put together her life in a way that gave it meaning. Furthermore, she discovered some leads about employment possibilities. All of this was evidence of her growing real capacity.

Her classes with Ms. Smith had also seemed to her to be expressions of her real self—until it became apparent to her, as well as to me, that they were interfering with real therapeutic change. Ms. Smith encouraged her to see herself as being disabled. Susan's "neurobiological wiring" meant that she was indeed stuck and that she should resign herself to her borderline plight. Susan's self-activation ceased—both in and out of session. She began collapsing in her efforts to make plans for her life and resumed her altogether passive and helpless stance with me in the office. It was another déjà vu, another verse of her old song. I was angry, but I was not really angry at Susan. I talked to Ms. Smith (who had given me no updates on medication changes) several times on the phone. It became clear that our notions of treatment were based on completely different models and that she and I would not be able to agree on a collaborative strategy. I informed Ms. Smith of this.

I wanted to alert Susan to what was going on, and I feared that she might decide that she was handicapped, rather than continue to make plans to support her life. But when I told Susan of these conversations, she fell silent. It was the first time in months that this had occurred in session. She was silent for 12 ½ minutes. I wrote it down because it was so unusual and, once again, difficult—to wonder what she was feeling and doing in that silence. Finally, I asked her, "What's up? Why are you so quiet?" Another 2 minutes of silence. I knew that I was trying to drive a wedge between her and her relationship to her new hope, her new rewarding unit. I also guessed that she was angry at me and that I was once again experienced as the withdrawing unit.

> SUSAN: I can't go through this again. You have to help me. I'm scared. I went to bed and prayed. I am sick. Coughed up blood. I hear voices again. I'm borderline, and it is my illness. It is a handicap that I must deal with. I've seen the MRIs. This is how I'm wired. You have to help me. I think that I need to be in the hospital.

> THERAPIST: This is exactly my concern for you. You seem ready to go from the frying pan into the fire. You are buying a diagnosis that traps you in an illness mentality again. The wiring in your brain is there, but that is what we are about. We, in this relationship, over time, are rewiring your brain. You can find out what you feel, what you want, and how to stay after it.

> SUSAN: [*After a brief silence.*] What I get mad about is this. I called you Saturday night. I was overwhelmed. I woke you from sleep at 1 p.m. You said, "We won't figure this out over the phone tonight. Do what you can to settle down, and we will talk when you come in tomorrow." After hearing what I have been through the last 3 weeks . . . I thought

you understood. Then I called Ms. Smith. She came over and sat with me until I quieted down. I thought you understood and cared, but now I see that she cares more.

At this point I got angry and said, with feeling,

THERAPIST: Bullshit! Coming to rescue you in the middle of the night has nothing to do with caring for you. My concern is for you to stop collapsing in on yourself again and looking for someone else to take care of you, no matter what you are feeling. It looks like this is exactly what is happening. Do you see this?

Susan left the session silently.

Amazingly, for a while she seemed to remember who I was and who she was, because in the following session, she reflected to me, "I always look to you for the answers, and you never give them. I don't ask Ms. Smith for answers. She offers them." But the siren song of the new relationship kept her moving in that direction. I began to feel very discouraged and ineffectual.

Predictably, Susan's clinging and her demands for time and attention eventually began to tell on Ms. Smith, who gradually withdrew. According to Susan, Ms. Smith became increasingly annoyed with her, decreasing the frequency of her appointments, limiting the frequency and duration of her phone calls, and asking her to talk less in the classes. Susan plunged into a severe abandonment depression.

Over these years of treatment, we watched and tracked her process together, noting over and over how self-focus leads to abandonment depression, which then leads to defense. We noted that her first line of defense against really experiencing herself and her pain was her angry silence, the sit-down strike. The next was her focus on me and others for advice and guidance. The third was her angry unwillingness to do what seemed too hard (like getting to class). Fourth, we explored the meaning of the voices screaming in her head and how her focus on the presence of the voices had kept her from hearing what they had to say—that is, from listening to her own feelings. Our fifth piece of work explored and confronted the effect on her self-esteem when she related to her family without self-clarity or self-support. Finally, we addressed the incredible strength of her habit of acting helpless or compliant and looking for someone to take over for her.

Now, during this difficult interlude in her treatment, I pointed out to Susan many times that her relationship with Ms. Smith seemed to be confusing her and interfering with her efforts to find herself. I confronted the way that she was acting out her helplessness again, but I added that I also felt (with her) her profound sense of abandonment. My confrontations and observations had not helped her resist this bright promise that had come to her. Once again, a magical hope had been offered and withdrawn, leaving Susan to reexperience the abandonment that she so feared.

Now faced in vivo with the reality of Ms. Smith's withdrawal, Susan began to deeply experience just how much she really did fear abandonment. The crisis became an opportunity to explore, with feeling, her rage and fury at Ms. Smith—and at her mother, father, and brother. Excruciating memory, grief, and regret followed. As the pain of this most recent rejection was felt, Susan was reminded of countless other such experiences over the days, nights, weeks, and years—specific and vital pieces of her life that she had distracted herself from—a life lived on a battleground, in a foxhole that she was afraid to leave because she would not be heard, not be believed, not be seen, only used by her brother. Once Susan understood this, she was at last able to confront her parents about the falseness and superficiality of the closeness between herself and each of them.

Once this rage was expressed in words, Susan and her mother were able to continue relating. An implicit repair was forged, and Susan began to feel that the relationship could now be real. And it was. As it became honest and more straightforward, Susan resumed, with fear and anger, her efforts to work on and support herself.

At that time, Susan had graduated from college. She was still speaking periodically to the families of psychiatric patients. She maintained a community at her church, where she continued to help in leadership positions. She was working part-time at a business that provided work opportunities for those with difficult vocation histories, a job that she had found through her networking with community advocates. All of these functions were practiced actively, despite the persistence of the underlying abandonment depression.

Now she repeatedly reflected on the relationship with Ms. Smith, feeling that it cast a constant and agonizing shadow on her life here. She began to wonder if it might be in her best interest to move back to the city where her mother and stepfather lived. We began to talk about this. Susan was sure that she did not want to live where Ms. Smith was, but she did want to continue therapy—and with another therapist who worked from a perspective similar to mine. She wanted someone who would not tell her what she felt or who she was or that she was not able, and she wanted to continue to take her regulating medications while looking at how to move forward. These were not regressive fantasies; they were informed by the complexity of her history and her present life. They were ideas that Susan could reflect on, knowing that old environments and relationships, home and family, exert a ponderous pull; yet, now, she had a new ability to speak for herself and support herself. So, I worked with her to plan her return home.

Susan was very sad to leave our relationship, and I was sad to have her go. She had taught me a lot about what people can endure and yet still use constructively, if they just think and feel about it with someone they trust. We had come to trust each other. It had been a long road from transference acting out to transference, from false-self relating to a real relationship. She talked in one of our last sessions about how important it had been to her to be able to be angry at me and let me know it. My repeated confrontations told her that I was strong enough to handle it—I kept saying more of the things that made her angry. She told me, too, that even when she didn't believe that she could do what I expected of her, she trusted me. When she tried and found that she could, self-esteem fueled further efforts. As for me, her anger had been so passively expressed in the beginning that it took a while for me to feel provoked by the gridlock. But when I did, I was usually able to not act out countertransferentially. It was incredibly helpful to me to have a good theory support me, as well as much supervisory assistance and correction. Somehow, mysteriously, we had those moments of promise, that light in her eyes, to guide us, even after a confrontation. They told me that we were on the scent of her real self.

It has been 4 years since Susan terminated her therapy with me. She sends me news of continued progress that is as astounding as it is satisfying. Upon return to her hometown, she did indeed contact a Masterson-trained therapist and resume her treatment. She is finishing a master's degree program, preparing to work with disabled children, for whom she has great empathy. She is employed while she goes to school, and she is singing in her church choir. She lives alone; she has lost weight. Most recently, her church offered her a full-tuition scholarship to go to theological seminary, with the promise of a full-time job working with the disabled upon completion of her studies. Her real self is alive and well, full of meaning and hope. Her indomitable spirit still evokes reverence and respect in me. Way to go, Susan.

9

Laura

Tormented and in Trouble

This is an unusual case because Laura was not my patient. I (DDR) met her when she was admitted to a residential treatment center where I was the psychologist consultant, about 20 years ago. I consulted at this treatment center for many years, and I supervised Laura's therapists there. I also followed patients of my own at the two local hospitals in the area that provided psychiatric care and where Laura was the subject of a number of case consultations. Through these channels, I was able to follow—although somewhat sketchily at points—Laura's treatment journey over the years. She was 15 when she was transferred to our center, after a 2-month stay in a psychiatric hospital.

Laura's borderline personality disorder was severe. In this, she was like many borderline-disordered individuals who are seen routinely and repeatedly in mental health facilities, from social service agencies to psychiatric hospitals. Her internal world was terrifying. She had far more bad objects than good ones. The bad ones were "badder" and the good ones less good, than, say, Terri's or Susan's. Furthermore, Laura had no family who could support her, either emotionally or financially, or help her through a hard time. She had a terrible history of trauma and an almost complete lack of experience of reparative relationships. This combination left her with a formidable handicap and an underlying abandonment depression so profound that her relatively underdeveloped ego could not contain and manage her seemingly intolerable affects in any adaptive way. Her story is a familiar one to psychotherapists who have to contend with the limitations inherent in state and municipal mental health systems, and it is a cautionary tale about what can happen when there is no therapy to offer a patient the all-important second chance.

Laura was originally admitted to the local hospital for severe depression and a transient psychotic-like episode in which she repeatedly cut herself over most of her body. She displayed paranoia, nightmarish fear, and, when she was afraid enough, violence toward others. At the time of her admission, the precipitant of her decompensation was a mystery, but several years later, she revealed that she was being sexually molested by a man, her high school volleyball coach. Laura seemed to respond well to the security and safety of the hospital environment and to a combination of antidepressant and antipsychotic medications; she found some relief from her fears, paranoia, and aggressive impulses. However, her depression persisted and so did feelings of hopelessness and suicidal preoccupations.

During the evaluation period, Laura's hospital team decided that she was a serious danger to herself. The involuntary treatment law in her state required a determination by a designated mental health professional that she was a danger to herself or others or was incapable of surviving on her own, to detain her involuntarily for psychiatric treatment. The facility to which she was assigned could be either a private psychiatric treatment setting or a public psychiatric hospital, and permission of her parents was not necessary. Having been found to be a danger to herself, Laura was transferred after 2 months in the hospital to the facility where I met her, a small residential treatment center for adolescents needing intense psychiatric treatment in a relatively restrictive environment.

At first, Laura was depressed, mistrustful, guarded, and passively resistant to treatment. There were occasional episodes of violent aggression, sometimes requiring physical restraint. But in time, her depression lifted a little, and she began to more actively participate in the center's various treatment modalities. She was seen in individual therapy twice a week and was followed regularly by a psychiatrist for medications management. She participated in weekly group therapy, attended the center's school, and took part in a daily recreation therapy program.

Conspicuously lacking in Laura's treatment, however, was a family therapy component. Her mother and stepfather at the time were living in a small rural community an hour-and-a-half drive from the treatment center. Although they had agreed initially to participate in weekly family therapy, they often didn't show up at the scheduled time or cited the cost of driving such a distance as a reason for not making the weekly trip. Her parents did visit her occasionally, but Laura consistently became severely depressed and made serious attempts to harm herself following her times with them. As a consequence, her treatment team decided that it was just as well if her mother and stepfather did not participate in her treatment. No further efforts to involve them were made.

Laura did form a few warm and trusting relationships with the staff, and by the time that she was discharged, a year later, she was only mildly depressed. Her affective experience was bright, and she seemed to be optimistic about her future.

When discharged, Laura was assigned a caseworker by the state and placed in a group home for psychiatrically impaired adolescents. She was enrolled in the local high school. She had a mental health center psychiatrist who prescribed and monitored her antidepressant medications, and her caseworker visited weekly. There was no provision for psychotherapy, because state funds for mental health care in her community were depleted, but at first, it looked like she was making a good adaptation. There were no signs of deepening depression, and her positive outlook about her future was sustained. But this adjustment was short-lived: Laura became increasingly isolated (she had a room by herself) and mistrustful of the few people in her life, and she was soon overcome again by severe depression and despair. One night, she deliberately overdosed on a combination of her psychotropic medications and alcohol and was readmitted to the residential treatment center.

Laura responded to this second admission much as she had to the first; after a period of profound depression, self-hatred, and withdrawal, interrupted occasionally by violent outbursts, she settled into the treatment regimen. She became more activated, and her depression lifted conspicuously. After 5 months in the treatment center, Laura went back to the group home. This time, she had three roommates, which prevented her from withdrawing so readily. Again, the state could not provide psychotherapy or counseling, so Laura's only connection with the mental health system was through weekly visits by her caseworker and her monthly appointments with the psychiatrist who was managing her medications. Once again, following a few months' respite from her agonizing depression, the torment of her inner world overcame her. She plunged back into her old despair and self-loathing, and the self-mutilation resumed.

Now 18 years old, Laura no longer qualified for the state services offered to children and adolescents. She now belonged to the regular state mental health system for adults, which could offer little continuity with her past care. And, of course, she lost her caseworker and her psychiatrist. She was admitted to a state psychiatric hospital, where her medication needs were addressed regularly, but no psychotherapy or counseling was available, aside from a weekly therapy group—again owing to the fiscal restraints of the system. Still, her depression, paranoia, and aggression remitted over time, and after almost a year, Laura was again discharged. From then on, she lived in subsidized housing arranged by her various caseworkers. There were five different apartments over the next several years, each move a consequence of yet another hospitalization.

Over the years, Laura developed a predictable pattern: There would be a period of relatively adaptive, if tenuous, functioning, followed by a slide into depression, self-harm, suicidal thoughts, and rage. Hospitalization would be required. Laura would eventually recover her functioning and then be discharged, only to start the cycle again. For a brief while, it looked as though Laura might have a real chance to break the cycle. She was participating 5 days a week in a day treatment program provided by a community mental health center. She had a new caseworker, who met with her weekly and provided direction for her involvement in the treatment program. But in this program, in a striking exception to the usual state protocol, Laura was given a counselor and the opportunity for twice-a-week counseling. She became quite attached to her counselor, a kindly and compassionate middle-aged woman, and she seemed to benefit from the counseling experience. She was able to return to school and earn an alternative high school degree. She participated in a job preparation program, lived alone in her apartment, paid her own bills, and navigated a relatively complex public transportation system. In general, she was more stable than she had been for years, and she was becoming increasingly independent.

But after nearly a year of participation in the day treatment program, Laura precipitously plummeted into her, by now, familiar paranoid, suicidal, and violent depression. It was later learned that a man at her job-training site had approached her sexually, and this apparently precipitated the return to her internal world of danger and desperation. Even with a secure, stable, and supportive treatment program, her adjustment was too precarious to contain the activation of her toxic inner life. Another hospital admission was necessary.

RELEVANT PAST AND FAMILY HISTORY

Laura was the third of four children. Her biological father left the family when she was very young, probably under 2, and she had had only rare contact with him over the years. Shortly after the breakup of the marriage, Laura's mother remarried. By Laura's account, her mother and stepfather were both alcoholics, and during her early years, their lives revolved around the use and sale of drugs. Laura's sister, only 5 years older, provided what parental functions Laura received. The family milieu seemed to be one of emotional neglect and deprivation and, at times, physical abuse. There was no reported sexual abuse, but patterns of interaction within the family were typically acrimonious and stressful.

Laura's mother appeared to suffer from severe and chronic depression, but she was never treated for it. She medicated herself with alcohol and marijuana, at the predictable high cost to her family. Laura longed for acknowledgment, affirmation, and approval from her mother, and she tried desperately but unsuccessfully to please her. Furthermore, when Laura forsook her usual compliance and spontaneously or assertively expressed herself, her mother tended to respond with cold and sometimes sadistic rejection. (A member of one of Laura's treatment teams described Laura's mother's demeanor as "wild-eyed.") Laura became increasingly avoidant of such autonomous behavior. Over the long course of her hospital history, it became clear that visits with her mother were often followed by episodes of cutting, violence toward staff, and suicidal impulses. In fact, Laura's treatment staff in time concluded that she experienced her mother as being so malignant that visits with her were discontinued.

Laura's brother, the oldest of her siblings, ran away from home as an adolescent and had no contact with the family since. Laura's older sister, as Laura describes her, was hard-working, responsible, generally compliant in the family, and avoidant of conflict. Her younger sister, however, was rebellious, outspoken, and angry and abused drugs and alcohol. She experienced transient psychotic states that had been determined by a psychiatrist at the local community mental health center to be drug induced. As such, she was a source of discord in the family.

Laura and her siblings grew up without parental supervision, and once they reached puberty, they began to roam the streets and neighborhoods of their small hometown unmonitored. They became heavily involved in drugs and alcohol. Laura reported as well that she met a woman in the neighborhood who enticed her into a relationship that eventually turned sexual. The experiences of the sexual abuse she suffered were so painful that she struggled to obliterate them from her memory through the alcohol and drugs or, later, cutting herself.

In spite of this early history of disinterest, absence, and abuse, Laura displayed impressively strong attachments to her sisters and brother and, later, to her stepfather, who was neither abusive nor disparaging of her and, at times, was quite kind and concerned in relating to her. Interestingly, she feared for her brother and younger sister—she worried that they were living in self-destructive ways, and she felt a sense of responsibility about helping them, if possible. And the intense longing for a connection with her mother persisted unabated.

Despite an attachment history characterized by emotional neglect and radical misattunement, Laura (when functioning well) had a winsome personality and would periodically attach herself to people who were sympathetic to her plight and tried to be helpful to her. But they were not constant enough in her life to provide her with consistent experiences of disruption and repair to overcome her inner terrors. She was able to use such caring people for management of the abandonment depression when they were available to her, but they were not always, and at those times she could achieve affect regulation only through substance abuse and self-mutilation.

DIAGNOSTIC FORMULATION

Laura's diagnostic profile was consistently that of a severe borderline personality disorder. Her behavior displayed extreme versions of the two internal models, the two object relations units that are typical of borderline personality organization. (As we shall see, Laura also demonstrated real psychological and functional strengths, yet these were not sufficient to overcome her problems. Laura's story makes clear the ferocious undertow against which borderline patients are doomed to struggle.) When Laura's rewarding unit was activated; when people were warm and interested in her; when she felt connected, attuned to, cared about, and taken care of, she was affable, kind, thoughtful, and warm. However, when she was in the grip of the withdrawing, self-hating unit, she experienced psychotic-like symptoms of paranoia and out-of-control rage, at herself and other people. At her functional best, Laura took good care of herself. She kept herself well groomed and neatly dressed in clothing appropriate for a teenager. She was initially guarded with others and sometimes appeared sullen but was cautiously open to engagement. Even at those positive times, however, she was notably overfocused on others in her efforts to discern their expectations for her and to please them. She seemed to be emotionally hungry and fearful and willing to do whatever was needed to maintain connection. When she felt rejected, abandoned, or threatened, she experienced herself as being utterly worthless, ugly, and despicable. It would be accurate to say that Laura's withdrawing object appeared to her as a sadistic torturer who terrorized her. At these times, her experience of relationship was hopelessness, rage, and suicidal depression.

Laura never developed a false defensive self adequate to protect her from her terrors. Her story illustrates why borderline people hang onto their maladaptive defenses so fiercely; without them, they are at the mercy of terrors like Laura's. The combination of severe early neglect and scarce experiences of attuned and caring relationships apparently rendered Laura exceptionally vulnerable to activation of her bad objects. Furthermore, the lack of an internal model of disruption and repair gave her no way to alleviate the terror and pain of these experiences. She could not contain her fear and her rage; her internal tormentor was externalized, projected onto others, and then battled in vivo. Yet, when the withdrawing unit was activated, she experienced her own self as being evil and worthless, deserving of punishment and even death. She handled this experience with a variety of self-punishing behaviors, including self-mutilation and suicide attempts. The pain of cutting served as a distraction from her seemingly intolerable and interminable emotional pain.

LAURA'S LATER COURSE

Determined by the state to be functionally disabled, Laura was covered by government-funded disability insurance. Employment was not a necessity for her. Laura's financial dependence on the state did not reflect her wish or her motivation. She was always most satisfied when productive. She longed for a job, and on the occasions when she was able to work (at reduced part-time), she was responsible, disciplined, and tireless. But Laura had a fear that was more than the equal of her wishes—an intense fear of aloneness and a suicidal preoccupation with punishment, to which she desperately struggled not to succumb. When the darkness came back—and it always did—nothing mattered to Laura, not even work. So, she remained trapped in a vicious cycle.

Laura clearly needed consistent, reliable treatment in addition to the capable case management that she usually received. Repeated efforts were made by social workers and psychiatrists who knew her from her hospitalizations to establish such an opportunity, but the mental health system did not have the resources to serve Laura in this way. The local mental health center, because of funding cuts, could only provide medications management for even the most seriously disabled patients. Sliding-scale agencies required a minimum fee that was beyond her reach. And attempts to find pro bono services in the private sector were unsuccessful. Her experience in therapy in the day treatment program had been a positive one, and at times, she was able to see her need for counseling. Laura was motivated to improve her lot, to stay out of hospitals, to be happy, and to enjoy the goodness of life. She had one good experience of counseling in the day treatment program and could see her need for more. But this never came to pass.

When Laura was 27, she was functioning at her highest level ever: She was living in a comfortable apartment; she had a friend (a fellow patient from one of her hospitalizations); she was employed by a business that trained and hired people with varied disabilities; and she had been out of the hospital for over a year. But late one night, she overdosed on her psychotropic medications and alcohol. She then made a desperate phone call to arrange a crisis admission to a residential service, but there was no room for her. The following morning, Laura was found dead in her little apartment. What precipitated her suicide remains a mystery. We do know that over all those years, the endless effort to keep her body and soul together without any real psychological help periodically left her exhausted and despairing.

We tell this sad story for two reasons. One is to remind all of us who work with severely borderline-disordered people of the enormity of their handicap so that we may never become jaded about their suffering. Their agony is so immense, so unendurable, and so relentless that for some, the only peace imaginable lies in not being. Our second reason is to point out how desperately important it is that our profession learn to provide the kind of structure and treatment that can help people like Laura find a safe place—perhaps even another chance and a more hopeful kind of peace.

10

Practical Considerations

The borderline personality–disordered young women presented in the last two chapters resemble each other in some ways—both experienced serial psychiatric hospitalizations and transient psychotic-like episodes. But they also share distinct and significant differences in their early histories, in the resources that they had available for treatment, and in the eventual courses of their personality problems.

Susan had a bipolar mood disorder on top of her underlying borderline personality. The mood disorder was being effectively managed with medication; she was financially able to afford psychotherapy; and she was motivated to make use of it. Her level of adaptive self-management suggested that she was a candidate for a trial of psychotherapy despite her troubled history.

Laura managed her life as well as she was able, given her early experience of severe neglect and trauma. She, too, was intelligent and motivated, but her circumstances disallowed access to psychotherapy or even counseling. There is no way of knowing now how she would have fared had the possibility of psychotherapy been open to her. The exquisite vulnerability to abandonment, the depth of despair, the suicidal impulses, the shaky affect regulation, and the poor impulse control that were prominent in her history and presentation would have made it a rocky road. Would Laura have been able to pursue it?

There seems to be a spectrum of personality-disordered psychopathology. Cooper et al. (2005) suggest that there is a continuum of personality disorders ranging from the lower-functioning through the higher-level personality disorders and then to the personality disorder traits that may exist in those who do not meet the criteria for a personality disorder diagnosis. This is to suggest that all of us may find in ourselves or in others sensitivities that resemble the relational habits of personality-disordered people, while not actually being personality disordered.

With regard to borderline personality disorder in particular, Klein (1989c) suggests that some borderline personality–disordered people can and often do function quite well, whereas others have such a limited capacity to cope with the demands of living that they function very poorly. These are the people whom Klein describes as manifesting *DSM–IV* borderline disorder diagnostic criteria of impulsivity, recurrent suicidality and self-destructive behavior, interpersonal chaos, mood lability, feelings of emptiness and boredom, and unmodulated anger.

> The presenting picture with these patients is often psychotic-like rather than neurotic-like. Primitive ego defenses are coupled with defects in ego functioning. The result is poorer adaptive functioning and at times the appearance of frank, albeit transient, psychotic-like episodes characterized by infantile regressions, paranoid ideation, hostility, depersonalization and derealization, ideas of reference, illusions, obsessive-compulsive symptoms, and panic-like anxiety. (p. 148)

Laura met all of these criteria.

In our experience, not all people with the most severe borderline disorders can tolerate psychoanalytic psychotherapy without self-destructive regression. Although the second chance offered by traditional psychotherapy is the most promising approach for some patients, for others, supportive therapy, basic counseling, or even case management might be more appropriate. Counseling and psychotherapy are not synonymous, and for some of these patients, counseling is the treatment of choice. Psychotherapy assumes that the patient has the capacity for change and growth, the internalization of new objects, and the revision of internal working models of relationship. Counseling makes no such assumptions; rather, as Klein (1989c) says, it "assumes that a patient's ability to 'take in,' internalize, or build intrapsychic structure is transient and fragile at best—nonexistent at worst" (p. 152). He goes on to say,

> The goals and objectives of counseling are to reduce anxiety, depression, anger, and any other dysphoric affect or combination of dysphoric affects that are chronically interfering with the patient's capacity to function in the most adaptive and realistic manner possible. . . . The good counselor accepts an on-going role in helping the patient to identify and monitor feelings, direct actions, and sustain adaptive functions and defenses. (p. 152)

The therapist makes use of techniques of reality testing, encouragement, direction, and problem solving to serve this function of auxiliary ego; the therapist must abdicate therapeutic neutrality and so willingly resonate with the rewarding unit projection by being directive and taking responsibility for the patient's behavior. Confrontation is not a useful intervention; the patient's defenses may not be adequate to manage, in an adaptive way, the abandonment depression, separation anxiety, and trauma that inevitably emerge in psychotherapy.

In other instances, case management may be the most appropriate treatment approach. This requires a caseworker assigned to the patient to plan, organize, and monitor living arrangements, meals, and money management and to coordinate any services provided by agencies and medical care providers. This sort of approach to management of the patient's fundamental needs is more concerned with survival than with self-activation. But there are some borderline patients for whom this approach to treatment is indicated, because of circumstances or limited capacity to benefit from counseling or psychotherapy.

How does a therapist determine when to recommend counseling or case management over psychotherapy? Klein (1989c) suggests,

> The profile of the lower-level borderline patient, for whom counseling might be the treatment of choice, includes some or all of the following: (1) repeated, real abuse, neglect, or separation trauma early in life; (2) repeated, severe, prolonged psychotic-like regressive episodes that are secondary to minimal stress or anxiety; (3) a history of repeated serious (life-threatening) suicide attempts or serious homicidal or violent intent or actions. (p. 152)

Even when psychotherapy is impossible or inadvisable, the developmental and diagnostic perspective that we present is useful for assessing a patient's capacities and treatment needs. In evaluating an individual's early history, it is important to attend to the development of object relations and the resulting internal working models of relationships. Special attention to the quality of relationships experienced is often revealing. Who provided care in the child's early years? Were there significant separation experiences in the first 3 years? Was there emotional neglect? Abuse? If so, how early did the abuse occur, and how severe was it? Was it perpetrated by a parent, and how long did it endure? As a general rule, severe early abuse by a parent over a considerable period is likely to be associated with significant developmental arrest of the self and its capacities. However, there may have been other significant adults in the child's life—a grandparent, neighbor, a church community, a family friend—who was able to compensate to some degree for the parent's deficient nurturing and caregiving. The presence of such benevolent substitutes sometimes surface in early memories, and these may account for the unexpectedly successful development of some patients who had severely neglectful or destructive relationships with their parents.

The patient's report of childhood and adolescent separation experiences may also tell us something about the patient's sensitivity to disruptions in relationships. How did this person negotiate the start of school, overnights with friends, summer camp, graduation from high school? These questions are all part of any good psychiatric and developmental history and are not distinctive of any particular psychotherapeutic orientation. But once the diagnosis of borderline personality disorder has been made or is suspected, we focus carefully on the patient's attachment style and intrapsychic structure. What is her or his experience of attachment? Has it been secure? insecure? avoidant? ambivalent? disorganized? Is there a capacity for whole object relations, integrated experiences of self and other, or are relationships characterized by split perceptions in alternation?

Does the patient have a flexible repertoire for managing dysphoric affects, or must she or he resort to primitive defenses? If splitting, projection, projective identification, and homicidal or suicidal impulses dominate the clinical picture, the patient may not be able to tolerate the emergence of the abandonment depression without countertherapeutic regression. For example, Susan, for most of her life, had been able to keep her defenses fairly organized around compliance. Laura, however, did not have any such sturdily established defensive structure and was much more easily tipped into near-psychotic disorganization.

The patient's relationship history is another important consideration. Does he or she demonstrate at least a modicum of trust in others, as evidenced by the tendency to turn to others when in distress? Have others been used for soothing and regulation of disturbing feelings? Has the patient been able to establish and maintain any mutually gratifying and enduring relationships? Does the patient or anyone else report any stable relationships that are relatively free of persistent projections of the bad object? Is there evidence of some ability to sustain a commitment to a valued relationship, even in the face of disappointments, frustrations, and other attachment disruptions?

Susan was able to maintain several relationships over the years. Many of them were with older, mothering-type women friends to whom she looked for soothing. Laura, however, was not able to find relationships that felt safe. In fact, the one relationship that she looked to as a child became torturous. Laura had longings for a mother and thus leaned on her older sister, but during her periodic bouts of blackness, her paranoid projections definitively blotted out existing relationships.

This sort of evaluative process guides the therapist's recommendation for treatment. "Safety first" is an important axiom that must be kept clearly in mind with the severely impaired, poorly functioning, high-risk people who have lack a stable and cohesive self-structure and can manage intense affect only by self-destructive behaviors. The most effective treatment strategy for any given patient is based on an accurate clinical diagnosis that includes a formulation of the individual's adaptive capacities and a healthy respect for the fragility and vulnerability of those with borderline character organization.

COUNTERTRANSFERENCE

The theoretical and technical concepts that inform and define our approach to psychotherapy are challenging. Learning them is easier said than done, and they are more easily mastered in writing than in practice, when the therapist is besieged by the inexorable dynamics of borderline relationships. The borderline person will avoid the full experience of the abandonment depression in whatever way that he or she can find. In the therapy hour, this generally means activating the rewarding unit and looking to the therapist for support of helpless and incompetent behavior. When the desired response is not forthcoming, the projection of a harsh, critical, and depriving therapist is the second resort, to externalize the source of depression and anxiety. The patient subjects the therapist to pressures—subtle and not so subtle but always powerful—to collude with these projections. Especially early in treatment the therapist may be barraged by projections and projective identifications that are "designed" to induce resonance with the patient's expectations.

Furthermore, we all bring our own countertransference vulnerabilities, our own sensitivities, to the therapy relationship. Many borderline-disordered patients possess an uncanny psychic radar that identifies and targets the therapist's developmental residues and manipulates them to enforce collaboration with the projections of the rewarding or withdrawing units. Countertransference is everywhere in work with the borderline personality disorder, as we demonstrate in the brief examples that follow. Therapists must be aware of their own relational vulnerabilities and frailties, and they must continue to clarify their internal experience in the transference, using this awareness to inform their interventions and protect themselves, when necessary, from impracticable situations.

Therapist L., an attractive woman in her thirties, came to supervision feeling "creepy" and deeply confused about an initial interview. The patient was a man in his late thirties. He had been referred by his supervisor through the company's employee assistance program for difficulties with attention and focus. To the therapist's surprise and consternation, however, the patient focused throughout the session on a detailed description of his addiction to pornography, especially, his preference for sadistic content (as explicitly and graphically described). The therapist believed that she was being scrutinized by the patient and that there was a leering, almost invasive, quality to his presentation. Although she felt confident and "grounded" when the session began, by the time that it was over, she was upset and feeling shaky.

As the days passed, she noticed herself dreading this man's next appointment. Did she have issues with sexuality that she had not previously been aware of? As such, she began to doubt her preparedness to help patients deal with pornography, although she had done so successfully and with no distress in the past. She felt co-opted out of her role as therapist and into the role of unwilling participant.

In her supervision, she began to explore the circumstances of the referral. The patient had come to see her under some duress, not really for treatment, and he was likely resentful of his supervisor for putting him in the situation. In that context, she could recognize that he was likely to have come to his initial interview projecting the withdrawing unit—sadistically acting out his toxic anger on her, as he acted it out in his pornographic pursuits. When focusing on his sexuality in the session, he did not explore its vicissitudes or wish to manage it differently. He was engaging in retaliation by proxy and in vivo—verbally enacting his sadism as he watched for her tormented response. Indeed, she felt as though she had been violated and surreptitiously coerced into a sordid interaction with him.

In the following session, the patient remained implacably committed to his sexually sadistic acting out. The therapist could not ward off his projections; within herself, she was unable to prevent his projections from contaminating her experience, both of him and of herself, and she seemed at a loss regarding how to intervene effectively. In fact, she could not intervene effectively, because he was abusing her. So, she referred him to a colleague. When countertransference cannot be managed effectively, it compromises therapeutic neutrality and takes an emotional toll on the therapist. It is better for both parties if the patient is referred to someone whose different countertransference vulnerabilities do not resonate so easily with the patient's particular pattern of transference acting out.

Therapist J., a seasoned clinician, reported that his countertransferential Achilles' heel tends to surface when borderline-disordered women are acting out helplessness. Although he understands that this dynamic mimics his past relationship with his mother, he nevertheless experiences impatience and critical feelings when passive dependency is enacted in the therapy relationship. In his impatience, he sometimes finds himself detaching emotionally from the patient, and these tendencies predispose him to behaving—either in his words or in his actions—in ways that reflect the projections of the patient's withdrawing object relations unit. Predictably, the patient feels criticized, activates withdrawing unit projections, and the vicious cycle escalates.

To fortify himself to maintain neutrality with these patients, this therapist reminds himself before each session that although he may experience impatience with his patient's helplessness and passivity, this function involves his own unresolved issues. This helps him to hang onto his neutrality in the face of their projections.

Therapist M. reported that when she engages with a borderline patient who is projecting the withdrawing object relations unit, she feels like she's shaking internally, as though her thinking is frozen. This experience is most acute when the patient is acting out a withdrawing, angry object and projecting the frightened and bad self onto the therapist. She describes her reaction as "automatic" and acknowledges that her response relates, at least in part, to her own experience of having been emotionally assaulted as a child. But just knowing that doesn't seem to help when she is surprised by a patient's sudden split. She has learned to put a brightly colored note on the patient's face sheet to remind herself of her vulnerability to these attacks; it minimizes the element of surprise and helps her prepare for them. Rather than reflexively react to the anger directed at her, she can depersonalize it, observe it and reflect upon it, and so maintain her therapeutic neutrality.

Therapist K. is a less experienced clinician. She told her consultation group about a new patient. As the young woman's story rolled out, K. experienced a deeper and deeper kinship with the patient and her process, particularly with respect to her difficulties with self-activation; it was as if her own story were being told. "I felt like yelling 'Yes! Yes! Me too! Me too!'" If only she could figure out how to help the patient, the therapist thought, maybe she could resolve her own issues. She reported fantasies of becoming good friends with this patient, who experienced her self and life so very much the way that she herself did.

But although identification with our patients is a primary way that we engage interest and empathy, it can threaten therapeutic neutrality and the necessary therapeutic objectivity. Clinical consultation helped this young therapist reflect on her process and regain her therapeutic distance. Her colleagues helped her remember that the psychotherapy relationship and a conventional friendship are incompatible.

Therapist S., who had many years of clinical experience, told her supervisor that three of her patients seemed to be speaking directly to unhealed parts of herself. It felt to her as though the universe were offering her opportunities to complete her own psychological work—an opportunity that she was eager to take. After that session, she reentered therapy herself to complete the work begun in a previous therapy experience.

The patient is not the only vulnerable person in the therapeutic relationship. When 40-something-year-old Therapist P. found himself experiencing profound attachment and sexual feelings for a vulnerable young patient, he had to consider whether his feelings were confounding the therapy. His decision to refer her to a colleague was the right one. Not only had the therapy had come to a halt, but it was teetering dangerously close to impulsive acting out.

The highly competent Therapist C. told her consultation group about being so moved by the depth of her work with one particular patient that it guided her back into therapy herself. In the therapeutic hours, her patient was finding a way of being with herself that C. herself had never known. She realized that she was offering a presence that she had never consistently experienced. This recognition brought up her own abandonment depression and pointed her to the need for further grief work herself.

These brief examples of countertransference are just a few reminders of how many ways therapists can be drawn into complicity with their borderline patients' enactments of primitive models of relationship. These models were once constructed out of necessity to regulate affect through attachments to others. However, they do so at the cost of support and development of the real self.

How do we know when we are acting out our countertransference? Typical signals include any lapses in adherence to the frame of therapy. When missed appointments or delinquent accounts are not addressed, it is very likely that the therapist is colluding with the patient's projection of the rewarding unit. Allowing sessions to continue past their agreed-on end and prolonged telephone conversations are other frame violations that manifest a failure on the part of the therapist to resist countertransference pressures. Preoccupations with a particular patient or dreams about her or him signify a boundary disturbance in the relationship, an overinvolvement.

Throughout this work, we try to show how psychotherapy by this model is a way that people can reprocedure themselves in real relationships, an enterprise that provides conditions conducive to the relinquishment of habitual false-self defenses and to the support of real-self experience and expression. For this to happen, a real relationship must be established and nurtured. The therapist must bring his or her own real self to the relationship. But it is the responsibility of the therapist to do it in a way that is real and alive, while still avoiding collusion with patient projections.

As most experienced therapists, including ourselves, know well, personality-disordered people and the issues with which they grapple demand a kind of "being with" that takes us into their most disorganized places, disorganizing us in many cases and requiring a self-process that allows us to metabolize, neutralize, reflect on, and verbalize feelings that have previously been inaccessible. For this reason, we must be just as concerned about the care of ourselves as we are for that of our patients—this is a prerequisite for the emotional well-being of the therapist. We have known of therapists who closed their practices and segued into some other career because of the vicarious trauma experienced with borderline patients and because of the real trauma reenacted in the transference.

To maintain our effectiveness as therapists, we need to learn how to prepare ourselves and how to protect ourselves; we need to learn to take care of ourselves, to find and practice what we each need, to support our emotional and physical health. This may include such basics as healthy nutrition, adequate sleep, regular exercise, and spiritual practice. Sufficient recreation and the pursuit of interests other than psychotherapy contribute to a healthily balanced life. When we start to feel that the practice of psychotherapy is all there is to life, we are in trouble. Ongoing learning, the stimulation of new ideas and ways of thinking about what we're doing as therapists, can be an effective antidote to the intellectual stagnation that sometimes accompanies the practice of long-term treatment. There will always be more to learn about our patients, ourselves, and the practice of psychotherapy.

Regular time for self-reflection or meditation—whatever one does for self-regulation—may be useful. Unless we are able to observe our own minds and feeling processes in times when we're not in the middle of the therapeutic moment, we cannot count on the capacity to do so during those times. If we do not practice self-observation when not on the battlefield, it is highly improbable that we will observe ourselves in the heat of the moment. To do so takes time. It is important that there be enough margin in our daily lives to listen to ourselves and process and metabolize our experiences so that we don't become dysregulated when we ingest our patients' projections. Self-care may, at times, mean deciding to not work with a particular patient or to limit hours of therapy to ensure adequate time for rest.

Supervision or consultation may provide a necessary stabilizing influence. It is a real gift to have a colleague who will discuss knotty cases with us and offer us support. Of course, there is also the potential for further learning through supervision or consultation.

Sometimes, what the therapist needs most is personal therapy. When countertransference dynamics persist in interfering with therapy momentum or in disrupting the therapist's sense of well-being, therapy may be helpful in resolving the personal vulnerability that allows resonance with the patient's projections. Yet, even when the work is going well, it may be a safe-enough place that the therapist's own issues will come up and demand their due attention.

The personal challenge of staying emotionally available is a tough one, but it's one that we can't refuse. Our goals, like a mother's with her child, must include more than just accurate attunement and understanding. These are important, but they are not enough. We must also be honest and real—firm enough, calm enough, interested enough, with our issues managed well enough—so that we can be with our patients in a way that is restorative and empowering.

People with borderline disorders are real people, and so are we as therapists. The relationship is mutual and reciprocal; it is not just the patient who is touched and challenged and changed. When we care for ourselves in ways that enable this containing presence with our patients, we are changed, enlarged, and enriched, too.

11

Now and Then,
Here and There,
Change Happens

The real self of infant and child is built in secure relationships, relation-ships replete with moments of recognition and mutual knowledge. In the experience of being seen, known, and validated by a more mature other, somehow—spontaneously, mysteriously—the self emerges. These are the relational conditions in which the real self flowers and capacities for vital and self-supportive living grow.

When these relational conditions are absent, when this other person is not reliably available or is available only on condition of compliance and dependency, the conditions of attachment implicitly demand the devel-opment of a false defensive self to maintain interpersonal connections and ward off the abandonment depression. Although defenses like these certainly undermine the development of the real self, they also are neces-sary for survival. In lieu of a real-self attachment, the false self represents a creative, uncanny gift—a testament to the indomitable human hunger for attachment and an essential fear of life without it.

But there comes a time in life when these false selves exact a toll. Re-lationships are unsatisfying; jobs can't be held; there is no joy—life isn't working. This is when people come to us for help.

How can we as therapists offer them another chance? We have pro-posed a therapeutic procedure that is grounded in a technically informed, compassionately attuned relationship. That is, the psychotherapy of borderline personality disorder requires specific technical and structural parameters but in the context of a real relationship between the therapist and the patient. There must be an attitude of respect for the force behind these patients' self-defeating behaviors—an aberrant false defensive self designed to maintain attachment with others even at the cost of normal development of the real self. This way, the therapist can experience and communicate, implicitly and explicitly, empathy and understanding. Then the therapist's accurate attunement to the patient's affective experience and the resulting therapeutic space actively support the emergence of the real self. Repeated experiences of the disruption–repair cycle enable the internalization of a model of relational repair, an antidote to the model of abandonment fears and relational despair. Finally, the real-self-to-real-self relationship between therapist and patient procedures a new, healthier object relations unit, a new working model of relationships to be internalized, and affords a foretaste of more satisfying relational experiences ahead.

However, the therapeutic process must provide more than such a real relationship. It must be designed and structured in such a way as to support activation of the patient's real self. The therapist must expect self-experience, self-support, self-assertion, and self-soothing from the patient. In addition, therapeutic neutrality—the therapist's unwillingness to collaborate with the false-self projections that ineluctably occur in work with borderline patients—is requisite to the reproceduring of old relational habits and to the related restructuring of intrapsychic object relations units. That is, the therapist must, as consistently as possible, speak to the patient's real self and thus communicate a belief in its existence and in its capacities. To do so is always the most empathic and caring communication possible, even when firm limit setting is the first order of business. Finally, the psychotherapy endeavor must be structured in such a way as to provide a benchmark for real-self adaptive functioning and discourage the reenactment of archaic relational procedures that have undermined the development and activation of the real self.

In essence, this approach to psychotherapy of the borderline personality disorder is intended to provide both the compassionate attunement and the technical and structural factors necessary to reprocedure and rewire the impaired real self for experience and expression. In a sense, therapists, through explicit interventions, are showing what it means to activate the real self; through the therapist's stance and verbal interventions, through the frame and the tracking of the triad, false-self adaptation and real-self activation become defined. But it is equally likely and important that the therapist, through implicit communications in the real relationship, show how to be real. Through the relationship, real-self presence and activation are demonstrated.

As therapists, our beings speak. How we communicate is as important as what we communicate. But although we must be who we are, we must also say and do what must be said and done. Therapy involves both left brain and right brain, both head and heart, both technique and mystery.

Having said this, let us reflect for a moment on the change process and the outcomes described in the preceding chapters. What really contributed to the healing changes in Terri, Susan, and the others? Was it the relationship, the therapeutic alliance carefully forged? Was it the structural parameters of the treatment or carefully crafted and properly timed interventions? Was it help in discovering and observing their own triad and defenses, in the safety of not needing them? Furthermore, will they be able to maintain the changes? Will they be able to see and track their own defenses rather than be lived by them? Will the fire of vitality, ignited by affect in this process, continue to burn despite inevitable relationship ruptures? Will the light of self, now lit, grow recursively brighter, and will it sustain itself when the abandonment depression is triggered, as it will be at some point?

The answers to these questions about the endurance of change over time seem to be in the affirmative, based on the patients with whom we have worked. We find the earlier questions, about the ingredients of the change process itself, more intriguing.

Much, if not most, of what we have observed of the change process has been quite predictable, given the model of psychotherapy that we practice. When the patient's defenses are controlled, there is activation of affects of the abandonment depression, and further defense is mobilized. In this way, the dynamic of the disorders of the self triad became evident, both to the therapist and to the patient. Incrementally, the real self is re-procedured, and real-self capacities grow.

But some happenings were quite startling and inexplicable—seemingly spontaneous shifts in affect, memories suddenly evoked, flashes of profound insight, momentary alterations of the patient–therapist relationship, quantum leaps of self-growth. It can be speculated that these changes would have been predictable had our observational capacities been more precise. But there were times when such events appeared to be more than something that occurred in the therapy itself; they seemed to be, perhaps, a function of fate, serendipity, or grace. At the very least, they were mysterious.

The theologian Paul Tillich (1955) has written, "We want only to show you something we have seen and to tell you something we have heard . . . that here and there in the world and now and then in ourselves is a new creation" (p. 17). We firmly believe in the need for a sound theory of psychotherapy and for a treatment strategy based on that theory. We believe that we must all do our best to enlarge the potential for change to occur—that is, to reduce the mystery and to enhance the probability. Yet, mystery remains and, no doubt, it always will. When change happens, both patient and therapist feel wonder and gratitude—that change happened here and now, and we were there. We were both there, patient and therapist, watching.

References

Adler, G. (1985). *Borderline psychopathology and its treatment.* Lanham, MD: Jason Aronson.

Ainsworth, M. D. S. (1967). *Infancy in Uganda: Infant care and the growth of love.* Baltimore: Johns Hopkins University Press.

Ainsworth, M. D. S., Blehar, M. C., Waters, E., and Wall, S. (1978). *Patterns of attachment: A psychological study of the strange situation.* Hillsdale, NJ: Erlbaum.

American Psychiatric Association. (1994). *Diagnostic and statistical manual of mental disorders* (4th ed.). Washington, DC: Author.

Appelman, E. (2001). Temperament and dyadic contributions to affect regulation: Implications from developmental research in clinical practice. *Psychoanalytic Psychology,* 18, 534–559.

Auerbach, J. S., and Blatt, S. J. (2001). Self-reflexivity, intersubjectivity, and therapeutic change. *Psychoanalytic Psychology,* 18, 427–450.

Bateman, A. W., and Fonagy, P. (2004). *Psychotherapy for borderline personality disorder: Mentalization-based treatment.* Oxford, England: Oxford University Press.

Beebe, B., and Lachmann, F. M. (1988a). The contribution of mother–infant mutual influence to the origins of self and object representations. *Psychoanalytic Psychology,* 11, 127–165.

———. (1988b). Mother–infant mutual influence and precursors of psychic structure. In A. Goldberg (ed.), *Progress in self psychology* (Vol. 3, pp. 3–25). Hillsdale, NJ: Analytic Press.

———. (1994). Representations and internalization in infancy: Three principles of salience. *Psychoanalytic Psychology,* 11, 127–165.

Berlin, L. J., and Cassidy, J. (1999). Relations among relationships: Contributions from attachment theory and research. In J. Cassidy and P. R. Shaver (eds.), *Handbook of attachment: Theory, research, and clinical applications* (pp. 688–712). New York: Guilford Press.

Blatt, S. J. (1992). The differential effect of psychotherapy and psychoanalysis with anaclitic and introjective patients: The Menninger Psychotherapy Research Project revisited. *Journal of the American Psychoanalytic Association*, 40, 691–724.

Blatt, S. J., and Blass, R. B. (1990). Attachment and separateness: A dialectic model of the products and processes of development throughout the life cycle. In *Psychoanalytic study of the child* (Vol. 45, pp. 107–127). New Haven, CT: Yale University Press.

———. (1996). Relatedness and self-definition: A dialectic model of personality development. In G. G. Noam and K. W. Fischer (eds.), *Development and vulnerabilities in close relationships* (pp. 308–338). Hillsdale, NJ: Erlbaum.

Bleiberg, E. (2004). *Treating personality disorders in children and adolescents: A relational approach*. New York: Guilford Press.

Bowlby, J. (1969). *Attachment and loss: Attachment*. New York: Basic Books.

———. (1973). *Attachment and loss: Separation*. New York: Basic Books.

———. (1980). *Attachment and loss: Loss*. New York: Basic Books.

———. (1988). *A secure base: Parent–child attachment and healthy human development*. New York: Basic Books.

Bretherton, I., and Bates, E. (1979). The emergence of intentional communication. In I. C. Uzgiris (ed.), *Social interaction and communication during infancy* (pp. 81–100). San Francisco: Jossey-Bass.

Bruner, J. (1983). *Child's talk: Learning to use language*. Oxford, England: Oxford University Press.

Bruschweiler-Stern, N., Harrison, A., Lyons-Ruth, K., Morgan, A., Nahum, J., Sander, L., et al. (2005). The "something more" than interpretation revisited: Sloppiness and co-creativity in the psychoanalytic encounter. *Journal of the American Psychoanalytic Association*, 53, 693–729.

Buechner, F. (1991). *Telling secrets*. San Francisco: HarperCollins.

Cassidy, J. (2001). Truth, lies, and intimacy: An attachment perspective. *Attachment and Human Development*, 3, 121–155.

Clarkin, J. F., Yeomans, F. E., and Kernberg, O. F. (1999). *Psychotherapy for borderline personality*. New York: John Wiley.

Cohen, N. J., Muir, E., Parker, C. J., Brown, M., Lojkasek, M., Muir, R., et al. (1999). Watch, wait, and wonder: Testing the effectiveness of a new approach to mother–infant psychotherapy. *Infant Mental Health Journal*, 20(4), 429–451.

Cooper, G., Hoffman, K., Powell, B., and Marvin, R. (2005). The circle of security intervention: Differential diagnosis and differential treatment. In L. J. Berlin, Y. Zaiv, L. Amaya-Jackson, and M. T. Greenberg (eds.), *Enhancing early attachment* (pp. 127–51). New York: Guilford Press.

Dozier, M., Cue, K. L., and Barnett, L. (1994). Clinicians as caregivers: Role of attachment organization in treatment. *Journal of Consulting and Clinical Psychology*, 62, 793–800.

Dozier, M., Stovall, K. C., and Albus, K. E. (1999). Attachment and psychopathology in adulthood. In J. Cassidy and P. R. Shaver (eds.), *Handbook of attachment: Theory, research, and clinical applications* (pp. 497–519). New York: Guilford Press.

Fairbairn, W. R. D. (1952). *Psychoanalytic studies of the personality*. New York: Basic Books.

Feldman, R., Greenbaum, C. W., and Yirmiya, N. (1999). Mother–infant affect synchrony as an antecedent of the emergence of self-control. *Developmental Psychology*, 35, 223–231.

Field, T. (1981). Infant arousal, attention, and affect during early interactions. *Advances in Infancy Research*, 1, 58–96.

Fischer-Mamblona, H. (2000). On the evolution of attachment-disordered behavior. *Attachment and Human Development*, 2(1), 8–21.

Flores, P. (2004). *Addiction as an attachment disorder*. Lanham, MD: Jason Aronson.

Fonagy, P. (1991). Thinking about thinking: Some clinical and theoretical considerations in the treatment of a borderline patient. *International Journal of Psycho-Analysis*, 72, 1–18.

———. (1995). Playing with reality: The development of psychic reality and its malfunction in borderline patients. *International Journal of Psycho-Analysis*, 76, 39–44.

———. (1999). Attachment, the development of the self, and its pathology in personality disorders. In J. Derksen, C. Maffei, and H. Groen (eds.), *Treatment of personality disorders* (pp. 53–68). New York: Kluwer.

———. (2000, April). *Attachment and borderline personality disorder: A theory and some evidence*. Paper presented as visiting professor of psychoanalysis of the Michigan Psychoanalytic Institute, Farmington Hills.

———. (2001a). *Attachment theory and psychoanalysis*. New York: Other Press.

———. (2001b, April). *The roots of violence in the failure of mentalization: A psychoanalytic perspective*. Paper presented at the Seattle Psychoanalytic Society and Institute Conference on Disorganized Attachment, Youth, and Violence, Seattle, WA.

Fonagy, P., Gergely, G., Jurist, E. L., and Target, M. (2002). *Affect regulation, mentalization, and the development of the self*. New York: Other Press.

Fonagy, P., and Target, M. (1996a). Playing with reality: I. Theory of mind and the normal development of psychic reality. *International Journal of Psychoanalysis*, 77, 217–233.

———. (1996b). Playing with reality: II. The development of psychic reality from a theoretical perspective. *International Journal of Psychoanalysis*, 77, 459–479.

———. (1997). Attachment and reflective function: Their role in self-organization. *Development and Psychopathology*, 9, 679–700.

Fonagy, P., Target, M., and Gergely, G. (2000, April). *Attachment and borderline personality disorder: A theory and some evidence*. Paper presented at the Michigan Psychoanalytic Institute, Farmington Hills.

Fosha, D. (2000). *The transforming power of affect*. New York: Basic Books.

———. (2001, October). *The transforming power of core affect and its dyadic regulation in accelerated experiential-dynamic psychotherapy*. Workshop presented in Spokane, WA.

Fritts, K. D. (1989). Confrontation of the transference acting out of severe helplessness and hopelessness. In J. F. Masterson and R. Klein (eds.), *Psychotherapy of the disorders of the self: The Masterson approach* (pp. 251–262). New York: Brunner/Mazel.

Gelso, C. J. (2005). The interplay of techniques and the therapeutic relationship in psychotherapy. *Psychotherapy: Theory, Research, Practice, Training*, 42, 419–420.

Greenberg, E. (2004). The Masterson approach: Defining the terms. In J. F. Masterson and A. R. Lieberman (eds.), *A therapist's guide to the personality disorders* (pp. 23–34). Phoenix, AZ: Zeig, Tucker & Thiesen.

Greenberg, J. R., and Mitchell, S. A. (1983). *Object relations in psychoanalytic theory.* Cambridge, MA: Harvard University Press.

Guntrip, H. (1961). *Personality structure and human interaction.* New York: International Universities Press.

———. (1968). *Schizoid phenomena object relations and the self.* New York: International Universities Press.

Hahn, A. (2004). The borderline personality disorder. In J. F. Masterson and A. R. Lieberman (eds.), *A therapist's guide to the personality disorders* (pp. 55–72). Phoenix, AZ: Zeig, Tucker & Thiesen.

Hamilton, N. G. (1988). *Self and others: Object relations theory in practice.* Lanham, MD: Jason Aronson.

Hebb, D. O. (1949). *The organization of behavior: A neuropsychological theory.* New York: John Wiley.

Hoffman, K., Marvin, R., Cooper, G., and Powell, B. (2006). Changing toddlers' and preschoolers' attachment classifications: The circle of security intervention. *Journal of Consulting and Clinical Psychology,* 74(6), 1017–1025.

Holmes, J. (1996). *Attachment, intimacy, autonomy.* Lanham, MD: Jason Aronson.

———. (2001). *The search for the secure base.* Philadelphia: Taylor & Francis.

Horner, A. J. (1994). Visions of the self. *American Journal of Psychoanalysis,* 54(4), 359–362.

Joseph, R. (1992). *The right brain and the unconscious: Discovering the stranger within.* New York: Plenum Press.

Karen, R. (1994). *Becoming attached.* New York: Warner Books.

Kernberg, O. (1975). *Borderline conditions and pathological narcissism.* Lanham, MD: Jason Aronson.

———. (1976). *Object relations theory and clinical psychoanalysis.* Lanham, MD: Jason Aronson.

———. (1980). *Internal world and external reality.* Lanham, MD: Jason Aronson.

———. (1984). *Severe personality disorders.* New Haven, CT: Yale University Press.

Kernberg, O., Selzer, M., Koenigsberg, H., Carr, A., and Appelbaum, A. (1989). *Psychodynamic psychotherapy of borderline patients.* New York: Basic Books.

Klein, R. (1989a). Application to differential diagnosis. In J. F. Masterson and R. Klein (eds.), *Psychotherapy of the disorders of the self* (pp. 9–29). New York: Brunner/Mazel.

———. (1989b). The art of confrontation. In J. F. Masterson and R. Klein (eds.), *Psychotherapy of the disorders of the self: The Masterson approach* (pp. 215–230). New York: Brunner/Mazel.

———. (1989c). Diagnosis and treatment of the lower-level borderline patient. In J. F. Masterson and R. Klein (eds.), *Psychotherapy of the disorders of the self: The Masterson approach* (pp. 147–168). New York: Brunner/Mazel.

———. (1989d). Shorter-term treatment of the personality disorders. In J. F. Masterson and R. Klein (eds.), *Psychotherapy of the disorders of the self: The Masterson approach* (pp. 90–109). New York: Brunner/Mazel.

———. (1995). The self in exile: A developmental, self, and object relations approach to the schizoid disorder of the self. In J. F. Masterson and R. Klein (eds.),

Disorders of the self: New therapeutic horizons (pp. 100–106). New York: Brunner/Mazel.

———. (1998, October). *Understanding and managing transference/countertransference phenomena.* Presented at a conference sponsored by the Providence Health System, Portland, OR.

LeDoux, J. (2002). *Synaptic self.* New York: Penguin Books.

Lewis, T., Amini, F., and Lannon, R. (2000). *A general theory of love.* New York: Random House.

Lyons-Ruth, K. (1991). Rapprochement or approchement: Mahler's theory reconsidered from the vantage point of recent research on early attachment relationships. *Psychoanalytic Psychology,* 8, 1–23.

———. (1998). Implicit relational knowing: Its role in development and psychoanalytic treatment. *Infant Mental Health Journal,* 19, 282–289.

———. (2000). "I sense that you sense that I sense . . . ": Sander's recognition process and the specificity of relational moves in the psychotherapeutic setting. *Infant Mental Health Journal,* 21, 85–98.

———. (2001). The emergence of new experiences: Relational improvisation, recognition process, and non-linear change in psychoanalytic therapy. *Psychologist–Psychoanalyst,* 21, 13–17.

Lyons-Ruth, K., Bruschweiler-Stern, N., Harrison, A. M., Morgan, A. C., Nahum, J. P., Sander, L., et al. (1998). Implicit relational knowing: Its role in development and psychoanalytic treatment. *Infant Mental Health Journal,* 19, 282–289.

Mahler, M. S. (1968). *On human symbiosis and the vicissitudes of individuation.* New York: International Universities Press.

———. (1979). *Separation–individuation.* Lanham, MD: Jason Aronson.

Mahler, M. S., Pine, F., and Bergman, A. (1975). *The psychological birth of the human infant.* New York: Basic Books.

Main, M., and Solomon, J. (1986). Discovery of an insecure-disorganized/disoriented attachment pattern. In T. B. Brazelton and M. W. Yogman (eds.), *Affective development in infancy* (pp. 95–124). Norwood, NJ: Ablex.

Masterson, J. F. (1976). *Psychotherapy of the borderline adult: A developmental approach.* New York: Brunner/Mazel.

———. (1981). *The narcissistic and borderline disorders: An integrated developmental approach.* New York: Brunner/Mazel.

———. (1985). *The real self: A developmental, self, and object relations approach.* New York: Brunner/Mazel.

———. (1988). *The search for the real self.* New York: Free Press.

———. (1989). Application to the personality disorders. In J. F. Masterson and R. Klein (eds.), *Psychotherapy of the disorders of the self* (pp. 5–8). New York: Brunner/Maxel.

———. (1990). Psychotherapy of borderline and narcissistic disorder: Establishing a therapeutic alliance. *Journal of Personality Disorders* 4(2), 182–191.

———. (1992, March). *How differential diagnosis affects psychotherapy.* Paper presented at the conference of the Masterson Institute, San Francisco.

———. (1993). *The emerging self: A developmental, self, and object relations approach to the treatment of the closet narcissistic disorder of the self.* New York: Brunner/Mazel.

———. (2000). *The personality disorders.* Phoenix, AZ: Zeig, Tucker & Thiesen.

———. (2004). The self in the personality disorders: An integration of attachment theory, neurobiologic brain research, and developmental object relations theory. In J. F. Masterson and A. R. Lieberman (eds.), *A therapist's guide to the personality disorders* (pp. 13–21). Phoenix, AZ: Zeig, Tucker & Thiesen.

———. (ed.). (2005). *The personality disorders through the lens of attachment theory and the neurobiologic development of the self.* Phoenix, AZ: Zeig, Tucker & Thiesen.

Pearson, J. L., Cohn, C. A., Cowan, R. A., and Cowan, C. P. (1994). Earned and continuous security in adult attachment: Relation to depressive symptomatology and parenting style. *Development and Psychopathology,* 6, 259–373.

Phelps, J. L., Belsky, J., and Crnic, K. (1998). Earned security, daily stress, and parenting: A comparison of five alternative models. *Development and Psychopathology,* 10, 21–38.

Rinsley, D. B. (1982). *Borderline and other self disorders.* Lanham, MD: Jason Aronson.

Rogers, C. R. (1957). The necessary and sufficient conditions of therapeutic personality change. *Journal of Consulting Psychology,* 21, 95–103.

Rowe, C. E., and MacIsaac, D. S. (1989). *Empathic attunement.* Lanham, MD: Jason Aronson.

Sable, P. (2000). *Attachment and adult psychotherapy.* Lanham, MD: Jason Aronson.

Safran, J. D., Crocker, P., McMain, S., and Murray, P. (1990). Therapeutic alliance rupture as a therapy event for empirical investigation. *Psychotherapy,* 27(2), 154–165.

Sander, L. (2000). Where are we going in the field of infant mental health? *Infant Mental Health Journal,* 21, 5–20.

Schore, A. N. (1994). *Affect regulation and the origin of the self: The neurobiology of emotional development.* Hillsdale, NJ: Erlbaum.

———. (1997). Interdisciplinary developmental research as a source of clinical models. In M. Moskowitz, C. Monk, C. Kaye, and S. Ellman (eds.), *The neurobiological and developmental basis for psychotherapeutic intervention* (pp. 1–71). Lanham, MD: Jason Aronson.

———. (1999a). Commentary on emotions: Neuro-psychoanalytic views. *Neuro-Psychoanalysis,* 1, 49–55.

———. (1999b, May). *Principles of the psychotherapeutic treatment of early forming right hemispheric primitive emotional disorders based upon the interactional developmental models of Schore's "Affect regulation and the origin of the self"* (1994). Paper presented as part of the workshop "Attachment, the Developing Brain, and Psychotherapy: The Neurobiology of Emotional Development," Spokane, WA.

———. (2000). Attachment, the right brain, and empathic processes within the therapeutic alliance. *Psychologist Psychoanalyst,* 20(4), 8–11.

———. (2001a). The effects of early relational trauma on right brain development, affect regulation, and infant mental health. *Infant Mental Health Journal,* 22, 201–269.

———. (2001b). Effects of a secure attachment relationship on right brain development, affect regulation, and infant mental health. *Infant Mental Health Journal,* 22, 7–66.

———. (2003). *Affect regulation and the repair of the self.* New York: W. W. Norton.

Settlage, C. F., Bemesderfer, S., Rosenthal, J., Afterman, J., and Speilman, P. M. (1991). The appeal cycle in early mother–child interaction: The nature and implications of a finding from developmental research. *Journal of the American Psychoanalytic Association*, 39(4), 987–1014.

Siegel, D. J. (1999). *The developing mind: Toward a neurobiology of interpersonal experience*. New York: Guilford Press.

———. (2001). Toward an interpersonal neurobiology of the developing mind: Attachment relationships, "mindsight," and neural integration. *Infant Mental Health Journal*, 22(1–2), 67–94.

Siegel, D. J., and Hartzell, M. (2003). *Parenting from the inside out*. New York: Tarcher-Putnam.

Slade, A. (1999). Attachment theory and research: Implications for the theory and practice of individual psychotherapy with adults. In J. Cassidy and P. R. Shaver (ed.), *Handbook of attachment: Theory, research, and clinical applications* (pp. 575–585). New York: Guilford Press.

Spangler, G., and Grossman, K. E. (1993). Biobehavioral organization in securely and insecurely attached infants. *Child Development*, 64, 1439–1450.

Sroufe, L. A. (1996). *Emotional development: The organization of emotional life in the early years*. New York: Cambridge University Press.

Sroufe, L. A., and Fleeson J. (1986). Attachment and the construction of relationships. In W. Hartup and Z. Rubin (eds.), *Relationships and development* (pp. 51–71). Hillsdale, NJ: Erlbaum.

———. (1988). The coherence of individual relationships. In R. Hinde and J. Stevenson-Hinde (eds.), *Relationships within families* (pp. 7–25). Oxford, England: Clarendon Press.

Stern, D. N. (1985). *The interpersonal world of the infant*. New York: Basic Books.

———. (1998). The process of therapeutic change involving implicit knowledge: Some implications of developmental observations for adult psychotherapy. *Infant Mental Health Journal*, 19(3), 300–308.

Summers, F. (2001). What I do with what you give me: Therapeutic action as the creation of meaning. *Psychoanalytic Psychology*, 18, 635–655.

Target, M. (2001). *Attachment disorganisation and the emergence of violence in adolescence*. Paper presented at the Seattle Psychoanalytic Society and Institute Conference on Disorganized Attachment, Youth and Violence, Seattle, WA.

Tillich, P. (1955). *The new being*. New York: Charles Scribner's Sons.

Tronick, E. (1989). Emotions and emotional communication in infants. *American Psychologist*, 44, 112–119.

———. (1998). Dyadically expanded states of consciousness and the process of therapeutic change. *Infant Mental Health Journal*, 19, 290–299.

Vaughan, S. C. (1997). *The talking cure*. New York: G. P. Putnam's Sons.

Watt, D. F. (1986). Transference: A right hemispheric event? An inquiry into the boundary between psychoanalytic metapsychology and neuropsychology. *Psychoanalysis and Contemporary Thought*, 9, 43–77.

Winnicott, D. W. (1958). *Collected papers: Through paediatrics to psycho-analysis*. New York: Basic Books.

———. (1965). *The maturational processes and the facilitating environment*. Madison, CT: International Universities Press.

———. (1986). *Holding and interpretation*. New York: Grove Press.

Index

Abandonment depression, 36–37; case
    study of Susan, 143; case study of
    Terri, 121; unawareness of, 109
Affect regulation, 18–19, 55–56
Ainsworth, M. D. S., 14–16

Attachment, 13–16; Ainsworth and,
    14–15; Bowlby and, 14–15, 22–23;
    earned secure, 96,101; insecure,
    15–16; nonattachment experiences,
    22–23; secure, 16–19; separation
    and, 13–14; theory of, 6–7, 13–16
Attitude of the therapist. *See*
    Attunement
Attunement, 16–21, 54; affect
    regulation and, 18, 55–56, 112;
    attachment and, 16, 51–53; attitude
    of therapist and, 20, 52–53;
    compassionate, 52–53; empathy
    and, 90–92; internal representations
    of self and others and, 20; new
    object relations units and, 56–57;
    the real self and, 20, 54–55

Beebe, B., 17–20
Borderline personality disorder:
    abandonment depression and, 36–

37; false defensive self and, 44–46;
    impaired self functions and, 46–48;
    insecure attachment and, 34–35;
    maladaptive defenses and, 37–38;
    separation sensitivity and, 35–36;
    spectrum of, 153–154; split object
    relations units and, 40–44; triad of
    the disorders of the self and, 38–40
Bowlby, J., 14–15, 17, 22–23

Capacities of the real self, 25
Confrontation, 80–81, 111, 120;
    attunement and, 88–90; empathy
    and, 90–92; goals of, 83–84;
    maladaptive defenses and, 83–85,
    96; necessity of, 84–85; secure
    separation and, 95; struggle and, 92
Cooper, G., 35–36, 78, 153
Counseling, 154–155
Countertransference, 92–95, 157–160

Defenses, 90, 37–38; avoidance
    of self-activation, 38, 40, 45,
    49–50; clinging, 38, 45, 49–50,
    122; compliance, 38, 49–50, 122;
    containment of, 98, 99; ego-syntonic,
    108; helplessness, acting out of,

175

38, 40, 45; maladaptive, 28, 37–38; projection of object relations units, 42; rage, acting out of, 42, 45, 49

Diagnosis-specific interventions: borderline disorder, 79; narcissistic disorder, 77–78; schizoid disorder, 78–79

Disruption-repair cycle, 21, 59–62; disruption-despair and, 59; lack of, 59–60, 150; neurobiology and, 59

Earned secure attachment. *See* Attachment
Experience-dependent brain development, 10
Explicit semantic memory, 24

False defensive self, 31, 44, 46
Fischer-Mablona, H., 1–4, 6–7
Fonagy, P., 14, 21, 25, 34, 47
Fosha, D., 29, 61
Frame of psychotherapy, 70–75
Fritts, K. D., 109–114

Goals of psychotherapy, 97; adaptation, 99–100; containment, 98; learning, 99; reproceduring, 81, 100–102

Hebb. D. O., 11, 42
Hoffman, K., 21
Holmes J., 14, 59, 101

Impaired self functions, 46–48
Implicit procedural memory, 24, 44
Implicit relational knowing, 52
Interactive repair model, 22
Internal representations of self and other, 20
Internal working models of relationships, 23, 57, 155

Karen, R., 14–15
Kernberg, O., 7, 14, 23, 40–41, 104
Klein, R.: confrontation, 80–81; when counseling rather than psychotherapy is indicated,

154, 155; diagnosis-specific interventions, 78; differential diagnosis of personality disorders, 31–32; frame of psychotherapy, 72–74; goals of psychotherapy, 98; lower level borderline disorders, 154

Laura, case study of, 145–152
Lewis, T., 12, 17
Limbic brain, 11–12
Lyons-Ruth, K., 21, 24, 51–52

Mahler, M. S., 14, 20, 54
Maladaptive defenses, 37–38
Mary, case study of, 85–89, 94–95
Masterson, J. F.: abandonment depression, 36–37; capacities of the real self, 25; confrontation, 80; countertransference, 93; diagnosis-specific interventions, 77–78; differential diagnosis of personality disorders, 31–32; frame of psychotherapy, 71; integration of developmental theory, object relations theory, self psychology, attachment theory, and neurobiology, 7
maladaptive defenses, 37–38; object relations units, 23; real relationship, 62–64; real self, 12–13; split object relations units, 40–42; stance of psychotherapy, 67; therapeutic neutrality, 69; transference acting out, 103–108; triad of the disorders of the self, 38–39

Mentalization, 25–26
Misattunement, 22, 35; false self and, 67–68; intentional and unintentional, 60–61

Nature *and* nurture, 10–12
Neurobiology and personality development, 10–12
Nonattachment experience, 22, 44

Object relations units, 23–24, 52, 56–57; development of new, 56–57, 62

Obstacles to psychotherapy: ego-syntonic defenses, 108; reaction rather than reflection, 108–109; transference acting out, 103–108; unawareness of the abandonment depression, 109

Personality development: affect regulation and, 18–20; attachment and, 13–16; attunement and, 6–18; disruption-repair cycle, 21–22; insecure attachment, 34–35; internal representations of self and others and, 20
nature *and* nurture, 10–12
nonattachment experiences, 22–23
object relations units, 23–24
real self, 20–21
Personality disorders, 6–7, 14
Psychotherapy: capacity for, 155–157; goals of, 97–102; obstacles to, 103–111; process of, 102–103

Reaction vs. reflection, 108
Real relationship, 62–64
Real self, 12–13, 67–70; activation of, 39, 45, 70, 81; capacities of, 25; development of, 20–21; support of, 54–55
Recursive development, 12, 29, 165
Reflective function, 25–29, 47
Relationship templates, 20
Relationships internalized and generalized (RIGs), 23
Reproceduring, 81, 100–102
Rewarding object relations unit, 41–42, 45, 49
Right brain to right brain attunement, 15, 17

Schore, A. N.: affect attunement, 54; attunement experiences and structural change, 57; countertransference and neurobiology, 93; experience dependent brain development, 10–11; interactive repair and structural change, 59; internal working models and neurobiology, 24; plasticity of the brain, 11; reflective function and neurobiology, 27; right brain to right brain communication, 15, 17; self-regulation and the orbitofrontalcortex, 28, 29
Self-activation, 13, 70, 81
Self-care of the therapist, 160–162
Separation: attachment and, 13–14; secure separation and confrontation, 91, 95; sensitivity, 35–36
Siegel, D. J.: affect and neurological change, 62; attunement, 54, 57; experience dependent neural development, 11, 19; "feeling felt," 18, 21–22, 28, 54, 112; "mindsight," 25; nature *and* nurture, 10; plasticity of neural structure, 11; right brain to right brain communication, 15; splitting and neurobiology, 42
Split object relations units, 40–44, 46, 120; case study of Laura, 150–151; case study of Susan, 136–137; case study of Terri, 49–50
Splitting, 28, 40–44, 156
Stance of psychotherapy, 67–69
Stern, D. N., 13, 17–18, 20, 23, 58, 91
"Strange situation," 15
Struggle and psychotherapy, 92
Susan, case study of, 125–144

Terri, case study of, 9–10, 32–34, 45–46, 49–50, 60–61, 117–124
Therapeutic alliance, 104
Therapeutic neutrality, 69–70
Therapeutic space, 57, 58–59
Transference acting out, 103–108, 113; rewarding object relations unit (Terri), 118–119; transference contrasted with, 103–104; withdrawing object relations unit (Terri), 119–120

Triad of the disorders of the self,
    38–40, 82, 84–87, 98, 109; case study
    of Susan, 142–143; case study of
    Terri, 123
Tronick, E., 15, 21–22

"Watch, wait, and wonder," 53;

cowatching, 100, 107; cowondering,
    111; process tracking, 115; signal
    wonderings, 110
Winnicott, D. W., 13, 57–58
Withdrawing object relations unit,
    41–42, 45, 49

About the Authors

Donald D. Roberts, Ph.D., has been conducting psychotherapy in private practice for thirty-five years. As a member of the faculty of The Masterson Institute for Psychoanalytic Psychotherapy, for the past fourteen years he provides training, supervision, and consultation for psychotherapists, leads seminars, writes journal articles, lectures at conferences, and teaches and trains psychotherapists in furthering their knowledge of psychoanalytic psychotherapy of the personality disorders.

In the private practice of psychotherapy for the past thirty-two years, **Deanda S. Roberts**, M.A., also offers supervision and consultation to individual psychotherapists and counselors, social service agencies, and college counseling centers. In addition, she leads seminars and study groups for those with an interest in psychoanalytic psychotherapy and attachment disorders.

Made in the USA
Columbia, SC
19 March 2022

57887027R00114